Books by F. S. C. Northrop

SCIENCE AND FIRST PRINCIPLES

THE MEETING OF EAST AND WEST

THE LOGIC OF THE SCIENCES AND THE HUMANITIES

THE TAMING OF THE NATIONS

EUROPEAN UNION AND UNITED STATES FOREIGN POLICY

THE COMPLEXITY OF LEGAL AND ETHICAL EXPERIENCE

Editor of IDEOLOGICAL DIFFERENCES AND WORLD ORDER

Co-editor with Mason W. Gross *of*

ALFRED NORTH WHITEHEAD, AN ANTHOLOGY

THE COMPLEXITY OF
LEGAL AND ETHICAL EXPERIENCE

The Complexity of Legal and Ethical Experience

STUDIES IN THE METHOD OF NORMATIVE SUBJECTS

by

F. S. C. NORTHROP

Sterling Professor of Philosophy and Law
in the Yale Law School

LITTLE, BROWN AND COMPANY

BOSTON   TORONTO

*Published simultaneously in Canada
by Little, Brown & Company (Canada) Limited*

PRINTED IN THE UNITED STATES OF AMERICA

The life of the law has not been logic:
it has been experience.

O. W. HOLMES, JR.

It is the business of philosophy to
analyze . . . experience.

C. I. LEWIS

It came into my thoughts that . . .
before we set ourselves upon [such
normative] inquiries . . . , it was
necessary to examine our own abil-
ities, and see what objects our under-
standings were or were not said to
deal with.

JOHN LOCKE

Preface

THE major theme of this book is that both legal and ethical experience are much more complex than any traditional theory of these subjects would lead one to suppose. Hence the first quotation in the front of this book. It might be supposed that the easiest way to show this would be to describe legal and ethical experience. Such, however, is not the main approach of this book. For "experience" is an ambiguous word. This ambiguity arises from the fact that experience is as much a product of theory as it is a criterion of the correct theory. Consequently, experience needs analysis, as the second quotation affirms. The safest way, therefore, to avoid oversimplification is to analyze the practical and the theoretical issues which concrete decisions and normative theorizing have generated. This analytic and problematic approach guides us to the theoretical traditions, hypotheses and methods which give our present legal and moral experience much of its meaning and content.[1] Also, since each particular theory owes its existence to certain facts in normative experience which any theory ignores at its peril, the pluralism of the theories, especially when supplemented with a description of the norms of different cultures, guides one to the diversity, the richness and the complexity of the facts.

Were one to use a merely empirical, descriptive approach, pushing all traditional and contemporary theory aside, one's method would leave one with merely a description of an "is." Yet it is the very nature of normative experience that it requires one to pass judgment upon what is. What ought to be normatively as well as what is in fact the case normatively is of the essence of concrete legal and ethical experience. For example, in their unanimous decisions in the desegregation cases, the Justices of the Supreme Court of the United States not merely described the de facto positive legislative educational statutes and social customs of the Southern States, but also evaluated them, declaring that they ought not to be. Since the "ought" involves in part at least the ideal as distinct from the actual and since the ideal requires normative theory for its specification, normative experience can be understood only by making evident through analysis the theories which it has generated as well as the facts which it exhibits.

The analytic problematic approach enables one also to avoid eclecticism, specifying the particular factors in experience for which each of the traditional theories accounts, yet at the same time relating the diverse traditional theories and methods to one another upon a basis of theory and principle which is not eclectic. For example, analysis shows that every legal theory, even those legal theories which would keep the judge's personal moral judgment out of his legal judgment, contain and presuppose a particular ethical theory. Conversely, the adequacy of any theory in personal ethics cannot be determined until its consequences for legal experience are faced. This is why we have put law and ethics together in our title. Similarly, every theory of law specifies (1) a given set of facts within the domain of human experience which comprises the subject matter of legal science and (2) a specific method for determining and passing judgment upon these facts. In fact, no theory of ethics or law is worth any more than the rigor of the method by which it is implemented. Hence the subtitle of this book.

No method for any subject can be stated correctly without specifying whether the conclusions drawn from its application refer to (1) immediately experienceable data, (2) inferred factors or (3) constructs introduced by contractual or other postulational techniques with their more indirect and pragmatic methods of verification. To distinguish these three factors with precision is to be concerned with epistemology. Consequently, as the chapters on the comparative legal and ethical norms of different cultures will show, the different normatively worded theories of legal and ethical experience and their respective methods for settling normative disputes concerning what ought to be, presuppose their particular non-normatively worded epistemological theories of conceptual meaning.

Clearly, the complexity of legal and ethical experience increases. Not only does any legal theory contain ethical assumptions, just as any ethical theory possesses legal consequences, but also any ethical and legal theory specifying its particular criteria of what the words "good," "ought" and "just" mean contains and requires for its validity a specific non-normatively worded epistemological theory of what any word in any subject means. For example, as Judge Learned Hand has made clear in his 1930 essay on Mr. Justice Holmes,[2] the legal positivists' theory of what the normative words "legally just" mean derives from the introspective psychological theory of ethics which identifies what is "ethically good" with private "preferences, arbitrary and imperative," and the latter ethical theory rests in turn on the non-normatively worded epistemological assumption (stated first for the modern world in Locke's *Essay Concerning Human Understanding* [3]) that no concept in any subject is meaningful unless its meaning is to be found solely in factors that are either directly inspectable with radical empirical immediacy or definable in terms of such factors. Reject or qualify the latter cognitive epistemological premise and both the psychological theory of ethics and the legal positivists' theory of law lose much of their plausibility.

Normative cognitivists and non-cognitivists alike agree that the non-normatively worded sentences of epistemology are cognitive and hence empirically or scientifically testable assertions. But since any normatively worded legal and ethical theory of what ought to be contains and presupposes for its validity its particular non-normatively worded epistemological theory of what is the case with respect to conceptual meaning, and since the latter assertions are cognitive, i.e., empirically testable, it follows that rival ethical and legal theories of what ought to be are cognitive also. Hence, though the scientific methods for determining descriptively the normative content of the positive law or the living law of any society differ from the scientific method for evaluating those de facto norms, once the latter are empirically determined, this book concludes, against the ethical non-cognitivists Stevenson and Ayer,[4] the legal non-cognitivists Hägerström and Alf Ross,[5] and the legal positivist Kelsen,[6] that not merely descriptive but also evaluative ethics and law are sciences. In other words, it is possible to pass a scientifically testable judgment not merely on whether the positive legal norms and the living law customs of a given society are descriptively such and such but also on whether they ought to be such and such. In short, evaluative as well as descriptive normative experience is cognitive.

Many previous legal and ethical analysts have held this position. In the opinion of the writer, their normative cognitivism suffered, however, from two fatal weaknesses. First, they failed to meet the arguments, recently emphasized by Alf Ross in his criticism of any "fait normatif" [7] and by Professor Ernest Nagel in his analysis [8] of the normative cognitivism of Professor Lon Fuller, that this theory is self-contradictory. Second, even assuming normative cognitivism to be theoretically self-consistent, the traditional cognitivists provided no method to implement their theory. Chapters XV to XX introduce the distinctions necessary to meet the first of these two weaknesses in traditional legal and ethical cognitivism. The final chapters of this book attempt to meet the second.

Two limitations of this book are to be noted by way of caution. Its problematic approach leads one to its positive conclusion. Nevertheless, by virtue of the emphasis upon the existential complexity of the problematic situation rather than on the linguistically analytic and precise statement of its own and alternative solutions of normative problems, this approach (a) leaves one *theoretically* without the analytically linguistic statement of its thesis which contemporary philosophical analysts have come to regard as essential and which even its author deems desirable, while also (b) *operationally* failing to provide the application to many cases which is necessary to show that the method specified in the last chapters is effective practically. Originally, the plan was to include (a) and (b) in this volume. When the attempt was made to do so, however, it was found that the woods became obscured by the particular trees so that the over-all thesis was thrown out of focus and that (a) and (b) were entirely too lengthy undertakings to include in this volume, requiring independent treatment, each by itself. Legal and philosophical analysts must not expect, therefore, to find here a linguistically precise analytic statement of the complex thesis. In this sense it is a prolegomenon to its positive conclusion rather than a linguistically rigorous, analytic statement of that conclusion. Similarly, followers of the case method in law, and operationalists generally, must not expect to find here the application to many concrete cases and contemporary evaluative normative problems. The writer hopes to eliminate these two limitations in future volumes.

The author is indebted to the editors of the following journals or publishing houses for permission to republish part of what this book contains: *Journal of Legal Education, Natural Law Forum, Yale Law Journal, University of Pennsylvania Law Review, Louisiana Law Review, Comprendre, Philosophy East and West, Northwestern University Law Review, Michigan Law Review, The Journal of Philosophy,* the University of Chicago Press, IVᵉ Congrès International des Sciences Anthropologiques et Ethnologiques, Harper and Brothers, the Antioch Press, the University of Hawaii Press and the Beacon Press. In most cases of republished material, deletions and revisions have been made to avoid repetition and to clarify points previously stated too briefly. This Preface, Chapter I and the final two chapters contain entirely new material. The book's most important conclusions — the analyses of contractual democracy, legal obligation and international law — appear in the last chapter for the first time.

The author is deeply appreciative of the patience and the care with which Mr. J. Randall Williams and his colleagues in Little, Brown and Company have taken in transforming the manuscript to the printed page. Without Miss Helen H. Livingston's patience and expertness in preparing the manuscript and making the index, what appears here would have been impossible. To be acknowledged also with deepest gratitude is a research grant made by the Wenner-Gren Foundation for Anthropological Research, Inc., to the Yale Law School which made Miss Livingston's assistance possible.

F. S. C. Northrop

The Yale Law School
September, 1959

Contents

THE COMPLEXITY OF
LEGAL AND ETHICAL EXPERIENCE

I

The Novelty of Legal Experience

To its practitioners, law appears as a sequence of cases pregnant on the one hand with principles and precedents and on the other with briefs and judgments that break at times with the past. To its subjects, law presents itself first as an unnecessarily prolix, dull and impersonal necessity, and finally in one's last will and testament as the trusted custodian of all that one can leave to those whom one holds most dear. But to the legal theorist and the philosopher, law is life itself.

For in law, as in the political institutions which law helps create, human experience presents itself at its worst and at its best in all its complexities. In medicine the main concern is with sickness and disease and with making the most of what one knows in the end, since all must die, will be a bad job. In literature and the fine arts, fiction and fancy probe the private and pursue the beautiful to find something that may well be more literal and less misleading than fact itself. In human relations without the presence of law, men argue, tempers flare, neighbors talk about their friends, when disputes arise, behind their backs and groups of men fight endlessly. It is as though where two or three are gathered together without a name that is legal, there worry and war are also. If the reader is inclined to doubt this, let him note how in even the simplest disagreements between friends over a wood lot in the country, each reports the worst about the other until appeal to a legal instrument is made, a few words on a single sheet of paper are written out with the lawyer's dull and perhaps prolix prose, and the official settlement is officially and publicly finalized. Then sleep returns to troubled and bed-tossed spirits and old friends can relax and smile again. Let no man say that war is inevitable and that peace is unnecessary. We all know peace on earth very well, and when we reflect a moment on even the most local and commonplace experiences such as the disagreement between friends over a wood lot, we know also what profession in our midst makes peace possible. In law the worst and the best in us come out, and in the end, unlike medicine, the better wins.

In natural science trustworthy theory about the "is" of non-manmade facts triumphs but there is no "ought." In religion and personal morality, the ideal and what ought to be are there, but all too often without either conclusions or conduct that come to terms with what is. In law, however, the "is" of the most sordid and vile conduct comes face to face in fact before a bar of judgment which passes a sentence in terms of norms with specific content that presuppose and prescribe an "ought." What the world would be were there no Sundays and what Heaven is where there are only Sundays combine in human legal experience. And in this meeting of the "is" with the "ought" in which the de facto sordidness of the defendant's act is measured against the normative "ought" of the law's prescriptive precedents and principles, for all the shortcomings and the miscarriages of justice, it is the "ought" that wins. In legal experience Cinderella wins her Prince. Thus legal experience combines within itself the ideal and the actual in a way that is not true either for natural science or for personal morality and religion. Precisely because this is the case one must expect, as the sequel will show, that an analysis of legal or political experience must take one to the sciences, social and natural, of what is, on the one hand, and to personal morality and to religion, on the other hand.

Legal experience has another dimension of complexity. Literature, as we have noted, psychology, personal ethics and much, at least, of religion probe the subjective and the private. Natural science and factual, or merely descriptive, social science exhibit the public. The finalizing of a will and the legal transfer of a wood lot suffice to show that in a very subtle manner law combines the public and the private within a single experience.

But although the life of the law is experience, as a great jurist has noted, it is also more than experience; for before experience can give anything as determinate, complex, particular and practical as law, it has to be analyzed. This becomes evident when one notes that medicine, literature, the fine arts, natural science, personal morality and religion refer also to experience. Evidently law and these other subjects derive from experience by way of different modes of analysis.

What is the mode of analysis that produces the subject called law? What is the method, given a correct analysis, by which knowledge of this subject is to be acquired? The initiation and partial prosecution of the inquiries necessary to answer these two questions are the major concern of this book.

Since the analysis of experience, which gives rise to law, is different from the analysis which produces medicine or natural science, the inevitable product of our inquiry will be a theory of law — a theory, namely, which specifies the factors in experience which are necessary and sufficient to account for what occurs in legal experience. Since legal experience is complex, especially so in the contemporary world, as the next chapter will show, we must expect to have to go where the specific character of the complexities takes us and to be led to a theory and method of law which is complex also.

Furthermore, even if, in the light of the analysis partially completed in this book, the method of law should turn out, contrary to the analyses of the Scandinavian and American non-cognitivists, to be a scientific method, it is the analysis of legal experience which must justify the scientific method; it is not scientific method as conceived in some other subject which determines the procedure that legal experience requires.

As noted in the second quotation on the motto page, the subject whose business it is to analyze experience is philosophy. Since law is not merely experience but also a particular mode of analysis of experience, legal theory without philosophical analysis and philosophical theory is impossible.

Scientific method is appropriate to a given experience only when philosophical analysis of the type of question the experience raises and the type of discourse it uses shows its questions to be those which scientific methods can answer and its discourse to be cognitive indicative sentences rather than ejaculatory or imperative statements. Since both the non-cognitive propaganda that characterizes so much of contemporary domestic as well as international legal and political experience and the challenge of the non-cognitive legal and moral theorists such as Alf Ross and Charles L. Stevenson raise the crucial question whether scientific method is either practical or meaningful in law or ethics, it would be both fact-begging and question-begging to make scientific method, as defined by some other subject, the criterion of our analysis of legal experience. Necessarily, therefore, both our method of inquiry and the legal theory at which we arrive as a result of our analysis of legal experience must be philosophical.

Even so, how shall we proceed? Without method there is likely to be madness, but with too much method, or, to speak more precisely, with an immature or doctrinaire method, there is sure to be simple-mindedness, and between the simpleton and the maniac there is little to choose.

Certainly experience must be allowed to speak for itself. But even lawyers and philosophers are not always good listeners. Furthermore, the minds of neither group, at least at the age when they have acquired sufficient experience to present something worth listening to, are not blank tablets. Instead, along with the richness of their legal, ethical and political experiences they have inevitably acquired certain fixed ideas with respect to how they think about their experience. Hence in our procedure we face a paradox. If we start with minds that are blank enough to allow legal experience to speak for itself, we have a mind without enough experience to report anything about it that is worth saying. If, on the other hand, we wait for a mind that has had enough experience to make what it says worth listening to, then one of necessity gets a mind which reports what experience tells it in terms of that particular person's theoretical and philosophical point of view.

To be sure, there are lawyers, judges and even law professors who tell us that they have no legal philosophy. In law, as in other things, we shall find that the only difference between a person "without a philosophy" and someone with a philosophy is that the latter knows what his philosophy is, and is, therefore, more able to make clear and justify the premises that are implicit in his statement of the facts of his experience and his judgments about those facts.

One resolution, therefore, of the paradox involved in choosing between the meager experience of a blank mind and the rich experience of a mature one which describes and interprets its rich experience from the standpoint of a particular legal analysis and philosophy is (a) to choose accounts of law by the latter type of richly experienced and analytically and intellectually mature people and then, by considering several of them, (*b*) to get their respective philosophical analyses and philosophical theories of legal moral and political experience out into the open. This book will pursue this method in part, but only in part.

Our reason for not carrying through a thorough analysis of all the major legal and ethical theories is twofold. First, such an excessively theoretical and analytical approach is an exceedingly lengthy undertaking and requires independent and full-time consideration by itself. Second, even such a full-dress approach along the lines of rival legal theories and philosophies may miss certain empirical factors in the complex which is legal experience. Hence, even at the inescapable cost of not giving a clear analytic statement and evaluation of the major contemporary ethical and legal theories, the more inductive and natural history approach to legal and ethical experience must come first. Only if such an empirical survey and sketch of the over-all terrain and its contemporary legal and political problems are made first can the clues to an adequate theory of legal experience and of legal method be discovered and can one avoid the very real danger of being bogged down in the morass of charges and countercharges between rival legal theorists to no decisive result. In a later, more theoretically analytic and linguistically precise work, the rigor can be added both with respect to the precise philosophical statement of the new clue and the critique of the traditional theories.

Furthermore, old theories of law mirror the day before yesterday's legal experiences. Since the character of legal and political experience, as of other experience, changes with time, it is well to begin with some of the factors that make the experience of contemporary man unique. Certainly both domestically and internationally he faces inescapable moral, legal and political problems. Little Rock demonstrates this domestically. The Cold War on the verge of hotness in an atomic age shows it internationally. In any event, problems are the best prescription for preventing law, ethics, politics and normative philosophy generally from becoming simple-minded.

II

Legal Philosophy in the Contemporary World

THE place of philosophy in law will depend upon two things: (1) the legal needs of contemporary society, and (2) the capacity of traditional methods and theories of jurisprudence to meet these needs.

Insofar as the legal needs of contemporary society are identical with those of the past, the traditional courses, methods and theories of jurisprudence will suffice. It is only when the contemporary legal needs of society are different from those of the past and call for a law, and a jurisprudence to define and sustain that law, different from those of the past, that jurisprudence becomes an absolute necessity in the legal curriculum. That such is the case at present the following considerations make clear.

Three facts make contemporary society unique. They are (1) the release of atomic energy; (2) the shift of the political focus of the world from Western Europe towards Asia; and (3) the inescapably ideological character of both domestic and international social problems.

The Release of Atomic Energy

The portentous consequences for good and evil of the release of atomic energy are reasonably well known. Two things are to be emphasized with respect to it. First, released atomic energy is not merely a bit more energy of the old type. Second, the release of atomic energy and the construction of the atomic bomb would never have been thought of even as a possibility had it not been for Einstein's theory of relativity. Both considerations have important legal implications.

The traditional method of obtaining energy involved merely moving energy from a relatively large store in nature to the place where man wanted to use it. The leverage involved in this mode of release was very small. It was merely the ratio between the quantity of energy taken out and the amount of the large reservoir of energy which remained after all dissipation in its release had occurred. In the case of atomic energy, however, energy is not derived from other energy but from matter or, to put it more exactly, from the bound matter of chemical atoms. In this instance the ratio of leverage is quantitatively larger to a degree measured by one over a number which is astronomical in size. The law which defines this leverage with mathematical precision is the mass-energy equation of Einstein's special theory of relativity. The leverage element in this equation is defined by a constant c^2. This constant c has the mathematical dimensions of a velocity and the numerical value of 186,000 miles per second. When this quantity is squared, a number astronomical in size results. It is the ratio in which this astronomical number functions that gives one the terrific leverage with respect to the amount of energy produced for human uses when one releases energy from bound matter. This mathematical fact means that an atomic war will be something quite different from a merely intensified traditional war.

It must be remembered also that an atomic bomb releases not merely astronomically greater amounts of energy than a traditional bomb but that the released atomic energy is accompanied by intense radioactivity. This means that even though the damage produced were equal merely to that produced by heavy saturation bombing, the defender, because of the radioactivity, could not immediately proceed to repair the damage. Whether anybody could go near a vast region of iron mines after its ore had been made radioactive by the dropping of a large atomic bomb upon it, short of several years after the bomb had been dropped, is still, to put the matter conservatively, very questionable. With iron mines untouchable by human beings, it is not clear how an industrial society could live very long even in times of peace.

These facts are relevant to legal theory for one very obvious reason. They drive home the point that a law which meets the greatest social need of the contemporary world must be one which puts forth all the reflection and research of which we are capable to create a truly effective legal world order. That the traditional international law and the traditional theories of jurisprudence are quite incapable of doing this is obvious to anyone acquainted with them. In an atomic age civilized men simply cannot afford to have war. International as well as domestic disputes must be brought under the rule of law. It would be an ironic tragedy indeed if a faulty legal theory prevented this from occurring. Yet more than one generally accepted philosophy of law have such a consequence.

The fact that the release of atomic energy is a consequence of Einstein's theory of relativity has another implication with respect to the legal needs of contemporary society and the type of jurisprudence required to meet these needs. Einstein's theory of relativity is an experimentally verified, deductively formulated theory of mathematical physics. It arose because of certain inadequacies which Einstein noted to exist in the basic concepts and postulates of physics as formulated for mechanics by Newton and for electromagnetics by Maxwell. The Michelson-Morley experiment in 1885 presented a fact which simply should not exist if the basic assumptions of both Newton's mechanics and Maxwell's electromagnetics are correct. This caused Albert Einstein to see that a reconstruction was required in the fundamental theoretical concepts of mathematical physics. Analysis showed him that the difficulty centered in such abstract theoretical notions as space, time and the relation of matter to space and to time.

It is to be noted, therefore, that Einstein's difficulty was a theoretical one. The fact is that he never performed an experiment in physics in his life. He was a theoretical physicist. Nonetheless, his sensitivity to the theoretical difficulties raised with respect to traditional physical theory by the Michelson-Morley experiment enabled him to make one of the most remarkable discoveries in the history of Western science and to place modern physics upon new and experimentally more valid theoretical foundations.

These considerations indicate that Einstein had no concern with engineering or with explosives. It happened, however, when his theory was verified and when he pursued its assumptions to their deductive consequences, that a certain theorem followed necessarily by the rules of formal logic. This theorem is the aforementioned mass-energy equation. Thus, it was by pursuing an abstract theoretical question, involving the basic concepts of space and time at the foundations of theoretical physics, that Einstein came, as a by-product of his investigations, upon the discovery of the possibility of deriving energy not from larger available pools of energy but from bound matter itself.

The social and legal implications of this fact have not been noted previously but are nonetheless important. What it means is that men must now order themselves socially with respect to a new nature — to the new nature which is designated by Einstein's experimentally verified theory of relativity. This experimentally verified, theoretically known nature is quite different from the one which we directly observe. Directly observed nature is the same today as it was when the ancient Greeks looked at it. But the experimentally verified, theoretically known nature of Einstein's mathematical physics is a nature radically different from any in which previous men have lived and with respect to which they have had to order their social relations.

Consider for a moment what law is. Law is an ordering of human beings with respect to one another and to nature. A law is good if it orders these human beings with respect to one another and nature in the light of a true, and as far as possible complete, knowledge of what men and nature are. A law is bad not because it is naughty but because in its ordering of men with respect to nature it puts them together in relation to nature in a way that is contrary to what true scientific knowledge reveals both men and nature to be. It follows from this that when physics places men, as it does at present, in an entirely different nature from the one in which they lived previously, the law, if it is to order men properly with respect to nature as scientifically known, must set up legal rules and create "living law inner relations in society," to use Ehrlich's language, quite different from the traditional ones.

A key to this difficulty can be grasped if we compare nature as known by contemporary mathematical physics with nature as known by nineteenth-century physics. The conception of nature of nineteenth-century physics which was most relevant to the legal and social ordering of men with respect to nature was thermodynamics. This science made it clear that human beings with bodies could not be human beings unless they obtained energy in a form available for work from a source in nature outside their own bodies. These sources as then known were limited. Thus it was that the major social problem for a man living in nature as known by nineteenth-century physics was the problem of finding and equitably dividing the limited available pools of energy. The great merit of the Marxist-Communist ideology, with its emphasis upon the production relations which joined men to these pools of energy in nature, is that, more than any previous economic and political theory, it took this conception of the relation between man and nature of nineteenth-century physics into account. In the twentieth century, however, the social and legal problem is the reverse of this. Now, instead of having too small available bits of energy for human use, we have too dangerously big amounts of energy — amounts so dangerously big that no individual or nation can afford to allow laissez-faire circumstance to determine who gets control of this energy.

These considerations indicate that the release of atomic energy entails the construction of a new domestic as well as a new international law. Moreover, it requires that a legal education which is to provide the knowledge necessary to see the need for this new law and to specify and construct it must have at least one course in its curriculum which directs the student's attention not merely away from the legal cases and the positive codes in the casebooks to the social sciences, but also away from even the social sciences to the experimentally verified theories of contemporary mathematical physics.

The implications of this conclusion are somewhat surprising but nonetheless inescapable. To say that a law which provides rules for properly relating men to one another and to nature in the contemporary world must ground itself in the experimentally verified, deductively formulated theory of twentieth-century mathematical physics is to assert that contemporary jurisprudence must return at least in part to the Greek and Roman Stoic doctrine of a *jus gentium* grounded in *jus naturae*. Moreover, this *jus naturae* must be taken in its original Greek and Roman Stoic meaning, as literally a law of nature verified by physics. In other words, the philosophy of contemporary law must be a philosophy of nature as well as of culture, a *jus naturae* as well as a *jus gentium*. Also this philosophy of nature must take as its basic concepts and postulates, just as did Greek and Roman Stoic philosophy drawing upon Greek physics, the primitive concepts and postulates of experimentally verified, deductively formulated physics. By so doing, one obtains a philosophy of law which is verified in a sense that holds for everyone, since its basic assumptions are those of mathematical physics, which the physicists have verified by scientific methods which give results that are the same for all men.

In returning thus to the Greek and Roman Stoic doctrine of the natural law of contemporary Roman Catholic law schools, it is to be noted that the content of this natural law cannot be that of the natural philosophy and physics of St. Thomas and Aristotle. Its content must be that of the experimentally verified physics and attendant philosophy of natural science of the twentieth century — not that of the thirteenth century, or the fourth century B.C.

A contemporary jurisprudence grounded in natural law and its scientifically verified philosophy of contemporary mathematical physics has one other merit which is required, as noted above, to meet the legal needs of an atomic age. The requirement is that we have a truly effective international law. As Roscoe Pound has noted in a paper entitled "Toward a New Jus Gentium," [1] such an international law entails the return to the concept of a universal law. It is precisely this universality which a philosophy of law, grounded in a scientifically verified philosophy of nature, provides, since all men, regardless of the diversities of humanistic laws of their different cultures, live in the same nature or are capable, as they acquire scientific knowledge, of so living.

It does not follow, however, that adjustment, upon the part of legal theory, of its concepts and norms to the experimentally verified, universally valid theories of contemporary mathematical physics is a sufficient as well as a necessary condition for an adequate legal philosophy and method. The extent to which this is the case will concern us in later chapters.

It is relevant, however, at this point to note that scientifically verified philosophy of natural science has two parts. One is its ontological part, the other its methodological or epistemological part. The ontological philosophical assumptions of any scientifically verified, deductively formulated theory are found by examining the theory to determine its basic or primitive entities and relations. The epistemological part of any experimentally verified scientific theory is found by exam-

ining the scientific method by means of which the theory is verified
and determining the relations which join the basic concepts and postulates of the verified theory to the directly observable data to which
they refer for their empirical verification.

The Shift of the Political Focus of the World from Western Europe to Asia

In its issue of November 13, 1948, *The Economist* of London re-
ported as follows: "There have been signs for some time that the
storm centre of world politics might shift from Europe to the Far
East." *The Economist* then goes on to point out that this shift is
already here.

Although it has not received the attention which it deserves, this
shift of the focus of world politics from Western Europe to Asia is
the major political fact of our time. It should have come home to citizens of the United States on December 7, 1941, when they were
brought into the second major war of this century, and its first *truly*
world war, by the attack of an Asiatic rather than a European power.
Everywhere throughout Asia peoples are arising and insisting not
merely upon the self-determination of their social institutions but also
upon the principle that international decisions must take Oriental
peoples and values as well as Western ones into account.

The full implications of this rise of Asia are yet to be appreciated.
A majority of the people on the surface of this earth live in the Orient.
This means, if political power goes where the majority of the people
are, that the control of world affairs will inevitably and eventually
pass to the Orient.

The first legal implication is equally obvious. It is that any law
school which is to train men competently in a nation which is one
of the two major powers in such a world must pay attention to the
codified law and the living law of the major peoples of the Orient
as well as to that of the traditional and contemporary West. No longer
can a legal curriculum adequate to the social and legal needs of the
contemporary world be concerned solely with Western social and
legal institutions, cases, principles and theories.

For the same reason, a course in jurisprudence which teaches theories of jurisprudence derived almost exclusively from Western law is an inadequate, contemporary jurisprudence. A jurisprudence which faces the legal needs of the contemporary world must derive its method and its theory from a study of Oriental as well as Occidental law.

The method which it must use is also clear. The great sociologist of law, Ehrlich, has shown in his *Fundamental Principles of the Sociology of Law* that no codified law of any people or culture is understood or effective unless the underlying, living law to which it corresponds is also known and present. Once this is grasped it becomes evident that a jurisprudence which meets the social and legal needs of a world in which Oriental as well as Occidental peoples are playing a major role must go behind the comparative studies of the codified, positive laws of the different peoples and cultures of the world to their underlying living laws. These living laws are exhibited by cultural anthropology and cultural sociology.

Recently these sciences have found, however, that their investigators do not understand any foreign culture which is observed objectively until they stay with that culture long enough to discover the particular concepts and assumptions used by that people themselves in conceptualizing the facts of their experience and ordering their lives morally and socially. Moreover, it has been found that these key concepts, indigenous to a given people and culture, are always philosophical in character. In fact the word "philosophy" is nothing but a name for the basic concepts which a person or people uses to conceptualize the facts of experience. This means, therefore, that a jurisprudence which would find the living law beneath the codified law of any one of the world's cultures must pass through cultural anthropology and cultural sociology to the comparative philosophy of culture. Thus, just as the first unique fact of our age, the release of atomic energy, entails that an adequate jurisprudence must ground itself in the basic concepts — that is, in the philosophy — of experimentally verified twentieth-century natural science, so this second fact of our time, the Oriental focus of international politics, entails that an adequate contemporary jurisprudence must ground itself in the basic concepts — that is, in the philosophy — of the world's cultures.[2] This also will require our attention in subsequent chapters.

The Inescapably Ideological Character of Both Domestic and International Social Problems

The foregoing considerations prepare us to recognize the third unique fact of our time. A study of the key basic concepts of any culture, without which the living law underlying the codified law of that culture is not understood, reveals that these key concepts not merely provide the ideas in terms of which the people of that culture conceive the facts of their experience but also define their values. Each people regards the social ordering of people with respect to nature in society as good insofar as that ordering fulfills and gives expression to the conception of themselves and nature which their particular key philosophical concepts prescribe. Furthermore, each people judges the social and legal institutions and moral conduct of any other people or nation from the standpoint of its own basic ideological or conceptual assumptions.

That the ideological assumptions of the traditional cultures of the Orient are different from those of either the medieval or modern cultures and nations of the West has been obvious for a long time. This difference in ideological outlook created no social problems, however, as long as the Oriental peoples were docile or were incapable or undesirous of insisting upon determining international policy. But the moment the Orient arises, as it has arisen, this ideological conflict between traditional Western and traditional Eastern basic concepts and values becomes inescapable. In fact, the major problem of our time is that of putting together the quite different ideological and cultural values and legal institutions of the Orient and the Occident.

In this connection a frequent confusion should be avoided. Many people speak of the issue between Soviet Russia and the traditional democracies as an issue between the East and the West. One may use the words as one chooses, provided one makes clear one's usage and does not surreptitiously shift to a different meaning. The issue, however, between Soviet Russia and the traditional democracies is an issue purely within modern Western civilization, between the West of Europe and the East of Europe; it is not an issue between the East in the sense of the traditional Orient and the West in the sense of the traditional Occident.

It would be a mistake, however, to suppose that the only ideological social and legal problem of our time appears in the shift of the political forces of the world toward Asia and in the evident conflict between the Soviet Russians with their Marxist philosophy and France, Great Britain and the United States with their pre-Hegelian modern natural and legal philosophy and its attendant social and legal institutions and practices.

Nor is there identity of philosophical and legal outlook between the Continental European modern liberal democracies and those of Great Britain and the English-speaking world generally. Chapter X will document this particular complexity of contemporary legal and political experience. Another ideological conflict exists between the more emotional, aesthetic, voluntaristic values of any Latin people, such as the Spanish and the Latin Americans, and the more empirical and more rationalistic values of the peoples of the North of Europe and North America.

But domestic social problems are fast becoming equally ideological in character. This shows most obviously in China, where one group was dominated by the Marxist-Communist doctrine and the other group, under Chiang Kai-shek, was guided by a somewhat ambiguous ideology which attempted to combine classical Chinese Confucian and Western Christian and laissez-faire free enterprise capitalistic values. For centuries domestic Latin American politics has been characterized by inescapable ideological conflict. There different political parties would have different legal constitutions. It is for this reason that Latin American elections tend so frequently to be revolutions rather than merely the peaceful casting and counting of ballots. When the parties to a domestic election differ upon the basic ideological legal and political rules according to which the game is to be played, then domestic politics becomes as inescapably ideological as is international politics at the present moment. Contemporary French politics is an additional example. As was written in 1949, when most of this chapter was first published, if either the de Gaullists or the Communists were to come into power, the change would probably occur more by revolutionary than by constitutional means, and in any event a new constitution would result in fact if not in name.

Let us not miss the full implications of facts such as these. They mean that in most of the nations throughout Asia, Africa, Latin

America and Continental Europe there is at present not merely no effective international law, but also an ineffective domestic law.

Nor is the domestic politics of the United States as far from this type of situation as one might suppose. In the presidential election of 1948, there were eleven political parties — at least three or four of which had radically conflicting economic and political ideologies affecting individual civil liberties as well as economic and political social relations. Suppose that in some subsequent election the Dixiecrats and the Wallaceite liberals should increase their ratio of the total votes; then very easily the United States might find itself in the predicament of contemporary France, where no party represents more than a minority. When this happens governments cannot function, since any statute they attempt to pass fails to have the living law, majority support necessary to make it effective. Since 1948 events at Little Rock have made evident to everyone the seriousness of the domestic conflict that arises when a Supreme Court makes a decision expressing one philosophy of a just educational system, which affects an Old South whose positive legislation and social customs express a different philosophy. This means that legal research concerning the criteria for affirming one legal or moral philosophy rather than another has become as imperative for domestic law as it is for international law.

The failure of our law schools and of our departments of economics, political science, ethics and philosophy to face and meet this most pressing social need can be truly serious. The contemporary tendency of a majority of the people to break into embittered factions with respect to their legal and moral philosophies, if coupled with the failure of research in legal and moral philosophy to provide a more adequate philosophy upon which a majority of men can agree, may be fatal not merely for democracy, but for any ordered society, domestic or international. For there is no ordered society except as a majority of the people in it agree upon at least some ideological principles; that is, some specific economic, political, moral and legal rules that they are to use to order themselves normatively with respect to each other and to nature.

This inescapably ideological character of both the domestic and international social problems of our world is another evidence of the inadequacy of the traditional theories, methods and courses in jurisprudence, for the traditional theories in jurisprudence reflect the old ideologies. When ideological issues become the key social and legal problems of society, to appeal to the old jurisprudence is to beg the basic social questions at issue.

Also, to teach the technical branches of law in the present manner is similarly to beg these questions or to answer them inadequately. This is the case because the present content and organization of these technical courses in law are but a reflection of the last popular traditional theory of jurisprudence, say legal realism. A new jurisprudence and new courses in the technical branches of law based on this new jurisprudence are required. This jurisprudence must be one which provides political and legal norms which resolve the inescapably ideological domestic and international social problems of our time.

Does any recent theory of ethics, law or politics provide the method for doing this and specify the result of applying this method to particular legal and cultural philosophies? The answer would seem to be in the negative.

Certain general characteristics of an adequate normative theory can, however, be noted. First, it must face the question — the most difficult in science and philosophy — of whether there is any method valid for all by means of which a theory specifying determinate goal values can be shown to be true or false. The problem, at bottom, is whether personal ethical or social normative statements are cognitive or merely emotive and hortatory. Second, if it can be shown that normative sentences are cognitive — that is, it is significant to say that they are true or false — then the scientific method which provides the criteria of this truth and falsity must be specified. It is with these matters that the following chapters of this book are concerned.

III

Some Philosophical Issues in Anglo-American Law

PHILOSOPHY is the name for the basic methodological and theoretical assumptions of a subject. Since every science uses some method of investigation and any scientist who reports its facts to his colleagues must express these facts with words and, hence, introduce concepts and theory, it follows that any science whatever is also a philosophy. When no facts arise, however, to bring the traditional theory or methods of a subject into question, its problems are not philosophical. Then to be a scientist one need not also be a philosopher. Mathematics and physics were in such a state during the two hundred years following the publication of Newton's *Principia* in 1686. American law thought it was in a similar condition when, following Langdell, it introduced the case method and identified its science with the empirical study of cases. But whenever any facts arise in any subject which bring its traditional theory or methods into question, at that moment its problems become philosophical. Then to be an effective scientist one must also be a philosopher. Such has been the state of mathematics and physics since the end of the nineteenth century. Such, as this essay indicates, is the state of law at the present time.

The philosophical problems of contemporary law are in part the consequence of the impact upon it of the new philosophy of mathematics, physics and language. The late Walter W. Cook, an influential professor during the 1920's, had studied mathematical physics as well as law. If, he reasoned, a science as established as physics, with its

Reprinted by permission from *Natural Law Forum* — 1957, Vol. 2, No. 1.

relatively simple subject matter, has been forced, not merely to re-
vise its basic assumptions as introduced by the great Newton, but also
to re-examine the conception of its method as suggested by Newton,
how much more is the need for a similar revision of theory and re-
examination of method likely in such a complex subject matter as
that of the social sciences and law.[1] Forthwith a new spirit entered
American legal thinking, and at least one portion of that new legal
philosophy called legal realism was born.

A similar phenomenon has occurred in Great Britain. To understand it we must examine one of the factors in the late nineteenth
century which turned mathematicians into symbolic logicians and
philosophers. Scientists like Dedekind, Cantor, Frege, Russell and
Whitehead discovered that supposedly rigorous proofs in their science are far from rigorous. They found also that part of the trouble
centered in the fuzziness of the dx/dy symbol of the infinitesimal calculus, the main symbolic instrument of modern physics. This obscur-
ity in their key symbol forced them to pursue a thorough philosophical inquiry into the nature of symbolic meaning generally. Before
their scientific problem was solved even partially, three things had
happened. First, every one of the aforementioned mathematicians
found that in order to be a mathematician he had to investigate philosophical problems. Second, the technical concepts of mathematics
became defined in terms of those of logic; only then did the aforementioned proofs become rigorous. Third, an entirely new logic,
called symbolic logic, within which traditional mathematics and traditional logic are but special cases, had to be invented. The present
result is that the Chairman of the Department of Mathematics at
Dartmouth College and many of the research men engaged in the industrial building of calculating machines and in the military leaders'
study of strategy have Ph.D.'s in philosophy and logic rather than in
mathematics. These developments remind us that as the problems of
a subject become philosophical, thereby turning its experts into philosophers, and as new philosophical solutions of these problems are
found, novel practical consequences ensue. The fourth, and perhaps
most far-reaching, result of these developments in mathematics is
the discovery of what Whitehead and Russell have called the "incomplete symbol." [2]

Such symbols have been described by Lord Russell as those which

"have no significance in isolation, but only contribute to the significance of whole sentences." [3] This failure of symbols to possess a
meaning when considered by themselves means that any science containing incomplete symbols cannot be understood if it uses only the
method that is appropriate for determining the meaning of its ordinary, or complete, symbols. It is now known that not merely mathematics and mathematical physics, but also common-sense language
and, hence, in all likelihood, law, contain many incomplete symbols.
This discovery constitutes the major thesis and method of Cambridge
and Oxford analytic philosophy today and of the younger generation
of American philosophers. It has already been introduced into the
study of law in Britain by Professors Glanville Williams and Gra-
ham B. J. Hughes and by the newly appointed Regius Professor of
Jurisprudence at Oxford, Mr. H. L. A. Hart, who, although he was
trained as a lawyer and practiced at the bar, was at the time of his
appointment Lecturer in Philosophy, undoubtedly on incomplete
symbols, at Oxford University. [4]

Why are incomplete symbols likely to become important for lawyers? The answer is simple. Failure to recognize them will result either in the filling of one's subject matter with nonexistent objects or
in the erroneous conclusion that because many abstract nouns of legal
science, such as "right," "duty," "obligations," "justice," do not refer
in isolation to concrete objects for their meaning, they therefore have
no scientific meaning whatever. It is the great merit of the American
legal realists, in their emphasis upon concrete cases, facts and the
prediction of facts as a necessary criterion of conceptual meaning in
law, to have avoided the first of these two errors. It is their weakness,
in the opinion of contemporary Scandinavian and British legal scientists, to have fallen into the second of these errors because of their
failure to note the existence of incomplete symbols.

Consideration of the aforementioned dx/dy symbol of mathematical physics as it functions in the notation of the differential calculus
will show what is meant. Taken in isolation from the other symbols
in this notation, it might seem to mean a certain number dx, referring, say, to distance, divided by another number dy, referring to
time. As it functions, however, in the notation of the calculus, dx/dy
is the symbol by means of which the physicist expresses the velocity
of an object at a given instant of time t. Put in more concrete terms,

this means that dx/dy is the symbol by means of which the mathematical physicist expresses the velocity of a train as it passes, let us say, the Bridgeport station at the instant 8:00 A.M. sharp. Yet, clearly, there cannot be a velocity at an instant since an instant has no temporal extension, and any velocity requires a stretch of time in order to be. The question, therefore, arises, What is the meaning of the symbol dx/dy? If one treats this question with the scientific method the scientist uses to define the symbol "train" — that is, the method of ostensive definition or denotation in terms of empirically verifiable and, hence, existent objects — one fills the universe, as did the early modern mathematicians, with an infinite number of nonexistent objects called infinitesimals. Clearly, this is nonsense. Yet, equally clearly, the dx/dy symbol has a very precise scientific meaning, for without it the state of a physical system at a given time cannot be expressed, and, forthwith, the entire exactness and predictive power of physics collapses.

This problem was resolved by distinguishing between complete symbols such as "train," "station," "case," "courtroom," "judge," which do have a meaning in isolation that is determined by ostensive reference to, or by definition in terms of, empirically observable and, hence, existent concrete objects, and incomplete symbols such as dx/dy, which, as their name implies, require their relation to other symbols of the expressions in which they occur to be specified before their precise scientific meaning is made evident. Thus, in his analysis of the notation of the differential calculus, the mathematician G. H. Hardy writes that "dy/dx does not mean 'a certain number dy divided by another number dx': it means 'the result of a certain operation Dx or d/dx applied to $y = \phi(x)$,' the operation being that of forming the quotient $\{\phi(x + h) - \phi(x)\}/h$ and making $h \to O$." [5] If the Regius Professor of Jurisprudence at Oxford is correct, most of the abstract nouns of law, such as "right" and "obligation," are incomplete symbols, and legal science, consequently, needs a quite different method of analyzing its cases and elucidating its subject matter from that of either the classical British legal positivists or the American legal realists.

In any event, two things are clear: (1) The issue between the American legal realists and Professor Hart's theory of the method appropriate for the determination of the meaning of legal concepts takes one to very technical philosophical distinctions and methods. (2) The impact upon British law of the philosophical solution of the basic problems of mathematics which arose at the end of the nineteenth century has resulted in at least one person, Professor Hart, finding it necessary to become a philosopher in order to understand his own science of law.

Within American legal science other developments enforce a similar conclusion. In a recent lecture Professor Arthur L. Corbin described legal education during the first two decades of this century and his discovery that its conception of the subject matter of law was erroneous. This conception was that of the natural law thinkers such as Blackstone and Simeon Baldwin. According to this philosophy, legal science possessed certain fixed and eternal principles which supposedly could be found and memorized, and the practice of law consisted in bringing any concrete case under these principles. With Langdell at Harvard the case method had been introduced into American legal study. As Professor Corbin made clear, an examination of the cases failed to make them fit the traditional Blackstonian natural law formulae. Had you been in the legal philosophy seminar just previous to Professor Corbin's lecture, you would have heard Professor Wesley Sturges describe the same phenomenon and his similar reaction to it. Note the questioning of traditional theoretical assumptions and scientific methods, a sure sign that the basic problems of one's subject are becoming philosophical.

Surprisingly, however, or perhaps not so surprisingly, the conclusion at which Professor Sturges arrived in his seminar lecture immediately preceding the public lecture by Professor Corbin was the direct opposite of the conclusion reached by Professor Corbin. For the latter the application of the empirical method to the study of statutes and cases takes one to new principles of law, replacing those of Simeon Baldwin and Blackstone; [6] for Professor Sturges it results in the conclusion that legal science contains no principles, either new or old, and that the search for principles is merely an emotive hang-over from the past which one should get rid of as quickly as possible. Professor Sturges' work in the field of arbitration [7] and the late Professor Shulman's recommendation of arbitration rather than litigation under legislative statutes and legal principles in the field of labor law [8] support this existentialist philosophy of law — the philosophy which affirms that it is of the very nature of any concrete case of ethical or legal judgment that it is particular and unique, and that, hence, one falsifies the very nature of any dispute if one attempts to resolve it by recourse to universal principles, thereby treating it as if it were like other disputes.

Why this radical difference in the results of the application of the empirical scientific method to legal cases upon the part of Professor Corbin and of Professor Sturges? At least three factors enter into the answer to this question: (1) the plurality of empirical scientific methods; (2) the impact of sociology, particularly that of Sumner and Keller, upon Professor Corbin's thinking; and (3) the importation into the United States from Great Britain of Austin's positivistic philosophy of law. Let us consider these three factors in turn.

The method of mathematical physics is certainly empirical. Yet it gives general principles and universal laws. Hence, empirical physical science is not existential, after the manner of Professor Sturges' legal science. No physicist supposes that his scientific task is completed if he merely finds a particular fact in its unique particularity; he must also find the general principle or universally quantified law of which this fact is an instance. These universally quantified theoretical principles are, to be sure, never eternal, absolute and final with respect either to their content as humanly knowable or to their empirical verification. Nonetheless, there are universal principles, and it is the business of empirical physical science to find them. Professor Corbin's theory of empirical legal science clearly fits this conception of scientific method. The philosophy of law and its method which his procedure rests upon and presupposes is, therefore, essentialism or universalism, rather than existentialism.

In Professor Corbin's lecture there was more than an occasional reference to the mores of society. This is the language of sociological jurisprudence and of Professor Corbin's Yale teacher and friend, the sociologists Sumner and Keller. Their word "mores" refers clearly to the normative ordering relations of the individuals in society and is equivalent to what the anthropologists call "the pattern of a culture" [9] and the Austrian sociologist of law, Ehrlich, termed "the living law." [10] Henceforth, we shall follow Ehrlich's usage, calling Professor Corbin's cases and induced principles "the positive law," and his mores of society "the living law."

In any society there are always deviants from the normative ordering relations of its living law; these deviants, however, constitute a
minority. As the anthropologist Professor E. A. Hoebel has pointed
out recently, the living law of any people is in part a qualitative, and
in part a quantitative, or statistical, concept, because a large percent-
age of the people, but not all, habitually follow common qualitative
normative principles for ordering their social relations.[11] Otherwise
there would be anarchy rather than society or culture. This, again,
supports Professor Corbin's thesis that, although it is impossible to
find, by an empirical study of legal cases, a single set of principles
which will fit every case, nonetheless at any given time a tentative
set of such principles covering the majority of cases can be found.
These principles which must be induced afresh in each generation reflect the changing mores of the society.

The latter thesis unequivocally connects the positive law with the
living law. Nevertheless, Professor Corbin's description of the legal
student's subject matter restricted it to the positive law alone. The
task of legal science is to take the statutes of the legislature, together
with the cases provided by the courts, and to arrive, by inductive
generalization from such materials, at tentative general principles
which define the law. In short, the living law belongs to social and
political science, not to legal science; law is the empirical science of
the positive law.

But why, if the law is so essentially connected to the mores of society, is not its study as much concerned with the living law as with
the legislative statutes and the judicial decisions of the positive law?
This question brings us to a third legal philosophy within recent
American law: legal positivism. It derives by way of Thayer of the
Harvard Law School from Austin in England. Professor Corbin and
the Yale Law School of Dean Swan's régime were profoundly influenced by it, as were Judge Learned Hand and Justice Frankfurter.
According to Austin, the subject matter of legal science is the positive
law alone.

In his law journal articles on Justice Stone and Judge Swan,[12]
Judge Learned Hand describes (a) how Thayer of the Harvard Law
School had become, in the early decades of this century, "the prophet
of a new approach" to the judge's concept of his role in interpreting
the Bill of Rights, and (b) how this new approach captured "young

Stone" as a law student, dominated Dean and Judge Swan's thinking and, after spreading from the Harvard of Thayer's time throughout the United States, finally became the opinion of the majority on the Supreme Court. According to this new legal philosophy, as described by Judge Hand, "the Bill of Rights could not be treated like ordinary law; its directions were to be understood rather as admonitions to forbearance" to the electorate and the legislators. Dominated by this Austinian legal positivism of Thayer, which equates the legally just with the will of the legislature, the majority of the new Court found it not merely possible but also necessary in principle, if they were to be jurists of scientific integrity, to depart from the older Court's precedents in which majority-approved social legislation was declared to be unconstitutional because it conflicted with "the due process clause" of the Bill of Rights; thereby the new social legislation became law. Justice Douglas, who participated officially in these events, refers also to Thayer in support of his and the majority of the Court's action.[13]

These historical events, explicitly mentioned and described by Judge Hand and Justice Douglas, demonstrate that a shift in the basic philosophy of law — in this instance the shift from the natural law philosophy of Blackstone, Simeon Baldwin and the Old Court to the positivistic philosophy of law of Austin, Thayer, Judges Hand and Swan and the majority of Justices of the New Court — results in an epoch-making difference in the way a concrete case is decided. Clearly, cases alone, or even cases, the Bill of Rights and the legislative statutes together, are not enough; the philosophy of law which the judge or the legal scientist brings to the cases, the Constitution, the Bill of Rights and the legislative statutes is equally important. In fact, it is all-important since it determines the interpretation that is put upon the Bill of Rights, the legislative statute and the case.

Why does the positivistic philosophy of law have such an effect? To answer this question we must go back beyond Thayer to Austin.

Law, according to Austin, is identified with the commands or will of the sovereign,[14] where this will is indivisible and legally unlimited.[15] It follows that legal sovereignty cannot be divided between the executive, legislative and judicial branches of government, but must be located completely in one of them. In a society, therefore, whose living law is monarchical, this definition of law requires the placing of the whole of the government's sovereignty in the executive branch;

that is, an absolute monarch. In a society where living law is democratic, it necessitates similarly that the whole of political sovereignty must be placed in the legislative branch. From this, three things follow. (1) The executive becomes merely the spokesman for, and executive officer of, the majority in the legislature. This is the case in Great Britain and in Free India. (2) The judiciary becomes merely the instrument for taking the will of the legislature as expressed in its statutes as the sole meaning of law and for applying this purely statutory positive law to the settling of disputes; all previous judicial decisions, if scientifically correct, being such applications of the legislature's absolute and legally unlimited will. Hence, the epoch-making effect upon recent American politics and United States Supreme Court decisions of the British positivistic philosophy of law which came into this country through Thayer.

Austin's legal positivism has one other consequence. Since it equates the whole of law with a sovereign will which is legally unlimited, thereby restricting, in a democratic society, the tasks of advocates and judges to the application of the legislative statutes to concrete cases, it follows that (3) the subject matter of legal science is nothing but the positive law. In all probability, it is the influence of legal positivism upon Professor Corbin and the Yale Law School of Dean Swan's era that led Professor Corbin in his lecture to equate the study of law with the inducing of general principles from the positive statutes and cases, notwithstanding his explicit recognition of the essential connection between the positive law and the living law.

In a society such as that of Great Britain or the United States where the positive law has arisen out of its own living law, such a training of future advocates and judges will result perhaps in but minor errors and inadequacies. Today, however, British and American law schools contain a large number of students from non-Anglo-American societies. Also, British and American lawyers are being constantly called upon to advise the political and legal leaders of such countries upon the effective introduction of modern Western positive law. The living law of these non-Western societies is not that of Great Britain or the United States. The task, therefore, confronting both these foreign law students when they return to their native people and American and British legal advisors to such people is that of applying modern Western liberal democratic positive law to peoples with a quite different living law. For such legal demands, a philosophy of law and a legal education which equates the whole of legal science with nothing but the positive law is quite inadequate. It appears, therefore, that a law school which provides its students with the legal skills for meeting the legal demands that are likely to be placed upon them in today's world must have a richer and more complex philosophy of law and its scientific methods than legal positivism provides. More specifically, three things must be taught: (1) the method of legal positivism for determining the positive law; (2) the method of sociological jurisprudence for determining the living law of any society; and (3) the method or art, yet to be specified, for making (1) effective in (2) when the norms of (1) and (2) differ.[16]

What is the method of sociological jurisprudence for determining the living law? A reading of the works of Dean Emeritus Roscoe Pound, who was the first to introduce this sociological philosophy of law into the United States, and of Ehrlich, who, following upon Savigny, pioneered in this philosophy of legal science in Europe, will show that they threw very little light upon the scientific method which the sociologically trained lawyer is to use to determine the living law.

It is the great merit of Underhill Moore that he saw this weakness in the traditional sociological jurisprudence and made the first constructive attempt to remove it.[17] Like Walter Wheeler Cook, he was aware that modern scientific method is a very much more philosophically subtle and complicated thing than many social scientists and lawyers realize. This led Moore to study the method of modern physics in its complexity and to bring philosophers of natural science into his seminar on legal theory and method to help him in this task.

Modern physicists had found it necessary to do the same thing. When the Michelson-Morley experiment of 1885 revealed an indubitable fact which simply should not exist on the theoretical assumptions concerning space and time of Maxwell's and Newton's physics, and Einstein became convinced that those assumptions must be modified in a fundamental manner, he was confronted with a methodological difficulty. Newton, when he suggested that he made no hypotheses and that he had deduced the concepts of his physics from the experimental data, left the impression that a proper conception of scientific method was one in which there were no theoretical assumptions which the experimental facts did not give or logically necessitate. On this conception of scientific method, Newton's basic theoretical assumptions simply could not be wrong. Thus, Einstein found himself forced to carry through a philosophical analysis of the relation between the data of experimental physics and the concepts of its theory.

Einstein once told me that it was his reading of the philosopher Hume which convinced him that Newton's conception of scientific method was false, and which, therefore, gave him the courage to suggest an alteration in Newton's basic assumptions. What Hume made clear to Einstein, and what Hume makes clear to anybody who reads him with care, is the restricted meaning of causality, different from that of physics, and the limited set of notions with which one would be left if one based scientific knowledge on nothing but the directly sensed facts themselves and what they logically imply. This reading of Hume convinced Einstein that modern physics is impossible unless certain concepts going beyond the observed facts are introduced speculatively and constructively and tested only indirectly by way of their deductive consequences.[18] Then it was not merely possible, but also methodologically proper, to replace Newton's theoretical assumptions with a different set from which Newton's theory derives logically as a special case, applying to certain of the experimental facts but not to all of them. In short, before Einstein had cleared up the problem raised by the Michelson-Morley experiment of 1885, the modern physicist not only found himself with a new philosophical theory of time and of space and of their relations to one another and to matter, but also with a new philosophical analysis of the complex nature of scientific method and the relation between its theoretical concepts and the observed data.

It was this enriched conception of scientific method which Underhill Moore introduced into sociological jurisprudence in order to provide not only the lawyer but also the sociologist with a trustworthy method for determining the living law of any culture. His use of this method was not born merely of the desire to ape physicists. There were reasons for it within the very nature of sociological jurisprudence itself. He reasoned that if the claim of sociological jurisprudence is correct it should provide a specific scientific method for determining what the living law is in an objective manner which is quite independent of the private preferences and enthusiasm for reform of the observer, and equally independent of the method used to determine the positive law. If it is to be of any practical use, it must also be applicable to the norms of social behavior near the Yale Law School on the streets of New Haven. Furthermore, if the living law has any relevance to the positive law, it ought to be possible, for example, by going into the banks of New Haven, New York, Pennsylvania and South Carolina, to determine the high-frequency order of the transactions between the people in these social institutions, and then to compare this normative order of the living law with that based upon the norms of the positive law to find out what this relevance is. In his earlier "institutional" studies, he used the common-sense terms of a merely inductive natural history science.[19] The results were sufficient to convince him in a rough way that the thesis of sociological jurisprudence was confirmed. He found, for example, in judicial disputes of three factually similar cases in commercial law appearing in the state courts of Pennsylvania, New York and South Carolina that the norms of the living law supported the judicial decisions of the three cases, in which two of the state courts gave the verdict one way and the third court gave it the opposite way. He became convinced, nevertheless, that the empirical method he had used involved too many intuitive judgments to be adequate as a method for sociological jurisprudence.

He then shifted his studies to car-parking habits of people on the streets of New Haven. He soon found that, when he allowed observers to use ordinary extemporized prose to describe such an apparently objective phenomenon, different observers failed to give similar descriptions of what occurred. This convinced Moore that extemporized prose will not do in sociological jurisprudence. By such means, in the name of the objective living law, a sociological investigator can smuggle in his own particular arbitrary normative preferences and prejudices. However human this may be, this clearly is not science, either social or legal. Thus, sociological jurisprudence itself called for the more philosophically subtle and conceptually precise scientific method which mathematical physics might provide.

A second consideration suggested the same conclusion. It has been noted that legal positivism identifies the legally just with the positive law. To say that anything is just is to say that it is either a statute of the legislature or a judicial decision or act which is in accordance with such a statute. From this it follows that there is no meaning in legal science for saying that the positive law is illegal or unjust.[20] Sociological jurisprudence has the merit of providing a criterion for judging the justice of the positive law. This is possible because of its extension of the subject matter of legal science from the positive law to the living law. This permits the sociological jurist to define good or just positive law as that positive law whose norms conform to the empirically determined objective norms of the living law. Positive law is bad when, with changes in the living law, the positive law, due to its principle of *stare decisis,* lags behind the evolving new norms of the living law.

Suppose, however, as was probably the case in Germany immediately before World War II, that the empirical study of its living law would reveal it to embody, with high statistical frequency, the norms of Hitler and his cohorts. Consider also the unanimous United States Supreme Court decision on segregation in education. The latter decision passed legal judgment not merely on the positive legislation, but also on the living law, of the Southern States. These considerations make it clear that an adequate legal science must provide a meaningful criterion for judging the legality of the living, as well as the positive, law. Can sociological jurisprudence do this?

Clearly, one cannot identify the criterion for judging today's living law with the "is" of today's living law itself. Such a procedure would make the "is" of the living law of Hitler's Germany or of the Southern States just.

Nevertheless, a sociological jurisprudential criterion suggests itself. This criterion is to identify the standard for measuring today's living law with the "is" of what tomorrow's living law is going to be. But if this criterion is to be scientifically specifiable, legal science must have a scientific method such that, given the objective determination of today's living law, this method enables one to deduce today what tomorrow's living law will be. This is precisely what the method of modern physics accomplishes. In Newton's physics, for example, given the positions and momenta of the masses of an isolated system today, the method and theory enable one to deduce what their positions and momenta will be tomorrow. This is the second consideration within sociological jurisprudence itself which led Moore to turn to the method of mathematical physics.

This method requires not merely inductive observation, experimentation and concrete operational definitions, but also abstract, axiomatically constructed, deductively formulated and indirectly verified theory. Moore went at least part way toward achieving a legal science with such a method by basing his sociological jurisprudence on the behavioristic psychology of Clark Hull,[21] which had been given a rigorous axiomaticized deductive formulation.[22]

When Underhill Moore's observers of car parking in New Haven described what they saw in terms of the concepts of this theory, they brought back similar reports of the situations which they observed. Thus, the first of the difficulties in traditional sociological jurisprudence — that of keeping the observer's subjective preference and normative prejudices out of his description of the living law — was removed. When, however, using the assumptions of this method and theory, Moore and his colleague Professor Charles C. Callahan attempted to find a mathematical formula connecting the present living law to the future living law, even for such a simple social phenomenon as car parking on the streets of New Haven, the theory did not give such a formula as a postulate or deduced theorem. Nor did Moore and Callahan succeed in finding even an empirically satisfactory formula.

It is one of the greatest tributes to Underhill Moore that he never fooled himself about what he did, confusing claims for sociological jurisprudence with its methodological achievements. He was one of the most honest men who ever lived, and, because of this honesty with respect to what he did achieve and what he did not achieve, he provides the touchstone for judging contemporary legal theory. His work showed that sociological jurisprudence did not have a method for judging the living law.

Since, as previously noted, most of the societies in the world today, including even the United States in the segregation case, are requiring their lawyers and judges to advise and pass legal judgment on both the positive and the living law, it appears, therefore, that contemporary legal science must embrace more than even legal positivism and sociological jurisprudence. One can no more get the criterion of the "ought" for judging the "is" of the living law out of the "is" of the living law of sociological jurisprudence than one can get the criterion of the "ought" for judging the "is" of the positive law out of the "is" of the positive law of legal positivism. In fact, there is a logical, as well as a methodological, block in the way. The logical difficulty is that the "ought" for judging the "is" of a particular subject matter cannot be found in the "is" of that subject matter itself. Sociological jurisprudence falls short when lawyers and judges are forced, as is the case today, to pass judgment on the "is" of the living law. Put positively, this means that legal science must affirm certain propositions to be true independently of and logically antecedent to both the positive law and the living law.

The problem, however, is to give methodological and objectively verifiable content to this thesis. The only factor in human experience and scientific knowledge fulfilling this condition is nature and natural man; that is, those facts in human experience, present in any society or culture, which are not the result of the beliefs of man and their deeds as directed by these beliefs. The thesis that there are scientifically verifiable theories of such facts and that such theory provides a criterion for measuring both the positive and the living law is the distinguishing mark of natural law jurisprudence.

The doctrine of natural rights of the Declaration of Independence and of the Bill of Rights as interpreted by the Courts before the advent of Thayer's legal positivism is one example of such a philosophy of natural law — the philosophy, namely, of Jefferson, who wrote the Declaration of Independence and who, because he was as fearful of a tyranny of the legislature as he was of a tyranny of the executive or the judiciary, insisted on a mixed form of government and upon adding a Bill of Rights to the Constitution.[23] To Jefferson's natural law jurisprudence we shall return in the sequel.

The limitations of the sociological jurisprudence of Underhill Moore showed in one other way. His grounding of it in the deductively formulated behavioristic psychology of Hull required a spatio-temporal description of the objective movements of every individual in a given social system in order to determine the living law of that system at a given moment. This was practical for the car parkings in a few blocks on the streets of New Haven. It is quite impractical for specifying the living law of 350,000,000 people in contemporary India. Thus, even for determining the "is" of the living law, to say nothing about providing a criterion for judging its justice and for reforming it, his method for sociological jurisprudence is inadequate.

Nonetheless, even with the method of natural law jurisprudence, a more adequate method for determining the living law of sociological jurisprudence is required. Otherwise the lawyer does not appreciate the living habits and customs of the people which must be reckoned with in an effective application of new positive law, or new natural law principles of reform, to a given people. There are reasons for believing that contemporary cultural anthropology and the philosophy of culture have found the required method for determining the living law of sociological jurisprudence.

Ehrlich defined the living law as "the inner order of the associations" of people in a society. Put more concretely, this means that the social norms with which law is dealing are not determined by any particular fact or factor in human experience, such as man's economic needs, his sexual desires or his physical power, but with the way in which all these and other facts are related and put together. It is not any particular fact, but the "inner order" of all the facts, that constitutes the living law. Ehrlich's "inner order," let it be recalled, is equivalent to what anthropologists call the "pattern" of a culture. Professor A. L. Kroeber, speaking for anthropologists generally, notes also that "values . . . are intimately associated with the most basic and implicit patterning of the phenomena of culture." [24]

The words "pattern" and "inner order" are, however, metaphors; they do not refer to concrete facts, nor are they scientific concepts with a literal meaning in isolation. The pattern of a culture is hardly something concrete which one can observe after the manner in which one sees the terrain of a river valley from an airplane. At best, the words "pattern" and "inner order" are incomplete symbols. Hence, the scientific method of determining the inner order or the pattern of a culture must be complex; it cannot be that of direct observation, even though empirical observation of a people and their culture is obviously required. What is this complex method? Anthropological science provides the answer to this question, as does independent work in the comparative philosophy of the world's cultures.

Anthropologists first thought, after the manner of those legal realists who rejected theory for the empirical study of cases, that the method of anthropological science consisted merely in going into the field to live with a particular people or tribe and to observe what one sees and hears. After many years of such observing and the writing of scientific reports, a few anthropologists suddenly awoke to the fact that they had been misunderstanding the facts which they observed and described. They discovered, moreover, that this occurred because they had been describing and conceiving of what they saw the native people doing in concepts brought to the observed facts by the anthropologist himself, instead of in the way these facts were thought of and, hence, understood and ordered by the native people. Paul Radin among the first and Professor Clyde Kluckhohn later discovered that in order to specify objectively the living norms and customs of a people, empirical anthropology has to determine their basic mentality. When Professor Kluckhohn did this for his Navaho, he found himself confronted with a complete Navaho philosophy.[25] The anthropologist Professor Cornelius Osgood found also that he had to attend even to the epistemology of the native people's way of knowing anything.[26] It is any people's sharing of their particular philosophical way of describing, ordering, integrating and anticipating the raw facts of their experience which makes their culture and its living and positive law what it is. Professor Hoebel comes to a similar conclusion in his study of seven different primitive peoples and their significantly different living laws. Methodologically he finds also that anthropological science and comparative sociological jurisprudence, in determining the pattern or living law of a given people or culture, must combine inductive observation of their features, ceremonies and behavior with a deductive specification of their common philosophical assumptions, these common assumptions differing from culture to culture and from tribe to tribe.[27] Studies in the comparative philosophy of the world's cultures lead to the same conclusion.[28] It appears, therefore, that not only are the basic and most pressing problems of contemporary law philosophical as well as scientific in character, but even the scientific method of sociological and anthropological jurisprudence is itself philosophical, being, in part at least, the method of the philosophy of culture.

It is not merely with respect to the general theoretical and methodological assumptions of its science that contemporary law faces inescapable philosophical problems and tasks. Philosophical issues appear also in technical portions of the positive law itself. Brief consideration of some recent decisions of the Sureme Court of the United States will make this clear.

It has been noted that the government of the United States is a mixed government and that the theory of law of its founding fathers was that of a natural rights and a natural law philosophy. According to this theory, certain things are true before the legislature, the courts or the executive come into existence. Hence, these truths, expressed in the Declaration of Independence and the Bill of Rights, provide principles for the courts to use in judging legislative statutes as to their justice or injustice and even for judging the living law from which these positive legislative statutes derive.

Jefferson tells us that his three gods were Bacon, Newton and Locke.[29] The presence of Newton in this trinity indicates that Jefferson drew from the theory of the natural philosopher as well as that of the social scientist and humanist for the criterion of his legal, moral, political and even religious thinking. The philosophy of nature and natural man as well as the philosophy of society and cultural man is functioning in his criterion of the morally good and the legally just.

For our present purposes, the most significant person in Jefferson's trinity is Locke. It was Locke who gave the natural law philosophy of Jefferson and our founding fathers its particular modern content. In his classic treatise *Of Civil Government,* Locke affirms that the sole justification of the existence of government is the preservation of the property of the individual.[30] In reading this statement today we must remember that he meant by "property" man's own body and person as well as what man has achieved by applying his labor to the God-given materials of nature. In short, Locke's concept of property includes personal rights, as well as property rights in the narrower sense. From this theory of government, Locke draws the conclusion that it would be a contradiction in terms for the government to take any property away from the individual, since the sole justification for the existence of government is the preservation of the property of the individual.[31]

Here we have a philosophy of government and law which provides a basis for judicial review of legislative statutes and for the interpretation of the Bill of Rights, not, after the manner of Judge Hand and the legal positivists, as merely "admonitions to forbearance" or "counsels of perfection" to the electorate and the legislators, but as legal principles to be used by the courts to judge the justice and legality of the statutes of the states and of Congress. Any legislation, regardless of the size of the majority behind it, which takes away from the individual any of the personal or property rights specified in the Declaration of Independence and in the Bill of Rights, violates the *raison d'être* of the legislature's very existence and, hence, is illegal. The dissents of Justices Black and Douglas in the Feinberg Law case [32] make such an argument and, hence, require such a natural rights philosophy for their justification. Undoubtedly, it was a natural law philosophy with Lockean and Jeffersonian content with respect to property rights that convinced the judges of the so-called "Old" Supreme Court of their rectitude in using the "due process" clause of the Bill of Rights to declare majority-approved social legislation unconstitutional.

Similarly, as noted above, it is the rejection of any natural law jurisprudence, whether of Locke, Jefferson, Blackstone or St. Thomas, by (*a*) the American legal realists and (*b*) Thayer and his Harvardian legal positivists that not merely freed, but also required, the New Court to depart from the precedents of the past and to declare the new social legislation legal. If, as legal positivism affirms, law is the will of the legislature as sole, undivided and unlimited sovereign, then the law of contradiction appears with new content, and it becomes self-contradictory to declare a legislative statute illegal. [33]

Curiously, not to say paradoxically, Justice Douglas, who presupposes a natural rights and natural law philosophy in his dissent in the Feinberg Law case, appeals to Thayer and legal positivism in justification of his position with the majority of the Justices on the new social legislation. [34] But if legal positivism is correct, then his dissent in the Feinberg Law case is an error, since according to legal positivism the content of the sovereign legislature's will as expressed in its statutes — whether they refer to social legislation or to personal rights is irrelevant — is the sole criterion of what is legal. The fact that it is the sovereign's will is all that matters.

The main point in this reference to Justice Douglas is not to point up the foregoing inconsistency. It should be evident at this point in this paper that no one has a single consistent theory of law that is adequate for all its needs and cases. As Justice Holmes noted, life is bigger than any legal theory. The point, instead, is to show that even a particular branch of positive law itself, namely, United States constitutional law, exhibits a problem which is inescapably philosophical in character, the philosophical issue, namely, between the philosophy of natural rights and natural law which Justices Black and Douglas and our founding fathers believe an adequate legal protection of life's civil liberties requires and the positivistic philosophy of law which these two Justices and the majority of the present Court believe an effective democratic solution of life's social problems calls for.

Let no one suppose that Justices Douglas and Black are the only people for whom this philosophical problem is real. Consider what happens, assuming a judge guided by legal positivism, if the majority in the legislature pass a statute making it a crime for an individual dissenter to practice his particular religious faith and convictions. Even Justice Frankfurter, notwithstanding his Harvardian and Oxfordian legal positivism, finds it difficult to stay with its implications at this point, as his dissent in the Feinberg Law case, even though on positivistic procedural grounds, shows.[35] Yet if, as legal positivism affirms, justice is equated with the will of the undivided sovereign, then whatever the will of the legislature is, whether its statutes refer to personal or to property rights, the legislative statute is just. The question, therefore, cannot be escaped: What is going to happen to American civil liberties, to the supposedly basic and inalienable rights of freedom of worship and freedom of scientific, philosophic, political or religious belief, if the positivistic legal philosophy, to which the present Supreme Court appeals to justify its decisions on social legislation, increases its hold upon legal education and lawyers and judges generally?

Consider also the recent unanimous decision on segregation in education. Insofar as there were any legislative statutes affecting the case, they were those of the Southern States which, if the legal positivist's identification of the legally just with a legislative statute be true, made segregation in education just in those States. Furthermore, Congress had provided the federal courts with no federal legislative statute making educational segregation in the positive or living law of any state a crime. Consequently, had the Supreme Court's Justices consistently applied the positivistic legal philosophy which they use to justify their decision on social legislation, they would have had to conclude that insofar as there was any law or justice relevant to the case, it was that of the Southern State legislatures, and that insofar as any federal court is concerned, since there is no federal legislative statute making segregated education in the positive or living law of any state a crime, the Supreme Court of the United States, or any other federal court, has no jurisdiction in the case. In short, the positivistic philosophy of law to which a majority of the Justices appeal to justify their decisions on social legislation is incompatible with their unanimous decision on segregation in education.

The situation is better, but still unsatisfactory, if one considers this decision from the standpoint of the sociological philosophy of law. An examination of the original living law of this country and of its Southern component enables us, at least, to understand what has happened — namely, the general approval of the decision from the country as a whole and the bitterness with respect to it in the Southern States.

New England was founded in major part by non-conformist Protestants who came to the western hemisphere to escape from the rule of the religious majority in Europe and who, like Jefferson, were heavily under the influence of the philosophy of natural rights and natural law of Locke.[36] With the opening of the frontier, this living law spread to the Middle West and the Far West. It is exceedingly unlikely that legal positivism has seeped down from Thayer to the masses to a sufficient extent to alter this original and basic philosophy of American culture. The coming of Roman Catholics in large numbers brought in a natural law philosophy also. These two portions of the living law of the United States constitute a statistical majority of the people. Sociological jurisprudence tells us that when a positive legal decision has such qualitative and quantitative support from the living law it can come into being and be effective. Hence, this legal philosophy enables us to understand why, even though there was no positive federal legislative statute on the matter, the unanimous decision of the United States Supreme Court has occurred without a bitter reaction from the majority of the people.

In the Southeastern States, however, an additional, quite different living law came into being through the founders of the Virginia Company and their blood and cultural descendants who spread out to the South and Southwest. The English scholar Mr. Peter Laslett has recently shown that this living law derives from the *Patriarcha* of Sir Robert Filmer,[37] instead of from Locke and Jefferson. According to this patriarchal ethics and law, good government is government by the first families, and a good educational system is one modeled after seventeenth-century Episcopal Oxford and Cambridge — a system in which the best education goes to those carrying the greatest familial and social responsibility, namely sons rather than daughters, the eldest son rather than the younger son because of primogeniture and, with few exceptions, the sons of the first families only. Equality of education for all, regardless of status and blood of birth, is foreign to the political, legal and educational ideals of such a society. Jefferson's Lockean democratic egalitarianism modified this aristocratic patriarchal Filmerian living law of the South, but it never removed it.

Sociological jurisprudence tells us that when a positive law decision resting on one norm conflicts with living law norms to the contrary, the positive law tends to be ineffective. The Prohibition Amendment is an example. Hence, the bitterness in parts of the South at the Supreme Court's decision.

Thus, although the sociological philosophy of law explains how the Supreme Court decision could occur without a federal legislative statute and indicates that it will have support from the country as a whole, it must also affirm that the decision is not law so far as the living law of the South is concerned. At the very least, a lawyer or judge guided solely by sociological jurisprudence might well have counseled living law changes from below rather than a positive law decision from above.

It appears, therefore, as with the dissents of Justices Black and Douglas in the Feinberg Law case, that the only philosophy of law which will justify the unanimous Supreme Court decision in the segregation-in-education case is one which affirms that legal science contains certain principles that are true independent of and antecedent to the positive or the living law, and that any positive legislative statute or living law custom which violates these principles is illegal. But, as noted above, the traditional philosophy of natural law of the United States is that of Locke, Jefferson, Blackstone and Baldwin. This theory of law produced the Old Court and would probably require the present Court to follow old precedents in declaring recent social legislation to be unconstitutional.

Again we see how positive legal decisions of one and the same set of Justices in one and the same Supreme Court exhibit inescapable philosophical issues and problems. In fact, on any existent theory of legal science, it is very difficult to make the specific decisions of the present Supreme Court of the United States on social legislation, civil liberties and segregation in education lie down consistently together.

Hence, the most pressing issue confronting positive American constitutional law and liberal democratic institutions generally is at bottom a philosophical as well as a legal problem. This problem is nothing less than that of so reconstructing the theoretical and methodological assumptions of legal science that a judge of scientific integrity will be free to allow the new social legislation, without which democracy will fail, to stand, while at the same time not so tying the hands of the judge that by default of jurisdiction he will fail to protect the natural rights and civil liberties of individuals without which, also, there is neither liberty nor democracy.

The foregoing analysis suggests that a natural law jurisprudence with a content different from that of Locke and our Founding Fathers is required for such an undertaking. Even so, if this new philosophy of natural law ignores the living law of sociological jurisprudence, it will fail. Similarly, a sociological jurisprudence which does not implement itself through a reconstruction of the positive law will betray mankind also by failing to bring the available living cultural and moral resources of the world to bear upon the peaceful resolution of the disputes of men and nations. In an atomic age, such a failure is a serious thing.

Law is, indeed, a complex subject — more complex than any traditional theory has supposed. It has at least three parts, each with its particular scientific and philosophical method: (1) positive law, (2) living law and (3) natural law.

In the Anglo-American common law world the scientific method for studying the positive law is inductive generalization, of the natural history type, from particular cases and statutes, combined with the elucidation of the resulting legal concepts by the method of contemporary analytic philosophy. The latter philosophical method is required because the most important legal concepts are incomplete symbols. In the civil law tradition of the Continental European nations, Scotland, Quebec and Louisiana, the method of determining the positive law is different. Instead of beginning with individual cases and applying to them the method of classification and case-by-case inductive generalization of the natural history type of scientific procedure, the civil law must be approached, in most, at least, of its parts, with the deductively formulated theory of the method and mentality of mathematical physics as one's model.[38] Our earlier references to Professor Sturges remind us that there is a third type of positive law with its still different method. Treating each dispute as unique, it dispenses with legislative statutes, legal principles and litigation, to settle disputes by the methods of arbitration and mediation.[39] This was the preferred method of positive legal procedure in classical Confucian China. Gandhi turned to it in his South African period.[40] With the present vogue of philosophical existentialism, nominalism and ethical subjectivism, accompanied by the increasing influence of Asia with its anti-litigational, mediational ethic of peace-making, this positive legal method is likely to take on increasing importance in the days to come.

The scientific method for determining the living law is that of deductively formulated and indirectly verified theory, as used in contemporary cultural anthropology and the comparative philosophy of the world's cultures. The scientific method of natural law jurisprudence is that of the philosophy of the scientifically verified theories of natural science, including psychology, when the latter science restricts itself to those facts about man that are logically antecedent to, and independent of, the cultural differences between men. Those psychological facts that are culturally relative belong to social psychology and to sociological jurisprudence, not to the psychology of natural man and to natural law jurisprudence.

Clearly, contemporary law is a challenging subject. Its challenge, moreover, appears to be inescapably philosophical with respect to both theory and method.

IV

Cultural Values and Recent Legal Theory

CONTEMPORARY legal science provides a convenient basis for giving an inventory of representative anthropological theories of cultural values. Law, like personal ethics, is concerned with norms. Since norms express the ethos of a culture, different theories of legal norms take one to the heart of the problem of cultural values.

Roughly contemporary legal theories of cultural norms fall into five groups: (1) Anglo-American legal positivism, (2) pragmatic legal realism, (3) neo-Kantian and intuitive ethical jurisprudence, (4) functional anthropological or sociological jurisprudence and (5) naturalistic jurisprudence. Each group contains different subspecies and varieties.

Legal Positivism

Legal positivism is the theory that cultural norms of justice are to be found and understood solely in terms of the positive legal constitutions, statutes, codes and institutions themselves, perhaps supplemented by police power or force. The main representative of this theory of legal values is the British jurist, John Austin. The designation of his legal philosophy as "positivism" is not an accident. It arises from the fact that this is the legal theory of traditional Anglo-American culture and that the philosophy of this culture is British empiricism, which is positivistic in its theory of scientific knowledge. Cul-

Reprinted from *Anthropology Today: An Encyclopedic Inventory*, prepared by A. L. Kroeber, by permission of the University of Chicago Press. Copyright 1953 by The University of Chicago.

tural values are positivistic in character when the meaning of the words "good" or "valuable" is given as a particular, inductively through the senses. This excessive emphasis on induction has the consequence also of making each science an independent science. Hence the restriction of legal education in any culture whose values are positivistic, such as modern England and the recent United States, to nothing but the positive institutions, statutes, codes and decisions contained in the books in the law school libraries. No further study of the relation of law to society is required. Law, like ethics, on this positivistic theory of cultural values, is an autonomous science; knowledge of economics, sociology or anthropology is quite unnecessary. To this Austin added the necessity of police power or force to give the law its sanction. The decisions and the constitutional norms were not law unless police power was added. Here again a factor derived from British empirical philosophy entered, namely the materialistic power politics philosophy of Hobbes.

Our designation of the first theory of cultural values in our inventory has revealed an additional fact. This theory is not merely culture-bound but also philosophy-bound. It holds only for that portion of Anglo-American culture which derives from an inconsistent combination of the positivistic British philosophy of Locke's *Essay Concerning Human Understanding* and the non-positivistic power politics realism and materialism of Hobbes.

Pragmatic Legal Realism

The contents of this paper were first presented at the international conference of anthropologists called in New York in 1952 by the Wenner-Gren Foundation for Anthropological Research to attempt an inventory of anthropological science. In a typically culture-bound manner, the American anthropologists who framed the program placed the inventory of the world's cultural values under the American pragmatic philosophical category "Problems of Process." This is an anthropological illustration of the legal philosophy called American legal realism.

According to this theory cultural values are not given in the positive legal norms used to decide in a given dispute whether the conduct involved is to be permitted or prohibited; these norms of decision, the constitutional codes and statutes, are, instead, merely instruments for social change. Thereby positive legal norms and cultural values are transformed from ends into means. Furthermore, instead of the positive cultural norm, as expressed in a code, statute or constitutional principle, being the measure of the conduct, the solution of the dispute is made the measure of the norm. If traditional norms prevent disputes from being resolved or merely generate new disputes when they are applied, then they are instrumentally demonstrated to be bad. "Problems of Process" become the key to cultural values. At bottom, what this means is that cultural values center not in norms or propositions but, instead, in the problematic situation presented by men in society and in the process which brings the diverse competing and conflicting items in the social situation to a synthesis which produces an "equilibrium." The word "synthesis" is not a misnomer in this connection, since this legal and anthropological theory derives from the American philosopher, John Dewey. The last philosopher to influence Dewey before he created his instrumental pragmatism was Hegel.

It is not irrelevant to point out that the Yale Law School has been a center of this theory of law and that when students with law degrees, coming recently from Continental European law schools, are confronted with this legal philosophy for the first time, they are shocked. The shock arises not merely from the conflict with their European training but also because they come from areas where dictators have been rampant, and they fear a theory of law which makes cultural values an instrument of the decision-maker rather than a constitutional control of him. In any event, we see that the problems of process theory of cultural values is both culture- and philosophy-bound. This theory is seriously considered largely in the United States and derives from its pragmatic instrumental philosophy.

At bottom, this theory of cultural values makes the solution of the problem in what Dewey calls "the problematic situation" the criterion of the good. Or, to put the matter more practically, it makes the bringing to equilibrium of the diverse competing elements in the social situation the criterion of the good and of cultural value. But with a dictator in the social situation and with law made his instrument rather than a fixed norm to control him and with equilibrium made more easy by dictatorial than by democratic parliamentarian methods, what factor is there in this pragmatic instrumental theory of cultural values to insure that the cheap and easy way to the resolution of the problematic situation will not be taken?

The answer to this question as given by Dewey himself in his *Human Nature and Conduct* is that only that solution is a "true" solution which results from sensitivity to, rather than dictatorial blotting out of, all factors and interests in the problematic situation. This amounts, however, to the admission (*a*) that all values are not in process and (*b*) that there must be at least one constant non-instrumental norm even in an instrumental philosophy of cultural norms, the non-instrumental norm of objective sensitivity to every factor in the existential situation.

Even if this be granted, certain questions remain. To read the literature of the American proponents of this theory is to move in an aura of optimism. Values in process and problem-solving become uncritically identified with "progress." In Europe and Asia, to set norms and values in flux is all too often to create problems rather than to solve them and to produce demoralization and confusion rather than "progress," whatever that vague word may mean. In short, to the members of older cultures, this "problem of process" instrumental philosophy of cultural values has an aura of optimism which makes it seem artificial and unmindful of the stubbornness of normative problems in giving way to a solution.

The outstanding fact of our contemporary world is that its problematic international situation is characterized by conflicts between rival ideologies which are logically incompatible and hence not resolvable by the facile injunction to be sensitive to all the factors in the situation. Moreover, one major nation in the world has its explicit answer to the present problematic situation. Merely to counter with emphasis on problem-solving is not enough. The situation calls for a specification of what the answer is. But to specify an answer will be to specify the cultural norms according to which the decision-maker must operate. Again one has norms controlling the politician and the judge rather than norms which are merely his instruments. Moreover, the question arises: What are the specific norms which solve the problem in the contemporary international problematic situation? To answer this question, it is necessary to go beyond instrumental pragmatism and legal realism.

Even so this theory of cultural values has been necessary. We are

living in a world in which the traditional norms are being recon-
structed or giving place to new. Pragmatic legal realism is the necessary instrument for breaking from those values of one's past which
are outmoded.

Neo-Kantian and Intuitive Ethical Jurisprudence

The ethical jurisprudence of modern Continental legal theorists
derives from Kant and the modification of his philosophy which is
called neo-Kantianism. Kelsen is its leading contemporary representative. The ethical jurisprudence of contemporary Anglo-American
jurists derives from the British empirical philosopher G. E. Moore.
The late Morris and Felix Cohen are its most able proponents in law.

All these moral and legal philosophers have one assumption in
common concerning the nature of cultural values. This assumption is
that values always involve an "ought" which cannot be derived from
any "is." Put positively, this means that the basic norm of a culture
cannot be found empirically but must be assumed *a priori* as the presupposition of any ethical or legal judgment whatever. Empiricism in
cultural or legal science merely gives the materials to which the value
judgment refers, but not the value norm itself, according to this theory. The difference between Kelsen and the intuitionists centers
merely in the degree to which the *a priori* ethical "ought" of a society, which Kelsen calls "imputation," applies to the legal and social
order as a whole. For Kelsen most of the law is given inductively in
positive legal codes and statutes, as with the British legal positivist
Austin. To these codes and statutes of positive law, Kelsen adds but
one *grundnorm,* which is basically ethical and *a priori* in character.
This *grundnorm* is the *a priori* assumption that the positive laws given
inductively ought to be obeyed. It is, according to Kelsen, only because of this "ought," given as an ethical *a priori* and applied to the
concrete case imputatively, that the judge has the authority to use the
inductively given positive law to send a violator of the law to the electric chair. Kelsen believes that the codes themselves do not give this
"ought." With the Anglo-American intuitionists, on the other hand,
not merely one solitary *grundnorm* as the background and basis of
the inductively given positive law but every proposition and statute in
the entire positive law and in every instance of its application in-

volves a continuous exercise by the judge of the moral judgment. In short, whereas the ethical jurisprudence of the Continental Europeans is merely formal, that of the Anglo-Americans is substantive also.

That every culture is not merely the inductively given "is" of the behavior of the people in that culture but is also the culture itself, through its leaders, passing normative judgment upon that behavior in the light of certain norms which express an "ought" rather than a mere "is," cannot be denied. It is clear that man in society is not merely acting but also acting in the light of and under the control of both a personal and a social ought-to-be. There is, to be sure, the "is" of social action, but this "is," if scientifically complete, includes the behavior of the murderer as well as the behavior of those who do not violate the ethos of the society. Clearly, therefore, the "ought" which defines the ethos is true at best only of a part of what is and thus requires something more than the "is" of a culture for its own definition. To this extent, the ethical jurists are right when they say that a scientific account of cultural values cannot be determined in any given society by the inductive description of the observable "is" of that society. Otherwise, any behavior whatever in that society would be good, and there would be no need whatever for norms, legal institutions and the citizen's sense of having to reconcile what he can do inductively with what he ought to do. Upon this point everyone, including even the instrumental pragmatists when they resort to sensitivity to all the factors in the problematic situation, must agree. The cultural "ought" for any society is not to be identified with its inductively given "is."

Kant's ethical jurisprudence had one other characteristic: No conduct is ethical, embodying an "ought," unless it is the kind of conduct which can be generalized for all men in the form of a determinate, universal law. This is the point of Kant's categorical imperative. It is as old as the Stoic Roman legal and the Roman Catholic Christian thesis that moral, just and religious man is universal man, rather than patriarchal (or matriarchal) family, or color-of-skin biologically bred and genealogically defined tribal man.

Thus modern Kantian *a priori* ethical jurisprudence holds a thesis in common with classical Greek and Roman Stoic natural law jurisprudence. Both affirm that moral man and just man is universal man.

By this they mean that to be moral and to stand for the ethos of one's culture that ought to be, is to stand for certain determinate commandments, codes or principles which are such that, if anyone appeals to them as the justification of his own conduct, then he is obligated to accept their validity for any human being whatever. Any society which takes as its ethos the thesis that all men are equal under the law is one holding this moral and legal philosophy of cultural values.

This concept of cultural values has its basis in a particular conception of the method of scientific knowledge, namely the method of deductively formulated scientific theory. The reason for this is that in such a scientific method no fact is ever supposed to be anything more than an enigma yet to be scientifically accounted for, if it is given merely inductively. Before it can take on the status of a scientific fact, it must, according to this deductive theory of scientific method, be embodied in a deductively formulated theory. In other words, it must be shown to be an instance of a universal, determinate law. It is not an accident that Kelsen's neo-Kantian theory of positive law is that of a deductively formulated theory or that Kant, who is the author of the categorical imperative, was a physicist and philosopher of the deductively formulated mathematical physics of Galilei and Newton before he wrote his moral and legal philosophy. In fact, it is only in Kant's philosophy of mathematical physics, with its theory of any individual thing as an instance of a determinate universal law, that he can find the cognitive epistemological basis for his categorical imperative.

This theory of cultural values as things expressed in terms of determinate statutes and laws is also culture-bound. It characterizes the entire legal history of the Western world since the creation of Western law by the Roman Stoic philosophers. This concept of law, these lawyers tell us, derived by way of Greek philosophy from Greek physics. In fact, it was in ancient Greek physics that, for the first time, men on this earth arrived at the conception of man and nature in which every individual event and thing is thought of as scientifically known only when it is embedded in an abstractly constructed, deductively formulated theory.

To be sure, before this there had been codes expressing the cultural values of different societies in the world, but these codes were not technically formulated. They were expressed in concrete, inductively given language and they were codes which restricted citizenship under the law to membership in a patriarchal joint family or to membership in a village community of elders or to membership in a blood-bound tribe or to some other variety of what Sir Henry Maine called a "law of status" society.

Only following the discovery by the ancient Greek mathematical physicists of a new way of knowing man and nature as an instance of universal laws having nothing to do with inductively given family or tribal relations did the concept of cultural values expressed in terms of abstractly constructed constitutions, interpreted by means of a technical legal terminology, arise. As the student of ancient law, Sir Henry S. Maine, has put the matter, the shift was made from "status to contract." The significance of his meaning becomes clear if we express it as the shift from inductively given genealogically defined familial or tribal status to theoretically constructed status under universal law in a deductively formulated, contractually conceived written or unwritten constitution or theory.

Upon this conception of cultural values as things expressed in universal, theoretically constructed, determinate laws, the Greek and Roman natural law jurists and Kantian ethical jurists are in agreement. Clearly also, a legal philosophy such as this is required to justify the unanimous decision of the Supreme Court of the United States with respect to desegregation in education, in *Brown v. Board of Education of Topeka* (349 *U. S. Supreme Court Reports* 294).

But this conception of cultural values is restricted largely to the cultures of the West and to Islam insofar as it has drawn on Greek science and philosophy. In pre-Western Confucian Chinese culture, for example, there are, to be sure, codes, but they are of the inductive, natural history, concrete type. Furthermore, they are used frequently only as a last resort. Instead of being the good way to settle disputes, required by the ethos of their culture, they are used only when the "first-best" way prescribed by the ethos of a Confucian culture is not accepted by the disputants. The proper procedure for dispute handling in a Confucian Chinese culture is not the recourse to codes, after the manner of the Western concept of justice, but the softening of the insistence upon codified rights through the intervention of a mediator. Again we see the degree to which any theory of cultural values is bound both to a given culture and to the philosophy of that culture.

Notwithstanding the correctness of their thesis that the "ought" expressed in the ethos of any culture cannot be identified with the inductively given "is" of the total behavior of people in that culture, Kelsen's ethical jurisprudence and the intuitive theory of G. E. Moore, with their absolute insistence upon the impossibility of deriving the "ought" from the "is," have turned out to be incomplete and at bottom inadequate. This becomes evident the moment a judge in any court tries to use either theory. To tell him that he has to use an "ought" and that this "ought" must have the property of being expressible as a universal law is of little use to him in deciding a case; for the decision turns around whether this determinate, universal, propositionalized "ought" is to have one substantive content rather than another. To be more precise, is it to be given the content of a laissez-faire, a nationalized Socialistic, a Thomistic Roman Catholic or a Communistic communal ethos? To such a crucial question neither Kelsen's nor G. E. Moore's and Felix Cohen's theory of ethical, legal and cultural science can give an answer. In practice, therefore, it leaves judicial decision completely relativistic and arbitrary. It also leaves anthropological legal and moral science generally with little to say with respect to the solution of the normative domestic and international conflicts of the contemporary world.

Anthropological or Sociological Jurisprudence

The essence of this jurisprudence is that a distinction must be drawn between the positive law and the living law. By "positive law" is meant the inductively given constitution, codes and institutions and cases of Austin's and Kelsen's positivistic jurisprudence. By "living law" is meant the underlying inner order of the behavior of people in society apart from the statutes, codes and cases of the positive law. The thesis of sociological jurisprudence is that the good norm for selecting the positive law to be used by the judge in making his decision is to be found by identifying it with the "inner order" of the "is" of the living law. Positive law is good if it corresponds to the underlying inner order of society as given by sociology or anthropology; it is bad if it does not so correspond. Since the inner order of society has content and varies often from one society to another, this theory of cultural values has the merit of giving to the judge who is operating his positive legal institutions a norm possessing content. He is not left with merely an abstract, vacuous, empty universal concept of justice after the manner of the follower of the ethical jurisprudence of Kelsen or G. E. Moore, or with the irreducible *grundnorm* of Kelsen's first positive legal constitution.

It is to be noted that this sociological jurisprudential theory completely rejects the thesis of Kant (as usually interpreted), Kelsen and G. E. Moore, that the "ought" can never be identified with any empirical "is." Sociological jurisprudence shows the sense in which the neo-Kantian doctrine is true and the sense in which it is false. The truth of the doctrine consists in the fact that the "ought" of the positive law cannot be derived from the "is" of the positive law. The mere fact of the Constitution of the United States, with its particular norms and positive legal institutions, is no justification for the "ought" of that Constitution and its institutions. Generalized, this means that the "ought" of a given subject cannot be derived from the "is" of that same subject. But it does not follow from this that the "ought" of positive law cannot be derived from the "is" of something else.

It is at this point that the *a priori* Kelsenian and the intuitive theory of moral and legal values committed the error which left it with nothing but an abstract, empty *a priori*. To get content, one must go to some subject matter. The pure abstract *a priori* notion of a universal norm or a simple unanalyzable ethical predicate "good" can never give specific content. Specific content, by its very nature, has to be provided by an "is" that is substantively determinate and hence empirical.

Nor does this present any difficulty. Clearly it produces a problem only for a person who insists upon restricting cultural values to an autonomous science of ethics or law. Then, clearly, the "ought" for the subject matter of that science cannot be identified with its "is" and the theory of Kelsen and G. E. Moore holds true. But why suppose that the ethical and legal character of society lives in a hothouse isolated from the rest of society and culture? Why assume that the positive law must be separated from the living law of the society to which it refers?

To put the matter positively, let us assume that positive law can be constructed in terms of universal norms with any specific substantive content which the imaginations of men can conceive. Clearly the "ought" for any one of these normative hypotheses cannot be derived from the positive hypothesis itself. Thus in this sense the impossibility of deriving the "ought" of the positive law from the "is" of any inductively given positive law holds. But this does not prevent the criterion of the "ought" for the positive law from being derived from the inductively given "is" of the inner order of the behavior of people in society, quite apart from any given present or proposed positive law.

Prohibition legislation in the United States some few decades ago provides an instance. This legislation was legally passed. Hence, so far as the positive law was concerned, it was an "is." It happened, however, that it failed to correspond to the living law habits of the people of the community. The practical consequence was that, instead of reforming the living law habits of the people, both (a) the administration of the positive law by the legal and political officials and (b) the morals of the people with respect to law became corrupted. Hence the Prohibition Amendment was repealed. In short, the "is" of positive law was measured against the "is" of living law and found wanting. Thus sociological and anthropological jurisprudence teaches us that any adequate theory of cultural values must both distinguish the "ought" from the "is" and identify the "ought" with the "is."

This presents no contradiction or difficulty whatever provided that one distinguishes between the different social manifestations of the "is"; one, the "is" of positive legal constitutions, codes and institutions, and the other, the "is" of the de facto inner order of the behavior of people in a specific society independent of the positive law. To identify the "is" of the positive law with its "ought" is clearly a fallacy. But this in no way prevents the definition of the "ought" of the positive law in terms of the "is" of the living law. Put more concretely, this means that that positive law ought to be which corresponds to the living law of the society to which it refers, and that positive law ought not to be which does not so correspond.

In practice, however, this sociological or anthropological jurisprudence and the anthropology and sociology of which it is the expression have turned out to be harder to put into practice than to write about in theory. This weakness is not discovered by the sociologists or anthropologists who hold the theory, since they never become the judges who have to apply it. In the Yale Law School, however, holders of this theory have been forced to bring it down to concrete application. One person who has done this is the late Professor Underhill Moore. In practice, he found few sociological or anthropological jurists who agreed upon what the "inner order" or "pattern" of a given culture is, which the judge is to use in judging the positive law. All too often, as Underhill Moore showed, they identified the inner order of the sociological "is" with their own particular, pet theory of political and social reform. One suspects also that the intuitive pattern which one anthropologist "finds" in Japanese culture might not be that found by another.

As a result, Underhill Moore found himself forced to determine the inner order of society of the sociological and anthropological "is," which the jurist is to use to judge whether his positive law universal norms are good or bad, by throwing away the intuitive, synoptic method of describing society of the traditional anthropologists and sociologists who emphasized pattern and by introducing an analytic objective method grounded in the behavioristic psychology of Professor Clark Hull. He did this because he found, when he used the traditional method, that no two observers describing the same social pattern came out with the same description. To overcome this difficulty of the classical anthropological and sociological theory of cultural values, he introduced purely objective spatio-temporal descriptive concepts. When this was done, he found that different observers gave the same account of the inner order of the social or cultural phenomenon which they were describing.

The details of his system will concern us later. Suffice it to say here that it consisted in defining the "inner order" of society as the high-frequency portion of the objectively observed spatio-temporal total behavior of society. This provided a truly objective criterion of the inner order of the sociological "is," which is to be used by the lawyer to judge whether the positive law ought or ought not to be. That positive law which corresponds to the high-frequency behavior of the total behavior of people in society is, on this theory of cultural values of sociological and anthropological jurisprudence, the positive law that ought to be; the positive law that does not so correspond is the one that ought not to be. We have in this theory, therefore, the thesis both that the "ought" of one kind of law — that is, positive law — cannot be derived from the "is" of that law, but can be derived from the "is" of the underlying, empirically determinable, living law of an anthropological or sociological jurisprudence which uses an analytic objective method.

Underhill Moore saw, however, that even this is not enough to provide an adequate theory of cultural values. It is necessary, but it is not sufficient. In any society it is necessary to judge and to reform not merely the positive law but also the high-frequency behavior which is the inner order of the underlying living law. This is easy to see in the case of a foreign culture. The fact that the Germans with an overwhelming, spontaneous enthusiasm embraced and followed Hitler in their living law behavior will not be taken by most social scientists as a scientific justification for the thesis that such high-frequency behavior and the cultural norms which it embodied ought to be. *Brown v. Board of Education* makes this clear in the contemporary legal experience of the people of the United States, as the Court's decision in this case requires a reformation in the living as well as the positive law of the Southern States. In short, just as it is necessary to judge the "is" of the positive law against an "ought" beyond itself, so also it is necessary to judge the high-frequency behavior which is the "is" of the living law against an "ought" beyond itself.

Moreover, any society is not merely expressing its high-frequency living law behavior but also reforming it. An adequate theory, therefore, of contemporary legal and cultural experience must provide meaning for judging the "is" of the living law to be bad or in need of reform. This calls for something beyond the living law itself. At this point, therefore, anthropological and sociological jurisprudence points beyond itself. The "is" which it provides cannot pass the judgment which must be passed upon itself. Beyond society and culture, only one thing remains, namely nature.

Naturalistic Jurisprudence

The thesis of naturalistic jurisprudence is that, just as the positive law cannot find the meaning for its "ought" in the "is" which is the positive law itself but must be judged as to its "ought" against the "is" of the living law of anthropological and sociological jurisprudence, so similarly the living law of anthropological and sociological jurisprudence cannot find the criterion for its "ought" in the "is" which is the living law or pattern of culture itself but can be judged instead only from the standpoint of the "is" of something beyond itself, namely the inner order of nature as revealed by natural science. We have already found an illustration of this theory in the account of the concept of moral man as an instance of a universal law, as formulated by Roman Stoic lawyers and given to them through Greek philosophy by Greek natural science. Put more concretely, the theory is that, just as the "ought" for positive legal codes is the "is" of the inner order of society as specified by anthropological and sociological science, so the "ought" toward which this inner order of society is to be changed is the "is" of the empirically verifiable theory of the inner order of natural man and nature as determined by the philosophically analyzed and articulated, empirically verified knowledge of nature. It was, we have noted, the discovery by Greek mathematical physicists that true knowledge of any individual object or event involves understanding it as an instance of determinate universal laws in a deductively formulated theory that gave rise to the Western concept of moral and legal man as a citizen of nature rather than a citizen of a patriarchal joint family or of a tribe, which, in turn, generated Western Roman legal and religious universalism, with its thesis that all men, regardless of family, color, race or religion, are equal under the law. The favorable and vigorous initial response of the Roman Catholic Archbishop of Louisiana to the Supreme Court's decision on desegregation is interesting philosophically and anthropologically in this connection.

Roman Stoic legal universalism is something novel in the cultures of the world. Asian cultures, to be sure, also achieve universalism, but it is of a different kind, relating all men to nature by intuitive immersion rather than by technically constructed, contractually conceived constitutions and statutes in which all men are equal. Because this Asian way of conceiving nature is verified empirically, it is as much a scientific theory as are the theories of the West. Whether the moral or legal classics of a given culture do or do not describe its sages as physicists has little, if anything, to do with the question as to whether its values are verified by appeal to nature. The Chinese classics make little or no reference to scientists. Nevertheless, as Joseph Needham and Hu Shih have shown recently, the Chinese cultural values refer to nature for their source and verification.

A major consideration leading to a naturalistic theory of cultural values is the failure of recent attempts to find the "ought" for judging the high frequency of the living law of anthropological and sociological jurisprudence within the latter type of jurisprudence itself. Such attempts tried to identify the "ought" for judging today's scientifically determined inner order or pattern of culture with the "is" of tomorrow's inner order. To make such a theory succeed, it is necessary to be able today to determine what the inner order of tomorrow's society will be. For this an historical social determinism is necessary. This is the reason, for example, why the Marxist theory of cultural values employs and requires a deterministic theory of social evolution. Underhill Moore also attempted such a theory. Both attempts, however, fail, as Underhill Moore in his case recognized and as Chapters V and IX will show.

There are basic theoretical reasons why this must be the case. The attempt, therefore, to find the criterion for judging and reforming the inner order of today's society must be found in an "is" with content outside today's or tomorrow's society. This is why the sociological and anthropological theory of cultural values leads over inevitably into the naturalistic theory.

This does not mean that anthropology and sociology can be dispensed with. Quite the contrary. It means, instead, that there will be no adequate anthropological or sociological theory of cultural values and of the cultural methods for judging such values until anthropological and sociological science pays as much attention to the way members of any society know and conceptualize nature as it has given in the past to the inner order of the social relations and to the normative pattern of a culture. In fact, we shall find an essential connection to exist between a people's empirically testable theories of nature and the substantive normative content of their living and positive law. Upon this connection depends the fate of normative cognitivism and hence of scientific method in ethics, politics and law.

Some sociological and anthropological scientists have recently come upon some evidence in support of such a conclusion. It will be fruitful to approach their work from that of the sociologist of law, Underhill Moore. His method of determining the inner order of society even at the present time, T_1, of the system, by observing the spatio-temporal total high-frequency behavior of people in society is unworkable for a total culture. He applied it to simple cultural phenomena such as parking on a restricted block on a street in New Haven, Connecticut. To determine the inner order of the behavior of 400,000,000 Chinese in this manner is out of the question, and to do it for all the different cultures is even more impracticable. The same is roughly true of most of the other inductive methods of other schools of anthropological and sociological science, since they tend to be either so intuitive in their methods for determining the inner order of society that there is, as Underhill Moore noted, not sufficient agreement between them on what it is, or else their methods are so inductively piecemeal that the inner order of any society, culture or legal system as a whole is not exhibited.

At this point the cultural anthropology of Kluckhohn is exceedingly important. He found in his study of the Navaho Indians that no amount of inductive observation, however complete, gave him an understanding of their value system or their legal norms. It was not until he conceptualized the inductive facts which he saw in terms of the concepts which the Navahos themselves used to conceptualize these facts that their cultural values became evident and that the legal norms which they used for settling disputes followed logically and naturally. Furthermore, he found that, when their concepts were brought out into the open, he had a complete philosophy on his hands. Without this philosophy, the facts which he saw were not understood as the Navaho understood them, and the norms which they use for settling disputes were not grasped, nor did they make sense.

Sorokin found the same thing earlier in sociology. He showed that the inner order which defines the de facto living law of any society is determined by the philosophy of the people in that society. This is the point of Sorokin's thesis that causality in the cultural sciences is logico-meaningful rather than merely mechanical as in natural science. The meanings which its people bring to the raw data of their experience are what determine the inner order or pattern of any particular culture. In fact, there are no objective bonds between people observable from an airplane which give their culture a pattern. The word "pattern" is merely a figure of speech. Only when many people conceptualize the raw data of their experience with the same basic, consistently related concepts — that is, the same philosophy — does an "inner order" between them and what they do and create arise.

In other words, norms arise from knowledge and knowledge involves conceptualizing and propositionalizing the experience that is known. Now, philosophy is nothing but the name for the basic minimum and complete number of consistent concepts and propositions necessary to conceptualize the inductive data of experience. It appears, therefore, that the values of a culture are the fruits or application of living according to the basic philosophical assumptions used by a people in conceptualizing the raw data of their experience.

In short, the inner order of a given society is put upon an objectively determinable basis only when anthropological and sociological scientists not merely observe in the field as many facts as possible but also discover the philosophy used by the people in the culture in question to conceptualize those facts. If, moreover, as in the Hindu and Muslim communities in a village of India, two different philosophies are used, then to that extent one is confronted with two cultures rather than one.

It may be asked immediately: But how can one determine the philosophy of a culture in an objective way? To this the answer is twofold. First, the philosophy of the Navaho discovered and specified by Kluckhohn involves concepts quite foreign to those of the non-Navaho American culture from which he came. In this sense the philosophy of a culture other than one's own is surprisingly objective. Second, most cultures have their philosophy already present objectively in the basic treatises of the culture. Those of pre-Western Chinese philosophy are objectively present in the classics of Confucius and Mencius. Chiang Monlin has recently shown, through a description of his own childhood, the degree to which this Confucian philosophy infiltrated every nook and cranny of his early life. It appears, therefore, that an objective, workable anthropological and sociological science which can define the inner order or ethos of any culture must be not merely inductive with respect to the facts but also inductive with respect to the philosophical concepts used by the people in the society being studied for the conceptualization of those facts. In short, scientific anthropology and sociology must be an empirically verified, philosophical sociology and anthropology.

Kluckhohn and others demonstrate also that the inductive method must be that which supplements mere induction with deductively formulated theory. This is necessary because philosophical anthropology and sociology exhibit different cultures as different postulate sets for conceptualizing the raw data of experience.

But this philosophical sociological and anthropological science of cultural values leads to natural law jurisprudence and the philosophy of natural science as a criterion of cultural values. This comes out when Sorokin and Kluckhohn reveal that the concepts which the people in a given society use to define their legal and ethical norms and to generate their creatively constructed values arise from and are essentially connected with their inductive, empirically verified theories for conceptualizing nature.

If, for example, in the conceptualization of merely natural facts, quite apart from cultural and social phenomena, a people restricts itself only to those meanings given through the senses, then the cultural values of that people tend to be those of what Sorokin calls "a sensate culture." If, on the other hand, in the conceptualization of natural phenomena it resorts to what we today call "constructs" or to what Plato and Aristotle called "ideas" which are universals — that is, to concepts of individuals which have no meaning apart from universal scientific laws or postulates — then a people tends to free itself from family — or tribally — centered values of the more natural history mode of knowing nature of a more sensate or of a more Asian intuitive culture. Similarly, Florence Kluckhohn, in her attempt to obtain a scientific principle for classifying the diverse cultural values of the many different cultures, finds herself forced to use the concepts of space and of time. Now, these concepts are clearly concepts of natural science. More concrete examples can be given if one approaches nature restricting one's self largely to what is given purely impressionistically, or by what Chiang Monlin, describing Chinese mentality, calls "naïve observation." Then what impresses one is the sequence from darkness of night through dawn to the brightness of day, through dusk to the blackness of night again, the sequence of the seasons and of the cycles of human existence. Thus one is led by one's empirically verified, and hence scientific, theory to a cyclical theory

of time, in which time is regarded, not as something made quanita-
tively exact by astronomical measurements and calculations, but as
something intuitively and impressionistically vague. Then appoint-
ments are rarely kept in social relations with the precision that occurs in the United States. Also this impressionistic cyclical theory of
time in nature tends also to make the improvement of society point-
less, since reform and improvement merely hasten the time when
what is different from today becomes identical with what one has
today.

This inevitable intrusion of the empirically verified concepts of nature used by a people into their values and norms for culture appears
in our own time in another way. The Marxists and countless others
have pointed out the manner in which the social and political and
other values of society change with a change in technological instruments. But what is this but the effect of man's scientifically verified
abstract theories of nature upon the norms and inner ordering relations of culture?

It appears, therefore, that an inventory of the major theories of
cultural values as exhibited in contemporary legal, sociological and
anthropological science leads to the conclusion that each one of these
theories has something to say for itself and that none alone is the
whole truth. Unless cultural values are expressed in the positive law,
the anthropological and sociological jurisprudential theory of cultural
values can never be brought to bear in the concrete legal dispute or
case. But unless the positive law is referred to the living law of sociological jurisprudence, there is no criterion enabling the jurist to
choose between one content of the positive law rather than another
in his judging of any dispute. And unless sociological jurisprudence
becomes philosophical and its philosophy in turn is tested against the
concepts used by a people to know, integrate and envisage themselves
and nature, there is no criterion for judging or reforming the living
law of anthropological and sociological jurisprudence.

V

Legal Positivism, Intuitive Ethics
and Sociological Jurisprudence

LEGAL positivism delimits the subject matter of law to the cases and propositions in law books and to the legal institutions which apply those propositions. In domestic law this restriction of the law to the positive law has been found wanting. Dean Roscoe Pound's strictures against this "give-it-up" philosophy are well known.[1] Justices Holmes' and Brandeis' pragmatic conception of law as a social instrument for facing and resolving social problems rather than running away from them is now a commonplace. Increasingly important is Myres McDougal's observation that not merely British legal positivism but also American legal realism leave one with a type of law which is incapable of meeting either the opportunities or responsibilities of the contemporary world.[2] It has remained, however, for a legal positivist, P. E. Corbett, to give the final *reductio ad absurdum* to such a system of jurisprudence in his *Law and Society in the Relations of States*.[3] Consider, for example, the theory of auto-limitation introduced by Jellinek to account for legal obligation in international law. Corbett shows the "inherent absurdity" of this position by noting that it offers "no explanation . . . for the view that while the will of the State was essential to the birth of a rule, it was not essential for the purpose of keeping it alive."[4] He shows the same to be true of the theories of Kelsen and Lauterpacht.

The major problem confronting any legal theory is to account for social norms and legal obligation. At first the legal positivists and realists regarded their incapacity to account for the normative as an asset. Law, they said, does not involve value judgments; such judgments belong to philosophy and theology. Law is not to indulge in such supposedly speculative matters. Instead law is a science dealing with nothing but positive legal facts — hence the "realism" of the legal positivists, the early American legal realists and Corbett's description of his own approach to international law. But they never made clear how a subject such as law, in which even the judges of the positive law are inescapably engaged in decision-making, can thus separate itself in this ivory-tower manner from the ethical and ideological content of the concrete problems which judicial decisions are attempting to resolve. Finally even the legal positivists themselves were forced to face the fact of norms and attempt some theory of legal obligation. Kelsen, for example, saw (a) that there are no positive rules of law ever sufficiently positive to be effective which do not presuppose a legal norm carrying with it obligations; and (b) that consent and obligation are incompatible. Thus, as Corbett writes, "Kelsen and his school rendered the service of revealing . . . the hopeless inconsistencies of the doctrine that legal obligation can result directly from the will of the entity obliged." [5]

Strangely enough, however, this final admission by Kelsen and Corbett that law presupposes moral obligation and hence has an essential connection with ethics never caused them to question their legal philosophy. Instead they begin by drawing a distinction between legal rules and the normative ethical factor which they, following Kelsen's terminology, call a "jural postulate" or a "*grundnorm*." [6] This preserves the fiction of the independence of law from ethics providing one (a) identifies law with legal rules or with merely hypothetical propositions specifying the implications of the *grundnorm* for the legal rules and the judge's decision in applying them to a particular case and (b) assigns the *grundnorm* itself to some non-legal subject such as ethics or politics.

But even Kelsen could hardly be satisfied with a legal philosophy which restricted law to rules presupposing a jural postulate about which the science of law has nothing to say. No alternative remains, therefore, but to see what kind of content legal positivism can give to the primary and basic *grundnorm*. Without this, as Corbett notes, Kelsen's theory of law is "an empty dialectic," [7] and law "emerges, not as a method of social control, but as a system of thought which declares itself beyond criticism so long as its entire content is logically derived from one fundamental principle or postulate." [8] Lauterpacht and Kelsen sought, therefore, the type of content for the jural postulate or *grundnorm* which a positivistic philosophy of law can provide. Lauterpacht offers the proposition, "The will of the international community must be obeyed." [9] Kelsen comes forth with the *grundnorm*, "The states ought to behave as they have customarily behaved." [10]

To assert either of these *grundnorms* is to admit explicitly that the positivistic philosophy of international law can make no contribution to the bringing of disputes between nations under the rule of law to an extent greater than is, or has been, done. A more convincing demonstration of the impotence of legal positivism in international law can hardly be imagined. Curiously enough Corbett not only demonstrates these consequences, but also, because of his *a priori* assumption of legal positivism, acquiesces in the result.

This result is quite independent of the particular branch of law which Corbett has chosen to investigate. The demonstration that a theory of law which bases legal obligation on assent can never justify the application of law to dissenters holds as much for criminal law in the domestic field as it does for dissenters in the international arena. Hence, were this positivistic theory of legal obligation correct, domestic law which sends murderers to the electric chair without asking them whether they assent to the court's jurisdiction should not exist. A domestic law in which the individual reserves the right to decide whether the court has jurisdiction would place the private citizen in the same position in which nations now stand with regard to international law. And were this our present situation in domestic law, Corbett would undoubtedly have published a book called *Law and Society in the Relations of Individual Persons* and described himself as "realistic." In it he would have maintained that anyone who attempts to achieve an effective domestic law of murder is misguided, building false hopes and doing more harm than good.

But competent legal thinking involves more than the capacity and integrity to pursue one's philosophical premises to their consequences. A student of law can hardly call himself scientific or realistic unless he also faces the question of the validity of his premises.

Apparently, this is precisely what Austin, the founder of English legal positivism, did before he died, with results similar to those of the foregoing analysis. In her preface to the posthumous edition of his *Lectures on Jurisprudence, or The Philosophy of Positive Law*, his wife, Sarah, writes that Austin had refused to publish during his lifetime a second edition of this work, notwithstanding the demand, because he had become convinced of its limitations and inadequacy.[11] She adds the copy of an advertisement found in his notes describing his new position in part as follows:

> Positive law (or *jus*), positive morality (or *mos*), together with the principles which form the text of both, are the inseparably-connected parts of a vast organic whole. To explain their several natures, and present them with their common relations, is the purpose of the essay on which the author is employed. . . . He (author) had thought of entitling the intended essay, the principles and relations of law, morals, and ethics: meaning by law, *positive* law; by morals, *positive* morals; and by ethics, the principles which are the test of both.[12]

At times Kelsen seems about to make the same admission, only to withdraw again into the premises of his positivism. For example, the first sentence of the section on Nomodynamics in his *General Theory of Law and State* is: "The legal order is a system of norms." [13] A few pages later, however, he writes: "A norm is a valid legal norm by virtue of the fact that it has been created according to a definite rule and by virtue thereof only." [14] A page later one reads: "Law is always positive law, and its positivity lies in the fact that it is created and annulled by acts of human beings, thus being independent of morality and similar norm systems. . . . The basic norm of a positive legal order is nothing but the fundamental rule according to which the various norms of the order are to be created." [15] The latter statement suggests also that the solitary ethical proposition in legal science, which is its initial *grundnorm*, possesses little if any ethical content, but is instead merely a formal rule concerning how the more general and the more particular propositions of law are to be related when established in a scientific rather than a haphazard manner.

There are also suggestions that Kelsen's legal positivism is compatible with and even presupposes the living law of sociological jurisprudence.[16] This would be the case if the distinction between his pure theory of law and sociological jurisprudence were a purely verbal one, drawing the line between the activity of the jurist *qua* jurist and the activity of the sociologist of law *qua* sociologist. Were such the case, the relationship might be somewhat as follows: Any legal system is a system of norms. Furthermore, any system of norms derives its more particular norms from more basic general normative postulates which might appropriately be termed the *grundnorm*. This *grundnorm* of pure theory derives its validity and its ethical content, however, from the living law of sociological jurisprudence.

The method of validating a Kelsenian *grundnorm*, as illustrated in the location of the normative authority of his Austrian Constitution of 1920 in the earliest Constitution of 1867,[17] indicates, however, that such is not the case. Kelsen confirms this conclusion: "If we ask why the constitution is valid, perhaps we come upon an older constitution. Ultimately we reach some constitution that is the first historically. . . . The validity of this first constitution is the last presupposition, the final postulate, upon which the validity of all the norms of our legal order depends."[18] Clearly if law is nothing but positive law, then the assumption of an "ought" for some first positive law must be one's basic *grundnorm*. Thus he continues: "It is postulated that one ought to behave as the individual, or the individuals, who laid down the first constitution have ordained. This is the basic norm of the legal order under consideration."[19] Kelsen adds that this "basic norm is not created in a legal procedure by a law-creating organ. It is not — as a positive legal norm is — valid because it is created in a certain way by a legal act, but it is valid because it is presupposed to be valid. . . ."[20] This is another way of saying that legal obligation has its basis not in any act of assent but in a primitive and hence irreducible, hypothetically *a priori* moral presupposition.[21] Here the neo-Kantian character of Kelsen's legal positivism reveals itself.

But what is the validity of the initial presupposition? Why assume the validity of the first constitution? To these questions Kelsen replies: "That a norm of the kind just mentioned is the basic norm of the national legal order does not imply that it is impossible to go beyond that norm. Certainly one may ask why one has to respect the first constitution as a binding norm. . . . The characteristic of so-called legal positivism is, however, that it dispenses with any such . . . justification of the legal order. The ultimate hypothesis of positivism is the norm authorizing the historically first legislator." [22] Clearly, then, his pure theory of law does not presuppose the living law of sociological jurisprudence as a part of itself. In fact, it would be self-contradictory for the pure theory of law to derive its *grundnorm* from something outside itself. For the essence of the pure theory of law is that the *grundnorm* with its ethical "imputation" is not a mere hypothetical *a priori,* but is instead a primitive, and hence irreducible *a priori.*

At this point Kelsen's legal positivism becomes identical with the ethical jurisprudence of Morris and Felix Cohen. Nor is this an accident, for all three are neo-Kantians in their theory of ethics. They differ merely in the relation of their ethics to law. Kelsen would keep law independent of ethics except for the solitary "ought" of his basic *grundnorm.* The Cohens regard ethics as the essence of law. But for all three the ethical within law is an *a priori* which is a primitive and hence irreducible assumption. This follows from the basic philosophical assumption of neo-Kantianism that the "good" or the "ought" cannot be derived from the "is," and from the thesis to the same effect of the intuitive theory of ethics of G. E. Moore and W. D. Ross which Felix Cohen affirms.

Intuitive Ethical Jurisprudence

The jurisprudence of the Cohens [23] has two merits. It does justice to the inescapably ethical character of any legal statute; that is, its permission of certain and prohibition of other de facto conduct. Their ethical jurisprudence recognizes the futility of the attempt of Kelsen's pure theory of law to restrict the "ought" of legal science to a word in its first postulate referring to some present or past constitution of the positive law. In its place the Cohens introduce the richer basic ethical assumption which they term "justice" or "the good life." The remainder of law then becomes the application of this ethical ideal to the construction of the initial constitution, the legislator's creation of statutes under that constitution and the judge's application of both to the concrete cases in his decisions.

Were Soviet Russians, nineteenth-century American Republicans, Spanish Roman Catholics, Arab-bloc Muslims, New Deal Democrats and British Labour Party socialists in agreement on the specific basic ethical norm which defines "justice" or "the good life," the ethical jurisprudence of the Cohens would work and the basic problem of legal science would be solved. Unfortunately this agreement does not exist.

To provide any judge with a basic postulate of legal science containing the words "the good life" is of little use to him, since any case involving a moral issue results from a conflict between at least two different conceptions of what "the good life" is. To put the matter in terms of contemporary symbolic logic, the expression, "the good life," is a variable; it is not a material constant. An ethical jurisprudence is inadequate in theory or in practice until the criterion for determining the value of this variable in any instance is specified.

More explicitly, this means that an ethical jurisprudence will be adequate only when its basic ethical assumptions are spelled out in detail with content, thereby giving the judge a criterion for choosing one normative principle in deciding the case rather than another. Furthermore, an adequate ethical jurisprudence must include the scientific method for designating this specific ethical content. When the Cohens take the concept of the ethical as a primitive and hence irreducible concept in ethics and law, this specification of the methodological criterion and the attendant specific ethical norms which result from its application becomes impossible. As with Kelsen, it would be a violation of their concept of the ethical if such a criterion were found; for then the good or the legally obligatory would not be a primitive concept but would be defined in terms of the concepts designating the criterion. Such is the inevitable consequence of any theory of law or ethics which affirms the ethical to be a basic assumption which is irreducible. It merely indicates that there must be an ethical assumption of some kind without either giving a clue as to what it is specifically, or providing a successful method for testing any specific ethical and legal norm such as laissez-faire individualism, socialism, or communism. Notwithstanding the greater justice to the essentially ethical character of law which it promised, intuitive ethical jurisprudence, then, is as barren ethically and legally as is the legal positivism of Austin and of Kelsen's pure theory of law.

Law is always possessed of specific normative content. Since neither the positive law nor intuitive ethical jurisprudence gives any clue to why the content of positive law is what it is, positive law must depend, because of its specific content in any given society, on something beyond both itself and the ethically *a priori*. Here it is necessary to introduce sociological jurisprudence, with its thesis that the source of the content and the obligation of the positive law is in the underlying structure or living law of the particular society to which it refers.

Sociological Jurisprudence

The expression "sociological jurisprudence" will be used throughout this inquiry in its most general sense to include (*a*) the sociology of law, and (*b*) sociological jurisprudence in the more restricted sense; that is, the application of the living law as determined by the sociology of law to judicial decisions.

The earlier formation of this theory of law was given by Pound [24] and Ehrlich. Both failed to articulate clearly the precise manner in which the living law, as specified by sociology, determined the content of the ethical norms of the positive law. The tremendous erudition of Pound's jurisprudence with its sensitivity to all schools of legal thought and its attendant eclecticism left open the question as to whether the sociologist's contribution supplied the ethical norms in whole or part or was to be supplemented or even judged by ethical norms coming *a priori* from ethical jurisprudence proper. Ehrlich, particularly in his criterion of effective positive law as that which corresponds to the underlying living law of sociology, suggested that the ethical norms of the positive law might come from the sociological contribution alone. Even so, he specified no sociological method for localizing and determining the factor in society which provides positive law with its specific ethical content. He merely expressed the hope, in the concluding chapters of his classic work, that such a scientific sociological jurisprudence would be constructed and suggested the form, modeled on the economic science of the Austrian School, which it might take.[25] Speaking of this economic science which, although deductively formulated, is based on observation, he added, "And sociology also, including the sociology of law, must be a science of observation." [26]

But this type of scientific method raises a difficulty if sociological

jurisprudence is not in the end to be as barren with respect to the
specification of ethical norms as is legal positivism or the intuitive
ethical jurisprudence. Kelsen puts his finger on this difficulty when
he notes that contemporary sociology "is not a study which seeks to
determine how men ought to act, but how they actually do act and
must act according to the laws of cause and effect. . . . This transformation of the science of social relationships from an ethical science into a causal sociology, explaining the reality of actual conduct
and therefore indifferent to values, is largely accomplished today. It
is, fundamentally, a withdrawal of social theory before an object
which it has lost all hope of mastering. . . . [I]t abandons its essential problem as insoluble." [27] In his more recent paper, "Causality and
Imputation," [28] Kelsen affirms this situation to be inescapable, because the laws of any empirical science are of necessity laws of temporal cause and effect, whereas legal science entails "imputation" (that
is, a minimum *a priori* ethical *grundnorm*) and the freedom of the
moral individual from the empirical, temporal laws of cause and
effect.

But does sociological jurisprudence need to be so poverty-stricken
ethically? Before turning to recent developments to answer this question, one caution is to be noted. Even if the answer should be in the
affirmative, this would not establish the validity of Kelsen's pure
theory or the Cohens' ethical jurisprudence. The result would be
merely that sociological jurisprudence is as vacuous and inadequate
ethically and legally as is legal positivism or intuitive ethical jurisprudence. For let it not be forgotten that of Kelsen's *grundnorm* it
can always be asked by any person confronted with such a law: "Why
this particular *grundnorm* rather than one which I might suggest?
Why this particular content freely imputed by you rather than a different content which I freely will?" Similarly of the Cohens the question can be asked: "Why the specific content of 'the good life' which
you read into your otherwise vacuous ethical norm rather than the
different specific content which I might suggest?" To all these questions neither legal positivism nor intuitive ethical jurisprudence has
an answer. And without an answer, legal and ethical obligation is
meaningless and law and ethics are not merely relative but also
arbitrary.

However necessary it is in legal science, as Kelsen and the Cohens have correctly noted, to distinguish the "ought" and the "good life" from the "is," it is equally necessary to provide some sense in which they can be related to and thereby judged as to their truth or falsity with respect to some "is." Otherwise no reason can be given for the ethical postulates of legal science taking one specific ethical content rather than another, and both ethics and law become completely arbitrary with no meaning for either ethical or legal obligation.

Underhill Moore's sociological jurisprudence [29] represents a tremendous advance over both the pure theory of law and ethical jurisprudence. What he sought was a legal science which could not merely demonstrate that some *grundnorm* has to be assumed, but also specify its content and verify the one that is to be assumed.

His procedure consisted in accepting not merely the fact that the basic postulates of positive law are normative but also that they are norms with a specific content which is only one of many possible specific contents. From this it follows that the ethical postulates of positive law cannot be true *a priori,* but must find their content and validation in some subject outside both the positive law and an autonomous ethics. Following Pound and Ehrlich, Underhill Moore identified this subject with the living law of sociological jurisprudence; that is, the inner order of society as determinable empirically by sociological science.

His problem then became that of providing an objectively determinable specification of the content of the living law in any given state of any given social system. He believed, quite correctly, that previous sociological jurisprudence had failed, because, although it assumed the living law to be objective for a given community, its methods of determining it were so intuitive and various that little agreement existed among different sociological jurists upon what the objective living law is. Too often the objective living law of a given sociological jurist was nothing but the image of this jurist's pet, arbitrarily chosen, positive law reform. This made sociological jurisprudence as arbitrary as Kelsen's pure theory of law or the Cohens' ethical jurisprudence.

Underhill Moore achieved this required objective specification of the content of the living law by assuming that whatever the subjective ethical norms of the many individual people making up the living law may be, these norms, to the extent that they are socially and legally significant, will show in their overt spatio-temporal behavior. Spatio-temporal behavior is a publicly determinable objective thing quite independent of any observer's normative preference. Hence Underhill Moore solved the problem of providing an objectively determinable specification of the living law of a given society at a given time by identifying it with the high-frequency overt behavior of all the people in that society. This amounted to an identification of the living law with the common norms of the majority of its people. Thus, what Kelsen and the Cohens said sociological jurisprudence could not do was in part at least achieved: two meanings were provided for the distinction between the "ought" and the "is" — one of these two meanings centering in the relation of the positive law to the living law, the other centering in the living law itself.

The meaning which centers in the relation of positive law to living law is as follows: The positive legal norm which corresponds to the high-frequency behavior of the living law is the positive law norm which ought to be. The positive legal norm which does not correspond to the high-frequency behavior of the living law is the one which ought not to be. This provides the judge, confronted with a specific case and two possible norms for deciding it, with a scientifically verifiable and objective criterion of the norm to be chosen. A positive legal norm which exists but does not correspond to the high-frequency behavior of the living law is a positive ethical and legal norm which "is" but not one which "ought" to be. This makes the sociological jurist's criterion of good positive law identical with Ehrlich's criterion [30] of effective positive law.

The criterion for distinguishing the "ought" from the "is" within the living law alone is equally precise in Underhill Moore's sociological jurisprudence. The "ought" of the living law of a given society is its high-frequency behavior; that is, the common norms of the majority of its members. The immoral and illegal behavior of the living law is the incompatible low-frequency behavior, which, if allowed to persist and accumulate, would undermine the common norms of the living law defined by the high-frequency behavior.

In his seminars, Underhill Moore often pointed out one difficulty in the application of this distinction. It arises because there is nothing in the theory to indicate at what specific point in the continuous curve of total living law behavior, the line between high-frequency and low-frequency behavior is to be chosen. This difficulty, however, applies only to borderline cases. It does not arise if the extreme low-frequency behavior is compared to the highest point of the high-frequency behavior.

However, Underhill Moore saw that these two distinctions between the "ought" and "is" are not sufficient. The insufficiency appears when one questions, as one must, the ethical validity of the high-frequency behavior of the living law in any given society at any given time. The fact that the high-frequency behavior of a given society is what it is does not necessarily imply that it ought to be what it is. Rarely, if ever, are the high-frequency normative accomplishments of a people identical with their ideals. Also there clearly exist societies with high-frequency behavior which one must and ought to brand as evil. And in many societies there is high-frequency behavior which should be reformed, as in Africa and Asia today.

An ethical and legal science which cannot provide meaning and a criterion for designating the high-frequency behavior of the living law of a given society as bad or in need of reform is defective. Otherwise good law and conduct would always have to be the de facto high-frequency behavior of the present status quo. One can, of course, wait for the living law to change and then bring the positive law into accord with this change. This would provide a positive legal norm and also a new living law norm different from that of today's high frequency status quo "is." Even so, one would not be able today to say that today's society is "bad" or in need of "reform." Yet this is what every reformer and every moral man frequently does and must say. Furthermore, this is what the Supreme Court of the United States did say to the people of the Southern States and the country generally in *Brown v. Board of Education.*

The question, therefore, arose in Underhill Moore's mind: "Is it possible today to determine the content of tomorrow's high-frequency living law?" If so, the norm specified by tomorrow's high-frequency living law could be used today as the "ought" for evaluating and reforming today's high-frequency living law.

Underhill Moore went to the physicists for an answer to this question. The reason for turning to natural science at this point was that physics is a science in which, given the state of a system today, tomorrow's state can be calculated today. Study of the scientific method of physics showed that for such a sociological jurisprudence two requirements are necessary. First, the scientific theory must be deductively formulated. When physics remained in the purely inductive natural history stage it was unable to achieve this required predictive power. This made it quite clear to Underhill Moore that the traditional inductive descriptions of societies and the studies of social trends after the manner of the historical sociological jurists or even the policy-forming law of McDougal and Lasswell are quite inadequate. Such inductive studies merely throw arbitrarily chosen facts in one's eyes, rather than give one the over-all high-frequency ordering relations (termed by Ehrlich "the inner order of society" [31]) necessary to evaluate the facts by putting them in their true proportions. Second, the deductively formulated postulates of the theory must specify a small number of key variables correlated indirectly with inductively given operations such that, given the present empirical values of these few key variables, the inner order of the present state of the system is defined and the values for tomorrow's state can be deduced.

Sociological jurisprudence should be able to designate the normative element of the living law by determining empirically the value of the smallest possible number of variables, preferably only one. Otherwise before sociological jurisprudence can be of any use to the jurist or judge he must have the sociologist place an endless amount of inductive data on his desk. From this standpoint, the policy-forming law of Lasswell and McDougal [32] with some seven secondary and three primary value variables is most questionable, if not as ethically vacuous as legal positivism or *a priori* ethical jurisprudence. Have Lasswell and McDougal in practice done more than substitute several vacuous ethical concepts for the one vacuous ethical notion of the Cohens' intuitive ethical jurisprudence, thereby merely multiplying the vacuity of the latter system tenfold? Moreover, even if a non-arbitrary criterion is given of the particular inductive data selected to define operationally each of the ten value variables, the sociological jurisprudence of Lasswell and McDougal has not provided an objective determination of the living law until it also includes an invariant law or formula specifying the inner order of the ten value variables. This follows because, as Ehrlich made clear, the living law is not the observed facts of sociology but the inner order of the facts.

In any event, it was to avoid such weaknesses that Underhill

Moore's sociological jurisprudence took its final direction. He turned to a causal sociological jurisprudence not, as Kelsen suggests, because of an uncritical aping of the method of natural science or because of an admission of the incapacity of sociological jurisprudence to provide a meaning for the "ought" as distinct from the "is," but because it offered a possible way to provide meaning for such a distinction. If he were able by such a scientific method to deduce the norms constituting tomorrow's high-frequency behavior from today's high-frequency behavior, he would have today a meaning for the "ought" different from today's living law high-frequency "is" and hence an objective, empirically verifiable criterion of normative social reform.

Even though he chose the very simplest social system imaginable, where if anywhere a causal sociological jurisprudence might be possible, the result was a failure. After years of selection of every possible variable in the subject matter, Underhill Moore and Callahan [33] found that they could not obtain a formula connecting the high-frequency content of the present state of the social system to that of its future state without assuming the new norm as an independent variable. In short, the future state could be deduced only if the new norm were assumed. Hence it could not be used to define the new norm. There is no greater tribute to the integrity of Underhill Moore as a legal scientist than the fact that he not only saw this negative result but accepted it. This is the sense in which his own work ended in partial disappointment.

Nonetheless, he demonstrated that sociological jurisprudence can provide an objective, empirically verifiable criterion to distinguish the "is" of the positive law from its "ought" as identified with the high-frequency "is" of the living law. He showed also that it can provide within the living law for a similarly objective distinction between its "ought" as identified with its high-frequency behavior and immoral and illegal behavior as defined by that low-frequency behavior which, if not curbed, will make the norms of the high-frequency behavior impossible. The latter distinction makes clear how the "ought" of positive law operates to bring the low-frequency behavior of the minority into compatibility with the high-frequency communal behavior and inner order of society necessary for the community's existence. What he failed to achieve was a criterion equally objective for designating when the high-frequency living law is bad or in need of reform.

The simplicity of the social behavior which Underhill Moore studied (that is, the total distribution of parked cars on a street in New Haven) makes it highly probable that his negative finding with respect to the deduction of tomorrow's living law from today's is definitive for any sociological jurisprudence which identifies any society's living law with objectively determined, overt, high-frequency behavior. There is a theoretical reason, pointed out by Karl Popper [34] among others, for believing that such a criterion for the "ought" of today's living law would be incorrect even if it were achieved. It is that if such a causal determinism held for norms, then moral and legal reform would not only be unnecessary but also impossible. For if such determinism exists, on the one hand, man can do nothing about it; and on the other hand, the reform will come automatically without one's doing anything about it.

In accepting this negative result it is necessary to avoid the error of concluding that the meaning of the word "ought" as applied to the living law is an ethical *a priori.* This error concerning ethical norms with respect to the living law is similar to that of Kelsen and the Cohens with respect to the positive law. An abstract, vacuous, ethical "ought" is of no more use in distinguishing the good from the bad in the living law than it is in the positive law.

If it is meaningful to say that high-frequency living law behavior is good or bad, then content must be given to the words "good" and "bad." And an objective criterion for specifying this content must be indicated. Is there any way, other than that attempted by Underhill Moore, which ended in failure, for doing this? Recent developments in sociology, cultural anthropology and neurological behavioristic psychology provide part of the answer to this question.

These developments also specify the manner in which the psychological theory underlying the sociological jurisprudence of Underhill Moore and of Lasswell and McDougal must be supplemented. When this supplementation is made, a new and simpler objective method of sociological or anthropological jurisprudence becomes evident. It requires the empirical determination of but one independent variable in any society in order to specify the ethical and legal content of its living law. This new method has the merit also of avoiding the weakness, noted by Underhill Moore in his own system, of not being able objectively, rather than arbitrarily, to draw the line between high-frequency or ethical living law behavior and low-frequency or non-ethical living law behavior. And this new method, which we shall call that of philosophical anthropology, points the way beyond itself to another objective criterion for judging the living law in any specific instance to be "good" or "bad" or in need of specifiable reform. The steps leading to philosophical anthropology will command our attention in the next three chapters.

VI

Petrazycki's Psychological Jurisprudence

PROFESSOR BABB'S abridgment into one volume and his English translation of Petrazycki's mature legal works and Professor Timasheff's concise Introduction give the essentials of the context and content of Petrazycki's legal science.[1] The context is important for understanding the theory. The contents demonstrate Petrazycki's originality and establish him as a legal thinker of first-rate importance.

The physical context is that of Central and Eastern Europe between the latter part of the nineteenth century and the end of World War I. Petrazycki was born in 1867 in the predominantly Polish culture of the area which had been annexed by Russia in 1772. He first studied medicine and then took a brilliant degree in law at the University of Kiev. This degree won him admission to an advanced research seminar in law at the University of Berlin. There he mastered the traditional methods of legal scholarship and published in German two legal works in the traditional manner which he was later to refer to as the "dogmatic" method. Only in the appendix, entitled "Civil Policy and Political Economy," of the last of the foregoing works did he show signs of his dissatisfaction with the traditional legal science. In 1898 he was made professor of law at the University of St. Petersburg, where he developed his final theory and remained until the Bolshevik Revolution. In 1921 he emigrated to Poland, where he was professor of law at the University of Warsaw.

His intellectual context, therefore, was that of post-Kantian and post-Hegelian Continental Europe after certain very important epistemological and methodological lessons concerning the nature of sci-

Reprinted by permission from *University of Pennsylvania Law Review* — 1956, Vol. 104, No. 5.

entific knowledge had been learned from Kant, and when the development of cultural and legal positivism and experimental psychology had indicated certain weaknesses in the Kantian and Hegelian idealistic philosophy of morals and law. In his analysis of the mathematical physics of Newton, Kant taught Continental scientists and philosophers two things: (1) the necessity in science of theoretically contributed concepts specified deductively, as well as inductively given data; (2) the naïve realistic epistemological error of reifying the theoretically contributed nouns of scientific language into supposedly concrete, externally existing objects. This naïve realistic epistemological error is what Petrazycki meant, undoubtedly, when he described the traditional legal science, including legal positivism as well as the prevalent Hegelian idealistic philosophy of law, as "dogmatic." Petrazycki's problem became, therefore, that of finding the theoretically designatable and empirically verifiable concrete entities and relations to which the abstract nouns of law, such as "obligation," "right" and "sanction," refer for their scientific meaning. At this point the epistemological and methodological lessons concerning scientific method, which were learned from Kant, combined with the late nineteenth century's interest in experimental psychology.

English and especially American readers should find Petrazycki's final, mature legal science of considerable interest. It gives an insight into Russian scientific, philosophical and legal thought in the opening decades of this century immediately before the Bolshevik Revolution. Petrazycki exhibited at that time the same dissatisfaction with traditional legal science that appears later in the United States with the legal realists and Professor Roscoe Pound's sociological jurisprudence and in Austro-Hungary with Ehrlich. But, instead of turning primarily to social science, which he does secondarily, Petrazycki finds in psychology the basic facts and concepts in terms of which law is to be understood and analyzed. In this respect his legal theory is near to that of the psychologically grounded sociological jurisprudence of Underhill Moore's later work. Petrazycki is like Moore and Moore's colleague, the psychologist, Hull, in his insistence upon the importance of making explicit the basic concepts of his science and deriving all other concepts from them by the logical methods of definition and formal implication. But whereas Moore's psychological jurisprudence was behavioristic, following Watson, Pavlov's physiology and Hull, Petrazycki's is introspective. A reading of *Law and Morality* will show that it is nonetheless experimental or theoretically rigorous because of this.* Yet Petrazycki's introspective psychology is not that of Anglo-American introspective psychologists such as Locke, Hume, Bentham or James; nor is his psychological theory of morals and law like that of the psychological theory of interests of the Americans Ralph Barton Perry and Roscoe Pound, or the German Ihering.

Petrazycki's psychological jurisprudence differs from that of Underhill Moore in one other important respect. Whereas Moore left all strictly ethical concepts out of legal science, for Petrazycki the ethical concept of obligation is basic to both the theory of morals and the theory of law. At this point he is undoubtedly following Kant with the latter's emphasis upon obligation or duty as the basic concept in ethics. At this point also Petrazycki's jurisprudence is near to that of Morris and Felix Cohen. Nevertheless he does not agree with Kant or the Cohens and G. E. Moore in affirming that good is an *a priori* or primitive concept in legal science, thereby making ethics the foundation of law. Instead, obligation is an empirical concept finding its meaning in certain theoretically designatable and empirically verifiable factors in the psychological nature of any human being. At this point Petrazycki succeeds in constructing a logically precise and connected psychological jurisprudence which combines the psychological emphasis of Ihering, James, Pound, Perry and Underhill Moore with the ethical insights of Morris and Felix Cohen and the English empiricist,

* Professor Timasheff suggests, in his introduction to *Law and Morality,* that Petrazycki's introspective psychology is formally equivalent to the current behavioristic reflex theory. This judgment would seem to leave the "action ideas" of Petrazycki's psychology out of account. To establish a formal equivalence it is necessary to modify the Hull-Moore reflex psychology by adding (1) the conception of the human nervous system as a teleological (that is, negative feedback) mechanism as suggested by Rosenblueth, Wiener and Bigelow, and (2) the theory of cortically "trapped universals" as suggested by McCulloch and Pitts. The role of the "trapped universals" between sensory and motor neurons is formally equivalent to that of the "action ideas" between the "passive" and "active" components of "blanket impulsions" in Petrazycki's introspective psychology. For an exposition of (1) and (2) above and their application to legal science, see F. S. C. Northrop, "Ideological Man in His Relation to Scientifically Known Natural Man" in Northrop, ed., *Ideological Differences and World Order* (Yale University Press, New Haven, 1949). See also Chapters V and VIII of this book.

G. E. Moore, in a way that no other Continental, British or American legal thinker has done.

Also whereas Bentham, Ihering, Perry and Underhill Moore began with a specific psychological theory and fitted their analysis of the subject matter of law into this, Petrazycki begins with an inductive, empirical investigation of what distinguishes the subject matter of law from other somewhat similar subjects, such as morals and aesthetics, and then creates a new science of psychology to account for the unique character of legal phenomena. Thus Petrazycki has something exceedingly important to teach anyone about law quite apart from his psychology and his psychological jurisprudence.

The Unique Factor in Legal Phenomena

Petrazycki became convinced at Berlin that traditional legal science failed to be scientific because it lacked a clear concept of its subject matter. This showed in certain jurists who, seeing that law was normative, tended to identify it with morality without any clear conception of the difference between morals and law. It showed also in the jurisprudence of interests of Ihering and others who, noting that different interests came to expression in litigation, failed to provide the criterion which distinguishes economic wants or interests from legal wants and interests on the one hand or merely moral wants and interests on the other. It showed again in sociological jurists who, while finding the source of law in society, failed to provide a scientific concept distinguishing social phenomena which are legal from those which are economic, aesthetic or merely ethical in the generic sense of the word "ethical."

Petrazycki's positive solution appears if we concentrate on what distinguishes a merely moral relation of A to an object B, from a legal relation. His conclusion is that both impose an obligation on A, but that the obligation is unilateral in the case of a moral relation and bilateral in the case of a legal relation. The unilateral character of a merely moral relation between two persons A and B is shown by two examples from the New Testament to which Petrazycki refers: (1) Jesus' injunction to turn the other cheek, and (2) "But I say unto you: resist not evil." Why are these moral relations unilateral? Petrazycki's answer is that when A enters into a moral relation with B, by ascribing to himself the obligation to act in a certain way with respect to B, he does not ascribe the converse right to B to demand such action on A's part. In other words, in a moral relation between A and B, A is under an obligation to himself to behave in a certain way with respect to B without B having the converse right to such behavior from A. Legal relations, on the other hand, are bilateral because in them there is no such thing as A having an obligation to perform in a certain way with respect to B without B having the converse right to such performance on the part of A. Petrazycki uses the term "ethics" to represent any moral relation or experience in which an obligation occurs. When that obligation is unilateral, we have the branch of ethics termed "morals"; when it is bilateral, we have the branch of ethics termed "law."

It is to be noted that Petrazycki's distinction between law and morality reverses the usual conception of the ethical merits of these two subjects. It is customary to regard law as a weaker and lower form of ethics than morality. Petrazycki's analysis indicates that there is a sense in which law is a higher ethics than morals. This becomes evident when one notes that in a unilateral obligation one gives no right to the object of one's ethical act. If I in one instance, having been slapped on one cheek, turn the other in accordance with Jesus' injunction, I in no way give the other party the right to have me turn the other cheek every time or any time he may choose to slap me. In this sense morality is a cheaper ethics than law. For in law any time that I obligate myself with respect to an object B, I automatically ascribe * to B the right to have this obligation carried through by me. Thus legal obligation carries with it a price, if Petrazycki's analysis be correct, which moral obligation does not entail. This may explain why people are less willing to obligate themselves as fully in law as they may do in personal morals. It may also explain why morality tends to be associated with generosity, whereas law is on more of a quid pro quo basis. In any event, the present writer finds Petrazycki's analysis of the distinction between morals and law convincing.

Aesthetics falls outside ethics, according to Petrazycki, because aesthetic relationships and judgments, while normative, do not impose

---

* In this emphasis upon "ascription," Petrazycki foresaw much of what the Oxford philosophical analyst and legal positivist Professor H. L. A. Hart now emphasizes. Petrazycki was not, however, a legal positivist.

an obligation. Thus when A asserts B to be beautiful or that B be-
haves in accordance with good form, A in no way obligates himself
either unilaterally or bilaterally.

Having thus found both the generic and the differentiating properties of legal relations and experiences, Petrazycki then turns to the
question of the source of their authority. Why does any person A
enter into an obligatory relation to an object B for which A pays the
price of ascribing to B the right to specific conduct on A's part in
accordance with that obligation?

The traditional legal science in Petrazycki's time, as in ours, found
the answer in "power" or "the will of the sovereign." * Petrazycki
sees, however, that these words are merely metaphors. To suppose
that they answer the question of the source of bilateral obligation is
to be guilty of the naïve epistemological error of reifying an abstract
projected construct into a concrete entity or will. This clearly is scientific nonsense.

Where, then, is the source of moral and legal obligation to be
found? What are the concrete, empirically observable and precisely
conceptualizable phenomena from which the abstract nouns of moral
obligation and legal right derive their scientific meaning? Clearly it is
not from "society," since society itself is not a concrete entity but is
instead a theoretical construct. We do not see society after the manner of a person looking down on a geographical terrain from the vantage point of an airplane. Human beings do not have muscles and
bones tying them to one another to form a concrete social organism
with physical power after the manner in which the bones and tissues
of the person's body bind his anatomical parts into a physical organism with muscular power. Instead, the concrete and real facts at the
basis of both society and legal relations must be found in the individual person alone and in his relations to other concrete or subjectively
projected objects to which the concrete individual commits himself.
Hence psychology, rather than official positive law or even sociology,
can alone provide the basic facts and concepts of legal science.

* Even Kant, notwithstanding his emphasis upon the naïve realistic epistemological error of giving abstract nouns an external, objective, concrete existence, distinguished law from ethics by making the source of the sanction for
law external, whereas in morals it was private and internal to the concrete individual person.

The Basic Elements of Petrazycki's Psychological Jurisprudence

Empirical psychologists such as Locke, Hume and Bentham and Continental psychological jurists, such as Ihering, had tended to conceive of colors, pains, pleasures, interests and wants in merely their passive relationship to the self as presented data. Or if, after the manner of Ihering at times and the later pragmatic instrumentalists, they emphasized the activity of the person, then the passive component was overlooked, and all psychological and legal experiences were made instrumental to a future end and in this sense always teleological. Petrazycki noted, however, that either account gives only one facet of concrete, empirical personal experience, when in fact there are two. This passive-active character of any specific person's concrete experience Petrazycki terms an "impulsion." Impulsions, therefore, become the elementary entities of his psychology and legal science.

Impulsions fall into two major classes: (1) "specific" and (2) "blanket" or "abstract." An impulsion is specific if the effect of its passive component upon its active component is the fulfillment of a specific biological function. An example is when the passive sensation of hunger results automatically and unconsciously in the biological act of getting and eating food. An unreflective hateful response to a stimulus is another example. An unreflective benevolent response, which Petrazycki terms love, is a third instance.

In blanket or abstract impulsions, conscious awareness of what one is doing is present. The passive factor does not determine the active factor automatically. This additional factor Petrazycki terms the "action idea." Furthermore, the content of the active component is left open. Hence the word "blanket" or "abstract." Thus specific impulsions are passive-active experiences unaccompanied by action ideas. Blanket impulsions are passive-active experiences accompanied by action ideas. They are, in other words, passive-active experiences in which the idea of the conduct associated with the impulsion "defines the character and direction of our conduct." [2]

The error of the hedonistic psychological jurisprudence of Bentham and the jurisprudence of interests of Ihering or Pound in its more passive formulation now becomes evident. Such a jurisprudence tends to identify the psychological basis of law with a passively sensed datum such as pleasure or an inspected want or interest. Similarly the jurisprudence of interests in its alternative active, instrumentally teleological formulation has no passive component mediated to its active component by an action idea to provide the psychological basis for a person actively ascribing (*a*) to himself an obligation and (*b*) to an object other than himself the right to have a specified form of active behavior fulfilled. In short, the traditional psychological jurisprudence in either its merely passive or its merely active formulation, being without both passive and active components in the psychological nature of man and an action idea relating one component to the other component, is left, of necessity, without any psychological basis for either moral or legal obligation. Hence the necessity in traditional jurisprudence of committing the naïve realistic epistemological error of reifying abstract nouns like political "power" or "the will of the sovereign" into supposedly concrete entities in order to account for social or moral obligation or for legal obligation of any kind.

It remains to give the psychological definitions of those particular experienced impulsions which are legal experiences. When, in any blanket impulsion, given a particular passive component, a person A in the active component of the concrete impulsion commits himself to conduct guided by an action idea which imposes an obligation upon himself with no converse right of the object of the impulsion to that particular active response, the impulsion is that of a moral relationship and experience. When the action imposed by the action idea carries with it not merely obligation upon A but also the converse right of B to that type of active response from A, then the relationship is legal and the psychological experience is a legal one.

Impulsions accompanied by action ideas Petrazycki also calls "intellectual impulsions." These may be of two kinds: (*a*) teleological, and (*b*) non-teleological. A blanket impulsion is teleological when the action idea within it takes the form of "action in order that *x*," where *x* refers to something in the future. It is non-teleological when the action idea takes the form of "action because of *x*," where *x* refers to something in the past or present. Because of this distinction within possible blanket impulsions, Petrazycki affirms that those ethical or legal theories are erroneous which conceive of all ethical or legal norms instrumentally as teleological or purposive. Some ethical or legal relations are of the latter type, others are not.

So far Petrazycki's legal science is merely formal. It refers, to be sure, to concrete psychological experiences of any human being. In this sense it is concrete. But the content of the action ideas in any moral or legal impulsions varies from culture to culture and even, as Petrazycki notes, from person to person. All people in any culture or society are beings experiencing impulsions. All people, also, experience those blanket impulsions whose action ideas impose obligations on A together with the right of B to a fulfillment of that obligation by A. Hence every society and culture possesses law.

Although any legal relation involves a specific concrete person and his bilateral imperative impulsions, it by no means follows that the objects of legal relations must be such concrete persons. The action idea may take as its object inorganic nature, as it does in most primitive and Oriental societies where the people and their sages identify good conduct and good law with "harmony with nature." The action idea may also take as its object an animal other than man. When, for example, I take care of my dog in such a way that I obligate myself to feed him and accept his barking as the calling of my attention to his right to be fed by me, I am committing myself to a legal obligation. This example, which is the writer's, illustrates two important practical consequences of Petrazycki's legal science. First, it enables one to interpret official positive laws about cruelty to animals in their obvious meaning as a relation between a person and a non-human animal. Second, it shows that, as with the sociological jurisprudence of Ehrlich, seven-eighths of the law is outside official positive law.

Petrazycki expresses the latter consequence of his psychological jurisprudence by dividing law into (a) "positive law" and (b) "intuitive law." Positive law in his usage must not be taken to mean what it means for Ehrlich or for legal positivists such as Austin or Kelsen; instead, positive law in Petrazycki's sense is any bilateral blanket impulsion which, in any person's psychological experience of it, finds the justification for its action idea in some authority or reason outside that experience itself. Official positive law is but one small portion of such bilateral blanket impulsions. Intuitive law, on the other hand, is a bilateral imperative blanket impulsion whose action idea finds its justification solely in the immediate present experience of the impulsion itself. In other words, it is a bilateral imperative impulsion which to the person experiencing it seems to be immediately, and hence intuitively, self-evident.

Intuitive law, according to Petrazycki, may be ethically inferior to "positive law." This occurs frequently when the person is insensitive morally and legally or is less reflective with respect to the action ideas of his impulsions than the general run of people in his community or in other communities. What actually happens, Petrazycki notes, in most intuitive morality or law is that the person reflects in his immediately experienced intuitions the deposited cultural norms of his past when these norms have taken on a purely mechanical form without much sensitivity to the subtle factors in human experience which are their origin.

The action ideas in legal impulsions may take as their objects, however, theoretically constructed factors rather than nature or a specific concrete person or non-human animal. Hence arise legal concepts such as "corporate personality." In short, the object to which a person relates himself in a legal experience may be what Petrazycki terms a "phantasmic projection." Furthermore, even when the legal object is a concrete, external person or thing, the legal right ascribed to that concrete object is not an intrinsic predicate of the object, but is instead a phantasmic projection. Failure (1) to note, therefore, that all legal concepts are phantasmic projections and (2) to trace all phantasmic projections back to the action ideas of the passive-active blanket impulsions which are their concrete psychological basis is the error of traditional positivistic or idealistic legal theory; that is, of dogmatic jurisprudence.

Legal impulsions analyze further, according to Petrazycki, into four major factors: (1) action ideas, (2) subject ideas, (3) ideas of relevant facts and (4) ideas of normative facts. The nature of action ideas has been indicated above. Subject ideas refer to the action ideas as they bear upon subjects *qua* subject, and differentiate into the subjects of obligations and the subjects of rights. Ideas of relevant facts are ideas of events such as the moment I entered into a legal relation with my dog, the occasion when an official legislative statute was passed or the moment when the judge gave a specific decision. Ideas of normative facts, on the other hand, refer to relationships between the person who obligates himself and the right of the object which that legal obligation entails. Thus ideas of normative facts are legal propositions or rules rather than ideas of legal events. One of the main points made by the contemporary Scandinavian school of legal thinkers, who at this point agree with Petrazycki, against the American legal realists [3] is that, in the latter's conception of law as the prediction of future legal events, the American legal realists fail to distinguish "ideas of relevant facts" from "ideas of normative facts." Without the (a) ascription of the normative rule as well as the (b) legal event, there would be no such thing as the tie of obligation upon the subject and the converse right of the object; in short, there would be no such thing as either law or society. Again let it be remembered, people are not tied together to form interpersonal obligations and rights and social institutions by physical bones, rods or muscles; they only tie themselves together legally and socially by means of bilaterally imperative action ideas to which they commit themselves. To have seen this and to have shown how it can be made meaningful is certainly the great merit of Petrazycki's psychological legal science.

Some Queries

Even so, is not his psychological jurisprudence a purely formal theory — almost as formal as the legal positivism, to which he objects, of a British empirically minded Austin or a Continental rationalistically minded Kelsen? To be sure, it goes beyond legal positivism in not having to resort either to "power" on the one hand or to an historically or dogmatically assumed *grundnorm* on the other to get effective positive law into being. Petrazycki's psychological jurisprudence, like Ehrlich's sociological jurisprudence, finds the source of the sanctions and effectiveness of law within the basic concepts of legal science itself, not in something foreign to legal norms and concepts such as a naïvely reified "social power."

Even so, is there any method or criterion in Petrazycki's, or any other, psychological jurisprudence for telling us what the content of any specific action idea will be or whether the content of the normative facts of a given official positive law, a given de facto sociological living law (in the sense of Ehrlich) or a given person's intuitive law is in need of reform or, in other words, good or bad? Insofar as Petrazycki answers this question with respect to official positive law, it is by an appeal to the empirical living law of sociological jurisprudence. It is at this point that, after constructing his legal science primarily in terms of psychological factors, he turns implicitly and secondarily to sociological jurisprudence, without specifying the concrete factors by means of which the private bilateral imperative impulsions of psychological jurisprudence become shared to produce the social bilateral imperative impulsions of sociological jurisprudence.

Furthermore, if the "sharing" is not itself to remain a mere metaphorical phantasm, emphasis must be placed upon communication between people by means of symbols, whereby they convey the specific action idea content of their respective private and local bilateral imperative impulsions to one another. By this concrete means psychological jurisprudence becomes socially and culturally transformed into sociological and anthropological jurisprudence, and private local legal experiences become socially, officially and culturally imperative, effective and powerful. This means that both society and the law of a society get their unity, power and sanction not from an external physical force added to the normative content of their particular action ideas, but instead a nation and its official positive law are able to draw physical police and military power to themselves only because of the symbolically communicated sharing of common action ideas with specific bilateral imperative content by their several concrete individual psychological persons.

It is in clarifying the concrete instrumentalities of this communicated sharing that contemporary cybernetics and communication engineering become important for legal science.[4] It may be noted also that the foregoing analysis of the relation between psychological and sociological jurisprudence which was implicit, if not explicit, in Petrazycki's theory of legal science undermines not merely the legal positivists and Kant's theory of the external sanctions of legal obligation, but also the prevalent power politics theory of the nation and of international relations. All of the latter theories derive their plausibility from the naïve realists' epistemological error of confusing abstract nouns referring to phantasmic projections with concrete entities external to individual persons and individual bilateral imperative experiences.

Even with the foregoing clarification of the relation between Petrazycki's primary appeal to psychological jurisprudence and his secondary appeal to sociological jurisprudence, one final crucial question still remains which no contemporary legal thinker can escape: Assuming the content of the normative facts in the intuitive law of any person or in the living law of any society to be what they are, what scientific criterion is there for passing judgment upon them as good or bad, or in need of reform? Clearly people the world over today, especially in the so-called underdeveloped areas, are questioning and reforming both their intuitive psychological and their social living law norms. Petrazycki notes that the average person thinks he has a basis for judging both the official positive and the living law of his society or any other in terms of his own private intuitive law. Petrazycki adds, however, as previously noted, that often a person's intuitive, moral and legal convictions may be less sensitive morally and legally and of lower ethical quality than those of the general run of people in his community. Hence, to go to the psychological intuitive moral and ethical experiences of the individual will not do. It is Petrazycki's thesis, furthermore, that so-called natural law is merely intuitive law. Before noting this error, one conclusion may be stated. In Petrazycki's psychological jurisprudence, even when its reaction to sociological jurisprudence is clarified, one is left normatively with a merely formal system, the content of which is a cultural, historical or psychological accident. One has no criterion of when the content of the intuitive or the positive social living or official norms within the system is the good or the scientifically correct one. Yet this criterion must be specified by any science of law which aims, as Petrazycki aimed, to provide a scientific theory of legal reform.

Is it not clear that for such a criterion legal science must (a) develop a theory of how the action ideas within legal impulsions get their content, and (b) specify the scientific method of distinguishing between content which is good and content which is bad? * The latter method, if it is not to be circular and question-begging, must be such, moreover, as to escape both the sophistic relativism of psychological jurisprudence and the cultural relativism of sociological jurisprudence. To assert that such a non-relativistic criterion exists for judging (a) psychological intuitive law, (b) official positive law and (c) the living law of sociological jurisprudence is the thesis of natural

---

* Professor Pitirim A. Sorokin informs the writer that in lectures which he attended at St. Petersburg after *Law and Morality* was published, Petrazycki was concerned with this very problem.

law jurisprudence. Petrazycki's identification of natural law, therefore, with psychological intuitive law is erroneous. The specification of the scientific method by which the thesis of natural law jurisprudence is to be implemented is the major task of contemporary legal science. Petrazycki's psychological jurisprudence is a necessary, even though not a sufficient, condition for this undertaking.

VII

The Method of Recent Cultural Anthropology

ANTHROPOLOGICAL, or sociological, jurisprudence affirms the thesis that positive law cannot be understood apart from its relations to the particular culture or society out of which it grows or to which it is applied. When the content of the norms specified in the positive law is reinforced by the content of the norms embodied in the culture or the social behavior of the society, positive law is effective; when this is not the case, it tends, as Ehrlich emphasized, to become ineffective. Ehrlich called this underlying cultural or sociological factor the "living law" to distinguish it from the positive law. He defined the living law as "the inner order of the associations" of the individual people making up the society. What Ehrlich called the "inner order of the associations," the anthropologists call the "pattern of a culture."

One of the main problems of anthropological and sociological jurisprudence becomes that, therefore, of specifying the method by which the inner order of the living law or the ethical content of the pattern of a culture is to be specified. The first major contribution of Professor Hoebel's recent book, *The Law of Primitive Man,*[1] is that in its first chapter it describes this method. Quite independently, in his study of the living law of Continental Europe in its bearing on the proposed positive legal constitutions of Continental European Union, the writer came upon the same method.[2] This method involves a specification of the qualitative norms held in common by a given people in a given area and the quantitative support which each set of norms enjoys. Thus, the living law of a given society is specified by

Reprinted by permission from *Louisiana Law Review* — February, 1956, Vol. XVI, No. 2.

the method of sociological or anthropological jurisprudence when the set of postulates of that particular culture or society is indicated and that set is shown to enjoy the acceptance and support of most, but never all, of the people. Thus, Professor Hoebel points out that for an anthropologist, "the measure of integration of [any] culture" will be given by the "consistency between basic postulates and . . . the specific selected behavior patterns" [3] and that the norm as specified by the basic postulate set is both a description of what is and a quantitative concept. He writes: "Norm, in its statistical sense, is a strictly neutral term. It merely expresses what *is*, on the basis of a numerical count. It says nothing of what ought to be or what people think ought to be. It is a quantitative concept." [4]

It is in the quantitative component of the qualitative and neutral postulate set expressing an "is" that the oughtness of the norm finds its origin. When the normative content of a given postulate set becomes accepted by a statistically large portion of the people in a society, it transforms itself into an imperative "ought." Then, as Professor Hoebel writes, following Sumner, "in society what *is* takes on the compulsive element of *ought*. . . . What the most do, others should do." [5] In this manner contemporary anthropology and sociology show how their empirically verified indicative sentences, concerning the "is" of a given people's shared meanings, are turned into imperative sentences by the majority of the people in their relation to the minority. Sumner's theory of the relation between indicative and imperative does not explain, however, why the quantitatively large portion of the people accept the "is" designated by the postulate set of their culture as an "ought" for themselves. At this point anthropological and sociological jurisprudence need to be supplemented with psychological jurisprudence after the manner of Underhill Moore and Leon Petrazycki. [6] We shall return to this point later in connection with Professor Hoebel's use of the expression "social power" and his definition of law.

The second major contribution of Professor Hoebel's book is by way of illustration of this method of anthropological jurisprudence when applied to the study of seven specific primitive societies. In each case he spells out the specific postulates and their corollaries in terms of which the social relations of the people take on a normative inner order or cultural pattern. These seven primitive societies are the Es-

kimo; the Ifugao of the Philippines; the Comanche, the Kiowa and
the Cheyenne Indian societies of the American Plains; the Trobriand
Islanders of the Southwest Pacific; and the Ashanti of Africa. In each
instance the norms are unique, as are the procedures by which they
are applied. Some of these societies are patriarchal, others matriarchal,
in their familial living law. In some of these societies the normative
family ties between different generations are unilateral, moving
largely or entirely through the male members or largely or entirely
through the female; in one of these societies, they are bilateral. The
procedures for dispute settling differ also. In some societies mediation is never used — in others there is usually a "go-between" who
serves to bring the disputants together but does not pass judgment,
whereas in others the go-between may at first mediate and then enforce a judgment if the disputants themselves do not come to an
agreement.

The latter differences are important. They become accentuated
when one compares the patriarchal or matriarchal societies described
by Professor Hoebel with patriarchal or matriarchal societies of the
Buddhist or Confucian cultures. Then it becomes evident, as the
writer has indicated elsewhere,[7] that law falls into three major species, rather than merely the two noted by Sir Henry S. Maine in his
classic work, *Ancient Law.* These three species are (1) the mediational types of dispute settling, in which the resort to codes is regarded as immoral or as a second best, as exemplified by classical
Buddhist and Confucian teaching and by the later Gandhi in more
recent times; (2) dispute settling by law of status rules or codes in
which patriarchal or matriarchal familial relations play a major role,
as exemplified in all the societies described by Professor Hoebel; (3)
dispute settling by law of contract codes in which legal norms are broken free from color of skin, familial or tribal associations and expressed in terms of axiomatically constructed constitutional utopias
whose authority is not tradition but the consent of those to whom
they apply.

Professor Hoebel's anthropological findings show also that between
groups with different norms war occurs and behavior, which would be
outlawed if applied to one's own people, is accepted as quite proper
when applied to another tribe or nation. Also, some societies show
greater integration and harmony than others and succeed in settling

disputes with less rebellion and emotional disturbance on the part of the disputants. A comparison of these differences with differences in the respective postulate sets shows a dependence of the behavioral and practical differences upon the differences in the theoretical assumptions. For example, the Comanche tribe of Plains Indians fails to achieve the social integration and deference to individual feelings obtained by the Cheyenne Indians. An examination of their respective postulates shows the former to be excessively individualistic, whereas the latter have stronger interpersonal normative assumptions which prepare the individual members to accept the order necessary for greater social integration and stability with less inclination to private emotional psychological rebellion. The Kiowa tribe of Indians, on the other hand, are midway between the extreme individualism and lack of social coordination of the Comanche and the greater social sense and collaborative spirit of the Cheyenne. An examination of their postulate set of assumptions shows them to be ambiguous both with respect to individualism and to social collaboration. From this Professor Hoebel concludes, "When cultural goals are not clear-cut, it is not likely that social action will be either." [8]

These anthropological materials have several important implications with respect to legal philosophy. The Comanche Indians treat animals as legal objects.[9] This brings into question those legal theories which affirm every legal relation to be a relation between persons. There are natural law elements in many of these societies.[10] Professor Hoebel concludes also that primitive peoples legislate; [11] all is not mere frozen custom. He suggests in Part III that a sociological *jus gentium* — that is, what is common to all social systems — must be defined more in terms of function than in terms of common, normative content.[12] His description of a respected and able Cheyenne chief demonstrates that personality structure is a function of the postulate set of beliefs of a given people.[13] This shows that a natural law jurisprudence must refer to "the essential nature of man" with considerable caution. Certainly these case studies establish the main point of anthropological and sociological jurisprudence, which is that the positive law is meaningless by itself and can be understood only in connection with the implicit postulate set of the culture or the society which is its background.

Professor Hoebel's book as a whole divides into three major parts:

I, The Study of Primitive Law; II, Primitive Law-ways; and III, Law and Society. Part II contains the aforementioned anthropological materials. Part III draws several general conclusions. Part I includes, in addition to the aforementioned Chapter 1 on the method of determining the inner order of the living law, three chapters on (1) what law is, (2) the methods and techniques for studying its relation to the cultural assumptions of any people, and (3) the legal concepts of Hohfeld as a tool of the empirical anthropologist in his study of the law of primitive peoples. Some queries need to be raised with respect both to the definition of law in Chapter 2 and to the cultural anthropologists' application to primitive societies of Hohfeld's technical legal concepts which are described in Chapter 4.

The Hohfeldian concepts are the product of the abstract technical analytic form of scientific, philosophical and legal thinking which characterizes one particular group of legal philosophers in the Anglo-American modern West. If, as Professor Hoebel's empirical studies in Part II demonstrate, no people in any culture can be correctly understood in conceptual terms other than their own, is it not dangerous for the cultural anthropologist to approach primitive cultures through the Hohfeldian conceptual spectacles of traditional Anglo-American legal theory? As the anthropologist A. R. Radcliffe-Brown writes in his article, "Patrilineal and Matrilineal Succession," to which Professor Hoebel refers, "If we are to understand aright the laws and customs of non-European peoples we must be careful not to interpret them in terms of our own legal conceptions, which, simple and obvious as some of them may seem to us, are the product of a long and complex historical development and are special to our own culture."[14]

The aforementioned query becomes the more pointed when one notes Professor Hoebel's unexpected departure from his usual sober objectivity in his chapter on the Trobriand Islanders. Instead of proceeding to specify their basic postulate set and the way it operates in settling their disputes, he confronts us in the very first sentence of the very first paragraph with Malinowski rather than with Malinowski's anthropological subject matter, the Trobriand Islanders. As one reads beyond the first paragraph, the concern with Malinowski turns into a criticism and the criticism seems to be tinged more with emotion than supported by evidence. Something in Malinowski's account of the Trobriand Islanders seems to be emotionally disturbing Professor Hoebel for reasons that are not made clear. Why this, the only, departure from sober objectivity to be found in the entire volume?

Usually when anyone is emotionally disturbed by a professional colleague it is well to see if the colleague has not presented some evidence which brings into question certain assumptions of the disturbed person. What is the thesis of Malinowski, based on his study of the Trobriand Islanders, which Professor Hoebel criticizes with touches of feeling? It is that in Malinowski's book on these people, "the reader is definitely given to believe that law operates without the aid of physical force, although it does bind behavior." [15] The writer must confess that the evidence given by Malinowski seems convincing. Moreover, Professor Hoebel's own material in his chapters on other primitive peoples supports the Malinowski thesis that in some cases, at least, force is not the source of legal sanction. In the case of the Ashanti, to give but one example, Professor Hoebel writes that "the thought that his ancestors are watching him . . . is a very potent sanction of morality." [16] Many similar examples occur in Professor Hoebel's data.

Why, then, does he become so disturbed by Malinowski's similar conclusion? Why does he brush Malinowski off rather brusquely by quoting Seagle to the effect that Malinowski is guilty of "the pathetic fallacy of primitive jurisprudence" which consists in "transfer[ring] to primitive law the legal emotions of his own culture"? [17] The answer to these questions is not far to seek. It is to be found in Professor Hoebel's definition of law in Chapter 2, a definition which, like his Hohfeldian concepts, he brought to his anthropological studies. This definition he describes in the last paragraph of Chapter 2 as follows: "[L]aw may be defined in these terms: *A social norm is legal if its neglect or infraction is regularly met, in threat or in fact, by the application of physical force by an individual or group possessing the socially recognized privilege of so acting.*" [18]

The source of this definition is well known to students of modern legal theory. It is the basic thesis of both the eighteenth-century legal idealists, such as Kant, and nineteenth-century and early twentieth-century legal positivists, such as Austin or Hohfeld. According to these thinkers, what distinguishes law from morality is that whereas the sanction for morality is in the ethical content of the moral norm and the internal acceptance of that moral content as binding by the moral individual, the source of the sanction for law is external physical force or power. Naturally, therefore, Professor Hoebel was slightly disturbed emotionally when Malinowski brought forth facts which were difficult to reconcile with Professor Hoebel's preconceived definition of law. Having himself committed the pathetic fallacy by accepting a definition of law peculiar to his own Anglo-American culture and held only by some schools of legal thinkers in that culture, one need hardly wonder that Professor Hoebel was pushed out of his normal sober objectivity when Malinowski confronted him with facts that brought that definition into question.

Professor Hoebel's error is the more remarkable in that he is an anthropological jurist. Certainly the major contribution of anthropological and sociological jurisprudence to contemporary legal theory is its demonstration that instead of positive law getting its sanction from the power it attaches to itself, the positive law only succeeds in attaching power to itself when the ethical content of its norms corresponds to that of the inner order of the underlying living law. As the self-reformed legal positivist, Professor A. L. Goodhart, has recently written: "It is because a rule is regarded as obligatory that a measure of coercion may be attached to it: it is not obligatory because there is coercion." [19] In his first chapter and at many other places in his book, Professor Hoebel implicitly asserts this theory, only to allow his uncritical acceptance of the Hohfeldian and Austinian positivistic definition of law to force him to throw away this, the major contribution of anthropology to contemporary legal science.

Petrazycki has shown conclusively that the difference between law and morality does not center in the sanction for the former being external force and the sanction for the latter being internal personal commitment to the ethical content of the norm, but centers instead in the fact that ethical commitment to a moral norm is merely unilateral, whereas in the case of a legal norm it is bilateral. By unilateral, Petrazycki means that in the moral relation between A and any object B, A merely places an obligation upon himself while ascribing no right to B to conduct on A's part in accordance with the obligation which A places upon himself. By bilateral, Petrazycki means that when A commits himself to a legal obligation, this carries with it the converse right of B to demand behavior on A's part in accordance with the ethical obligation which A places upon himself.[20]

In any event, it is difficult to believe that, if Professor Hoebel had put his case studies first and allowed his findings as a cultural anthropologist to determine his definition of law instead of committing the pathetic fallacy of uncritically assuming a definition of law peculiar to one or two schools of legal thinking in his own Anglo-American culture, he would have come out with a different definition of law in Part III of his volume than appears at the end of Chapter 2 in Part I. Also, the chapter on the Trobriand Islanders could have been solely on the Trobriand Islanders.

The foregoing critique should be kept within a proper sense of proportion. It is likely that the ambiguity of the book with respect to what it means by the words "social force" or "social power" results from the failure of its author and most legal thinkers of the recent past to give a semantic analysis of these abstract nouns. Clearly the expressions "social power" or "social force" are metaphors. As Petrazycki has shown, their reification into a concrete entity is one of the major errors of the theory of law of Kant, the Hegelian idealists and the British legal positivists. Clearly society is not a concrete entity; it is a theoretical construct. The same is true of a society's "power."

This becomes evident when one recalls that the biological bodies of the individual person in any society are not tied to one another by rods of steel or bones or muscles or tissues to generate a single concrete entity or organism with its physical power after the manner in which the organs of the human body are tied together by bones and muscles and tissues to generate the concrete entity which is the individual person's biological body with its physical power. As Professor Hoebel's own studies make clear, there is no society or culture with power except as a statistically large majority of its members share common meanings and norms for ordering their relations to one another. From this it follows necessarily that power is an effect of these commonly shared meanings and norms, specified in Professor Hoebel's postulate sets of the cultures he describes. Furthermore, "power" receives its existence, effectiveness and sanction from those commonly shared meanings and hence cannot be the sanction for the ethical content of the positive or the living law.

These considerations show that nothing is more needed in the contemporary world than a semantic analysis of the words "social power" and "national power." Contemporary students, not merely of law, but of foreign policy and international relations, are still laboring under the semantic error of reifying these abstract words into a concrete entity, with results that may well be tragic for the whole of contemporary humanity. In his final chapter, "The Trend of the Law," Professor Hoebel points up the obvious need to extend positive legal norms and institutions from the domestic to the international field. "The science of comparative legal dynamics," he writes, "is called upon to add its catalytic effect to the crystallizing metamorphosis from primitive law to modern on the plane of world society." [21] If this "trend" is to reach "fulfillment," cultural and positive legal norms must find the source of their effectiveness and their sanction in their ethical content. Force between nations cannot be brought under ethical and legal control if the sanction for the ethical content of legal norms is force. Such a theory of law makes force King.

VIII

The Method and Neurophysiological Basis of Philosophical Anthropology

I T is of interest to approach this topic by way of the bearing of legal theory and method on international law. The sociological jurist contends that if any positive law is to be effective it must correspond to the underlying living law. To take this thesis seriously is to realize immediately one major reason (quite apart from the fact that it is so much the creation of legal positivists) why international law is so weak, calling forth such meagre living law sanctions for itself. Existent international law is the creation of but one historical portion of one living law culture of the world. More specifically it is the product of late medieval and early modern European jurists, watered down and weakened by later eighteenth- and nineteenth-century European positivists. Having thus its living law roots solely in one small historical piece of but one local culture of the world, is it any wonder that all the culturally diverse nations of the world refuse to grant to the international community unqualified jurisdiction over even a small piece of their particular national and international behavior?

Nor is there any need to wonder why even the recent modern portion of the West, whose legal jurists have created the existent international law, should have such little confidence in it. Rooted as the recent international law is, and its recent jurists have been, in either legal positivism or *a priori* ethical jurisprudence, the norms of international law of necessity have to be left either (1) at the mercy of the domestic political and Hobbes-Austinian power politics whims of the several absolute nationalistic political sovereigns whose power-implemented commands are alone "law, proper so-called" or (2) in the form of a vacuous ethical *grundnorm*. Under such circumstances not even a modern Western nation can trust its fate to such an international law, even though it be its own creation. For the moment a dispute arises, the *grundnorm* of this international law will be given specific normative content by the parties to the dispute and by the judges in terms of the living law of the culture of each. Hence, were any nation to accept such a vacuously defined international law without reservation, it would find itself judged from the standpoint of international normative rules with a specific content other than that of its own living law. Clearly no nation will put itself in such a position.

To look at contemporary international law, therefore, from the standpoint of sociological or anthropological jurisprudence is to realize why this international law is weak and devoid of living law support. Such will be the inevitable response to any international law grounded in but one culture of the world or in legal positivism, intuitive ethical jurisprudence or the traditional sociological jurisprudence, such as that of Professor W. Friedmann, which tends, while purporting to be giving an objective account of the norms of society, to base its findings and sociological legal judgments on the normative assumptions of but one political party (his own) in one European country, for example, the Socialist Party of Austria or of West Germany. One need hardly be surprised that such a "sociological jurist" (1) found it to be emotively disturbing to read the writer's study of Continental European Union, which took into account the different norms and their relative quantitative support of the major political parties of the six nations in this Union,[1] and (2) urged, consequently, that less attention be given to objectivity in the methods of sociological jurisprudence.[2]

There is no need, however, for international law to remain in its present somewhat ineffective condition. Nor is it necessary for sociological jurists to continue to confuse the norms of the living law with those of the political preferences of the investigator. Whatever may be its limitations, the sociological jurisprudence of Ehrlich and others has made it clear that, provided a new positive law comes to terms in its substantive normative content with the norms of the living law, drawing upon them for its moral sustenance and its moral sanctions,

that new positive law can be effective. Hence if sociological jurisprudence or cultural anthropology can find an objective method for determining the world's diverse living laws, an effective and meaningful international law is not ruled out *a priori* after the manner of
the legal positivists and the self-labeled "realistic" power politicians,
but is instead a scientifically realistic, practical possibility.

Given such an objective method, the first step would consist in determining the underlying specific living laws of each people or nation
or culture, and where the culture is heterogeneous, as is usually the
case, doing the same for each relatively homogenenous cultural component of any complex culture. Difficulties, which will concern us
later, will, to be sure, arise when this is done. But similar difficulties
present themselves even in the creation of a domestic legal system, as
Chiang Monlin came to learn in pre-World War II China [3] and as the
leaders of Pakistan, Free India, Indonesia and Ghana are now learning. Nevertheless, difficulties in the creation of effective positive law,
whether it be domestic or international, can be overcome provided
normative resources can be found in the living law for doing so. What
Dean Roscoe Pound has called the "give-it-up" philosophy is not a
moral or legal necessity for mankind in an atomic age.

The crucial question, therefore, is: Can a method for objectively
specifying the substantive normative content of the living law in any
relatively homogeneous component of any culture or nation be found?

Clearly this is a task for which the traditional lawyer or moral philosopher is quite incompetent. The living law of each of the many
cultures and peoples of the world can be specified only by a direct scientific study of these cultures. The sciences concerned with such a
study are cultural sociology and cultural anthropology. More, however, is revealed by these sciences than is necessary for, or relevant
to, the jurist's and moral philosopher's purposes. The relevant items
become evident when one notes that positive law is always concerned
with norms. Positive law specifies certain specific *grundnorms* and
particular statutes which serve as moral and juridical measuring rods
to distinguish in any culture the behavior which is legal from that
which is not.

What international law needs, therefore, from the cultural sciences is the specific normative factor in the specific living law of each
of the major cultures of the world. It is because of its concern pri-

marily with the normative factor in the living law of any society that sociological or anthropological jurisprudence distinguishes itself from sociology or anthropology proper. Thus, an adequate sociological or anthropological jurisprudence must first determine the key independent variable in any culture which, when its value is determined empirically for that culture, gives its specific living law *grundnorm*. What is this independent variable? Three independent developments in contemporary sociology, anthropology and psychology suggest an answer to this question. These developments are illustrated in P. A. Sorokin's concept of "logico-meaningful social causality," Clyde Kluckhohn's study of the Navaho Indian and Warren S. McCulloch and Walter Pitts' theory of neurologically trapped universals.

Logico-Meaningful Causality. Sorokin's inductive study of the major cultures of the world led him to the discovery that in the cultural sciences there are two types of causality.[4] In the natural sciences only one of these two types occurs. The type of causality common to the natural and the cultural sciences is the one noted previously by Kelsen in his criticism of sociological jurisprudence. This type we shall call mechanical causality.[5] Its essence is that given the determination of certain present facts, certain future ones can be deduced.

Sorokin agrees with Kelsen that were all sociology and sociological jurisprudence of this mechanical causal type, the sociology of law and sociological jurisprudence would be of no use in providing positive law with ethical *grundnorms* possessing specific content. What distinguishes cultural science, however, from natural science is that mechanical causation in cultural science applies only to isolated factors in the system, not to the over-all ordering relations of the cultural system as a whole. It was with this over-all "inner order of society" that Ehrlich identified the living law in his *Fundamental Principles of the Sociology of Law*. Sorokin adds that the sociological causality which defines this over-all inner order is logico-meaningful rather than mechanical.

The writer has described the matter elsewhere as follows:

> The nature of logico-meaningful causality begins to become evident when one pursues the analogy of Newtonian mechanics in the cultural sciences as far as it will go. Any natural system designated by Newtonian mechanics has its entities. They are the physical or scientific objects. The cultural systems also have their entities. They

are the human persons and their physical environment. When, in Newtonian mechanics, the postulates and values of the variables defining the state of any system are specified, the ordering relations of the system are made determinate. The mere specification, however, in any cultural system of the positions and momenta of the persons in that society is not sufficient to specify the ordering relations which define the culture of those persons.

An example will suffice to make this clear. In many village communities of India, Muslims and Hindus have lived together for centuries. Most of the Muslims are converts from Hinduism; thus racially the peoples are for the most part identical. Hence, the cultural differences between Muslims and Hindus which are so great as to necessitate the present division of the 19th century India into Pakistan and New Delhi's India are not to be explained by physical and genetic differences. The momenta and positions of the bodies of the Hindus and Muslims in any single village hardly account for the differences in their two cultures. The position of Muslims and Hindus is identical since both are located in the same village. If one watched both groups walking down the street there might be slight differences in their momenta, but hardly differences sufficient to account for the differences in culture. In fact we would suspect that where differences in momenta between Muslims and Hindus in the same village appeared, these differences would be the effect rather than the cause of the cultural differences. Clearly the cultural ordering relations are not given after the manner in which the ordering relations of natural systems exhibiting their mechanical causation are given.

What is the unique factor, in addition to the aforementioned physical factors, which must be determined in order to make the ordering relations, which incidentally define the ethos of a culture, determinate? Sorokin's answer is that this additional key variable, unique to cultural systems, is to be found in the meanings that the persons making up any single culture hold in common and use to conceptualize, order and integrate the raw data of their experience. It is because meanings are the key factor that Sorokin calls this unique causality of cultural science "logico-meaningful causality."

What this entails is that wherever there are two different cultures, the persons in those cultures are using different basic meanings or concepts to describe, systematize and integrate the data of their experience. The Hindus in the Indian villages are using those of Hinduism; the Muslims, those of Islam; and so we could go on beyond the Hindu villages to the rest of the world. Then we would say Soviet Russians are using those of Marx as interpreted by Lenin and Stalin. The traditional Chinese, those of Confucius; the Siamese, those of Buddhism, with a slight top layer of Hinduism; the Roman

Catholics those of St. Thomas; the Americans those of Locke and Jefferson and Adam Smith and Mill and Jevons, and more recently Keynes.

Our example of the Indian village suggests also another point noted by Sorokin. The meanings used by a given people to describe, organize and interpret the data of their experience determine the ethos of their culture. I would even go further and say that they are its ethos. The word "good" is literally nothing more than the name for the basic meanings of the hierarchy of all meanings used by a people to conceptualize themselves and their universe. This follows from what has been said. For if the basic meanings define the ordering relations of a culture, they automatically define its living law, and the living law of a culture is its ethos. To these basic conceptual meanings the word "good" adds but one thing in addition to its designation of them, *i.e.*, their application to, and use as a measure of, conduct. In short, ethics is the conceptualization of the data of experience, applied.[6]

And, it may be added, law is the application of ethics to society in the settling of its disputes.

But what are the basic meanings or concepts which define the living law ethics of a culture? The usual term for designating the basic concepts of any subject matter is philosophy. This is why the sociological jurist determines the value of the variable which specifies objectively the living law norms of a culture when he determines the indigenous philosophy of that culture. At this point Clyde Kluckhohn's anthropological studies become important.

Philosophy of the Navaho Indians. Kluckhohn's anthropological study [7] is especially significant because the Navahos have no written literature. Nevertheless, as noted in Chapters III, IV and V, he found that they use positive legal norms different from those of the surrounding American culture in settling their disputes. The reason for this difference became evident only after he teased out of them the concepts which they used for describing, integrating and anticipating the facts of their experience.

When their basic concepts were made overt and verified through conversation with them, Kluckhohn found that the Navahos have a complete, integrated and articulate philosophy. Once this philosophy was made explicit, not only did their particular positive legal norms follow naturally, but also the reason for the inner ordering relations of their society became clear. Again, this time through the eyes of the science of cultural anthropology, the living law of a culture is made explicit when its philosophy is specified.

Kluckhohn's study shows also that this specification can be made in a quite objective manner without the introduction of any arbitrarily chosen normative hypothesis upon the part of the investigator. Both the philosophy and the positive law which Kluckhohn found the Navaho to possess are different from the norms or the philosophy which he brought to the study from his own culture. Both the Navaho moral and legal norms and the Navaho philosophy came to him as a surprise.

But how can philosophy have this key significance in defining the specific content of the living law of a culture? Is not human, and hence social, behavior a mere response to the stimuli of sex or hunger, with philosophy a mere pseudo-rationalization after the fact? At this point it is necessary to introduce the recent investigations of the neurological and behavioristic psychologists, Warren S. McCulloch and Walter Pitts.

Neurologically Trapped Equivalents of Universals. One of the great merits of Underhill Moore's sociological jurisprudence was its analytic precision. It achieved generality because it treated the living law of a culture in terms of the overt behavior of all the individuals making up the culture. It had the precision also of being deductively formulated. Both of these sources of precision were present because Underhill Moore based his final legal science upon the deductively formulated, behavioristic psychology of his Yale colleague Clark Hull.

In Underhill Moore's use of this psychology, he treated all symbols merely as stimuli, ignoring their meaning. This tended to make it appear that all individual behavior and also the high-frequency group behavior which defines the living law norm is the mere effect of passing stimuli. On this basis it is difficult to understand how ideas and meanings, or, in other words, basic philosophical assumptions, can have the significance in defining the living law of a culture which Sorokin's sociology and Kluckhohn's anthropology demonstrate.

McCulloch and Pitts have shown,[8] however, that recent neurological research and theory necessitate the reconstruction of Hull's behavioristic psychology in crucially important ways. They noted that if the nerve cells or neurons of the human nervous system were ordered linearly, then the stimulus would completely determine the response, and philosophical concepts would have the irrelevance in human behavior which many previous thinkers have supposed to be the case. In technical terms, the stimulus of the sensory neuron would fire the intervening cortical neurons in the linear net, which in turn would fire the motor neuron, thereby producing the overt, muscular behavioristic response. Thus the stimulus alone would determine the behavior, the intervening cortical neurons being merely carriers of the impulse from the stimulus to the motor response. (See upper part of Diagram I on page 110.)

McCulloch and Pitts recalled Lorente de Nó's demonstration that cortical neurons are often arranged in a circle to which a sensory neuron comes and from which a motor neuron departs, after the manner indicated in the lower part of the diagram. These three investigators present experimental physiological evidence for believing that the firing of the sensory neuron fires one of the cortical neurons in the circle and that this cortical neuron in turn fires its succeeding neuron in the circle and so on. Suppose that the time it takes to pass this impulse, representing the stimulus, from one neuron to another around the circle is longer than the refractory phase required by any neuron in the circle to have its energy restored by the metabolic process of the body, after it has fired. Then the impulse will be passed continuously around the circle as long as the human being in question lives. Such a circular net, together with the impulse being permanently passed around it by the successive firings of its neurons, is a reverberating circuit. Assuming a one-one relation between the stimulus and the trapped impulse in the reverberating circuit (an assumption which is guaranteed if a sensory neuron responds only to a particular type of stimulus and but one sensory neuron relates the stimulus to the reverberating circuit in question); then the persisting impulse in the reverberating circuit formally "represents the stimulus that is gone." When something represents something else, it is a symbol. Thus McCulloch and Pitts noted that in the trapped impulses of reverberating cortical circuits one has the neurological correlate of what introspective psychology calls an idea. The writer then suggested:

> Suppose there are several such neurally connected circuits with their different trapped representatives of diverse stimuli or environmental facts. Connected meanings give propositions and connected propositions give theories. Suppose also that some trapped impulses

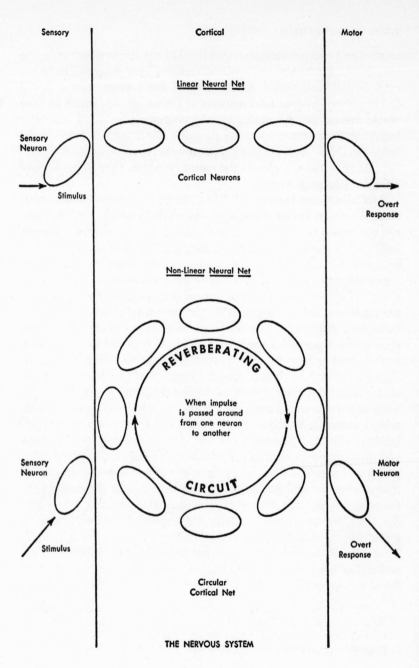

Diagram I

representing certain facts in experience (*i.e.,* stimuli) are used to define others. Then the trapped universals will be ordered hierarchically in the cortex. Thus the distinction between basic or philosophical concepts and derived, more inductively given, concepts will arise.

Suppose also that this hierarchy of meanings can both effect the firing of one motor neuron and inhibit the firing of another, as McCulloch shows to be the case. Then we see how philosophy not only can, but must, serve as the normative judge and censor of any stimulus striking a sensory neuron, defining what passes over into overt behavior and what does not. Thus, both law and ethics, as grounded in the trapped universals placed at the top of the cortical hierarchy because of their capacity to prepare the human organism for any stimuli hitting it, become intelligible. Neurological and introspective psychology hereby combine epistemically to affirm that behavior is a response not to stimuli alone, but to ideas found to be basic in remembering, describing and integrating the stimuli, and in enabling one to anticipate tomorrow's stimuli. When many people agree on these basic meanings, one has a single culture.[9]

One has also a communal, rather than merely a personal, ethics and living law. Then also the concept of "a legal system" or of "a nation" becomes meaningful in terms of concrete entities and events; that is, in terms of individual persons and specific events in their brains.

One caution with respect to the foregoing reduction to concrete persons and events of sentences referring to abstract nouns such as "a legal system" or "a nation" is to be kept in mind. The human brain undoubtedly achieves its capacity to remember past events by instruments in addition to that of the aforementioned reverberating circuits with their trapped impulses. As the late Professor John von Neumann has pointed out in his book, *The Computer and the Brain,*[10] there are several different classes of memory organs and a circuit is but one of them.[11] He immediately goes on to note that "the hierarchic principle" applies to memory organs both in the modern high-speed computing machines and in the human brain.[12] It is this hierarchical ordering of the differing trapped impulses in reverberating circuits, or their formal physical, chemical or neurological equivalents, which makes it possible for human brains to order the introspected concepts and meanings which are their epistemic correlates into defined and undefined concepts and into the postulates and theorems of (*a*) imaginatively constructed, merely descriptive or (*b*) axiomatically constructed, deductively formulated scientific and philosophical theory. This permits us to describe a legal system or the political abstraction which is called a nation as a group of people who share a common set of trapped universals for ordering their relations to one another and to nature. It is this hierarchic principle in the brain which makes possible the method of philosophical anthropology and of a scientifically objective, yet indirectly and experimentally verifiable sociological jurisprudence.

Contemporary sociology, anthropology and neurological psychology converge, therefore, upon the conclusion that Underhill Moore's sociological jurisprudence must be amended in the following manner: Between the stimulus which fires the sensory neuron and the motor neuron which contracts the muscles to produce observable overt behavior, there must be placed the reverberating circuits of the human cortex which contain the trapped equivalents of introspected ideas. It is reasonable to assume also that the correlates of these trapped impulses representing their respective sensory stimuli must appear in introspective consciousness and in linguistic communication as the directly inspected meanings and ideas of scientific and philosophical theory.

This reformulation introduces into sociological jurisprudence a much more simple, economical and effective way of objectively determining the living law of a given people or culture. One has merely to question them verbally to bring out their basic concepts and philosophy, as did Kluckhohn with the Navaho Indians, noting the consequences of this philosophy as it flows over into and is confirmed by their overt behavior, positive legal norms and decisions. In cultures which have a written literature one need merely study their basic scientific treatises concerning nature and their basic philosophical treatises to discover the underlying concepts used to describe and integrate the raw data of human experience, watching in turn their manifestations and confirmation in overt behavior, art forms, social institutions, positive legal documents and codes.

Unlike the sociological jurisprudence of Underhill Moore or Lasswell and McDougal, this is a workable method of determining the living law in any culture. To use Underhill Moore's sociological jurisprudence in the Hindu culture of India it would be necessary to determine objectively the spatio-temporal motions of some 350,000,-000 individual Hindus. Obviously, this is impossible. Yet without it the living law is not determined since high-frequency behavior has no meaning apart from the determination of the behavior of all. When one notes, however, the connection between neurologically trapped universals in the human cortex and introspected or linguistically and publicly expressed meanings, one can use these recorded meanings rather than the overt behavior of 350,000,000 individual Hindus to determine objectively their living law.

More specifically this means that instead of undertaking the impossible task of having sociological jurists, using behavioristic psychology, report the spatio-temporal motions of 350,000,000 Hindus, one will read the Vedic hymns, the Upanishads and the Bhagavadgita, together with the philosophical classics of Mimamsa and Sankara and Ramanuja. Then one must compare these philosophical treatises with an inductive inspection of the overt behavior of Hindus, their ritualism and the positive law in the Code of Manu and the other Hindu law treatises.

Another caution is necessary. The foregoing paragraphs refer only to the relatively homogeneous classical Hindu normative component of the cultural and living law complex which is contemporary India. To give the complex living law of the latter complex culture, the same method would have to be applied to its other relatively homogeneous components such as classical Muslim India, classical Sikh India, modern secular Congress Party liberal democratic India and Gandhi's mediational and pacifistic Mahayana Buddhist and non-dualistic Vedanta India. Also, as was made clear in the previous chapter, the relative quantitative support by the people of contemporary India of each set of norms has to be determined.

This scientific method of philosophical anthropology for defining the living law also avoids the weakness which Underhill Moore noted in his own sociological jurisprudence. This weakness consisted in his being unable to define, other than in an arbitrary way, the line which distinguishes high-frequency, and in his sense good living law, from low-frequency, or bad living law. In the philosophical jurisprudence based on the McCulloch and Pitts neurological behaviorism correlated with introspective psychology, the good living law is defined not quantitatively but qualitatively in terms of philosophical ideas and doctrines. Conduct within a particular living law is good if it corresponds to the philosophy of the community in question, bad if it does not. Quantity has nothing to do with the matter. What made the use of Hindu private law necessary in British India was not the fact that there are 350,000,000 Hindus, but belief in and practice of Hindu doctrines by Indian disputants in India's courts. Thus, it is not the high-frequency Gallup Poll statistics, which may express little more than a whim or hysteria of the moment, but the persisting philosophy of the community that provides the scientific basis for normative judicial decisions. The Feinberg Law passed hastily by the New York Legislature and upheld later by the United States Supreme Court [13] as compared with the philosophical basis of Justice Douglas' dissent illustrates this difference between a quantitative mood of the moment and qualitative sociological jurisprudence. No judge in finding the ground for his decision has to add up countless continuously changing, merely operationally determined quantities after the manner of sociological jurisprudence of Lasswell and McDougal or even of Underhill Moore. The basis for any decision is always some determinate proposition with substantive normative content. This follows from the method of sociological jurisprudence which requires for any living law that a qualitative set of postulates with substantive normative content be specified; the quantitative counting of noses becomes important only with respect to determining the portion of the population in the legal system and nation in question which supports this qualitative set of norms. For this reason also the scientific method of philosophical anthropology escapes the vacuousness of the intuitive ethical jurisprudence of G. E. Moore, W. D. Ross and Morris and Felix Cohen.

This does not mean that in determining the living law of any culture or people inductive studies may not be valuable. The more empirical the determination, the richer the content of the living law; hence the great importance of Underhill Moore's institutional studies and those of Lasswell and McDougal. Fully adequate inductive investigation must, however, supplement and simplify the latter by concentrating attention on the empirical determination of the logico-meaningful or philosophically basic doctrines held in common by large numbers of people in the particular society being studied. Otherwise, the inner order of the inductive data is not specified, without which, as Ehrlich has made clear, there is no specification of the living law.

The restriction to beliefs held in common by large numbers of people is justified because it is only common beliefs that are community beliefs and hence effective living and positive legal principles. There may be countless other philosophical beliefs differing from one another held by large numbers of people in the community but, precisely because any one of them is not held in common by a large number of other people, it is the living law belief of but one person, not the living law belief of the society. It is only living law philosophical beliefs held in common by large numbers of people in the society which give the society the inner order which is its living law.

The complex culture of India just before the partition into Pakistan and the present New Delhi India will serve as an example. This total culture exhibited three diverse and in part conflicting living laws. One was the living law of the pre-Western Hindu community. This is made determinate in an objective manner when the basic philosophical conceptions of nature and man in the fundamental scientific and philosophical books and commentaries mentioned above are studied. The Hindu positive law corresponding to this underlying Hindu living law is presented in an objective manner in the law books of Manu, Gautama, Apastamba and others. The second living law of the former India is that of the Muslim community. It is made determinate in an objective manner when the conception of man in his relation to the rest of reality, as rooted in the Quran and the attendant philosophical doctrines of Arabia and Persia, is made explicit. Given this philosophical determination of Islamic living law in India, the corresponding positive laws concerning marriage, inheritance, tithes, etc. become similarly determinate and intelligible. The third major legal factor in the old India is the modern Western political and legal institutions and doctrines. This came to India first as a positive law. When the British were there it was a living law to the extent that, because of their army and their jurisdiction, it had to be accepted. The extent to which it is a living law now that the British have left remains to be seen. The present Indian Constitution and Prime Minister Nehru's secular state measure the extent to which modern Western positive law has become India's living law.

In this connection, Pakistan has rejected a secular state for an Islamic one. This means that for the Muslim community of old India, which is now in Pakistan, the British positive law has been rejected in part as a criterion of the norms for Pakistan's present living and positive law. It is precisely because the philosophical beliefs which define the living law of the Muslim community are so different from and even antithetical to the philosophical beliefs specifying the living law of the Hindu community of old India that the partition into Pakistan and present India became necessary. These events and the determinate philosophical content of the diverse Hindu, Muslim and British living law doctrines are objective facts. What is true of the society which is India, is true of any society.

A philosophical anthropology, therefore, which identifies the living law of any culture with the philosophy of that culture provides a method [14] of specifying *grundnorms* for positive law which are not merely objective but also possessed of specific content which is the most likely to be lasting. Unlike the pure theory of law and *a priori* ethical jurisprudence, legal science is not left with a purely vacuous ethical postulate. Moreover, practical judicial, political and moral decisions based on such a science of philosophical anthropology are likely to be effective because positive acts whose *grundnorms* are specified in this manner will have the spontaneous sanctions of the living law behind them. No problem of legal obligation will arise.

Comparative philosophical anthropology makes it clear that the contemporary world does not have a single living law. Contemporary India has at least three major living laws and India is but one small portion of the world. Present China, apart from Formosa, has two major living laws, Taoist-Buddhist-Confucianism and Marxist Communism, both of which are in part at least different from any of the three living laws of India. Chinese Marxist Communism is in fact only a positive law used by President Mao and his colleagues in the hope of creating a new living law. Roman Catholic cultures in the West exhibit another major living law of the world. It is defined in major part by the philosophy and theology of St. Thomas Aquinas. Those modern nations of the West heavily under Protestant religious and modern scientific and philosophical influence illustrate a still different living law of which the United States is the purest case. The philosophy which specifies this living law is that of British empiricism as worked out by Hobbes, Locke, Hume, Adam Smith, Jefferson, Mill and Bentham, Jevons, Keynes and the Austrian school of economists. The legal theory of this philosophical living law oscillates between (1) the natural rights theory of the early John Locke, Jefferson and the United States Supreme Court in *Brown v. Board of Education*, and (2) the legal positivism of the John Locke of the *Essay*, Hume, Hobbes, Austin, Mr. Justice Frankfurter, during his frequent moments of nostalgia for the Harvard Law School of his day, and Judge Learned Hand.

Since the underlying living laws of the world are many in number rather than one, the way to an effective international law is to base it upon the world's living law pluralism. Only if this is done will positive international law be able to draw to itself the underlying living law support which sociological jurisprudence demonstrates that any positive law must have if it is to be effective.

What this means specifically will become clearer if the matter is first approached in a negative manner, by considering existing international law and more particularly the Charter of the United Nations. The Charter gives the impression that the world is in complete agreement upon a single set of determinate world norms. Did not each official representative of most of the nations of the world sign a document in which he dedicated his government to the building of a world order in which "freedom," "well-being," "economic uplift" and "the good life" would come to all men? This impression of a single world living law is, however, quite superficial and spurious, for the basic normative words "freedom," "well-being," "economic uplift" and "the good life" are left undefined. Nor is it difficult to find the reason for this lack of definition and the resultant vituperation which has followed when subsequent foreign ministers read the definitions required by their differing and often conflicting living laws into these otherwise vacuous words.

The existing international law and the United Nations Charter are the creation of traditional Western or Westernized Asian legal minds. Such minds tend to conceive of law in terms of legal positivism or *a priori* ethical jurisprudence. As the earlier portion of this study has shown, both of these schools leave indeterminate the substantive living law content of the basic ethical norms of any legal system. It is to be expected, therefore, that international legal institutions created by lawyers with either of these two philosophical mentalities will be ineffective and that their charters or constitutions will be filled with many high-sounding but normatively vacuous abstract nouns. The miracle is not, therefore, that the United Nations, for example, has failed to fulfill the hopes of mankind, but that it has been as effective as has been the case.

Even though Continental European Union has not received as much attention as has the United Nations, it is, nevertheless, a truly remarkable and much more effective international institution, as the writer has shown elsewhere.[15] The reasons for this will serve to illustrate the method of philosophical anthropology when applied to the complex culture and political climate of Continental Western Europe. The philosophically anthropological reasons for the success of Continental European Union will concern us in Chapter X.

IX

Cultural Dynamics and Historical Jurisprudence

RECENT findings in cultural sociology and anthropology converge upon the conclusion that the unity of a culture centers in the concepts and assumptions held in common by a given people in their conceptualization of the raw data of experience. The sociologist Sorokin found that cultures fall into groups depending upon whether the concepts used by a people derive all their meaning from sensuous immediacy or not.[1] When sensation is the sole source of meaning, then the values of a culture tend to be "sensate" in character. When, on the other hand, experience is known scientifically in terms of experimentally verified, deductively formulated theory, as occurred with the ancient Greek mathematical physicists, then the truly known individual becomes conceived as an instance of technically constructed universal laws and the Western Roman Stoic Christian concept of moral man as universal man comes into being, as Chapter XI will show in greater detail.

Similarly, as noted in the previous chapter, the anthropologist Kluckhohn has found that even the behavior of the Navaho Indians, who are devoid of a written literature, can be understood only when the concepts, or in other words the philosophy, in which they conceptualize their experience are determined and made explicit.[2] In short, a culture has unity when the people in the society in question use the same basic concepts or philosophy for describing and coordinating the data of their experience.[3]

This concept of the unity of a culture has important implications

From *Actes du IVᵉ Congrès International des Sciences Anthropologiques et Ethnologiques*, Vol. II, 1952, Vienna.

for historical jurisprudence and the problem of cultural dynamics. In fact, it enables us to understand why previous theories of cultural change have failed. The previous attempts to account for cultural change have been based upon the concept of causality. In other words, they have attempted to achieve a cultural dynamics by recourse to historical determinism.

When this way is chosen two possibilities present themselves. The causality or determinism can be conceived as obeying the logic of identity or the logic of negation, that is, the logic of dialectic. Hegelian dialectical idealism and Marxist dialectical materialism are examples of the latter alternative. The *Traité de Sociologie Générale* of Pareto [4] and the sociological jurisprudence of Underhill Moore [5] are examples of the former alternative.

Hegel and Marx's reasons for basing cultural dynamics upon the dialectical logic of negation are easy to understand. Both were members of Western civilization. In the Middle Ages the philosophy which defined the unity of Western culture was in major part that of Aristotle, St. Thomas, Hooker and Sir Robert Filmer. With the coming of modern science and its British empirical political and economic implications, the unity of some cultures of the West, such as modern parliamentary Great Britain and the United States, became defined by not merely a different but also an antithetical philosophy. With the advent of Soviet Russia since the time of Hegel and Marx, the logical incompatibility of the philosophies which define the unities of Western cultures which succeed one another in time becomes even more marked. Clearly, one cannot by the logic of identity deduce, from the philosophy which defines the unity of the culture of the Middle Ages, a later Western culture whose philosophical unity is the logical contradiction of that of the medieval world. Only a logic of negation can therefore meet the needs of cultural dynamics in Western civilization.

At this point, however, one other consideration entered into the thinking of Hegel and Marx. Both had identified what ought to be with the historical development of what is. Both, and especially Marx, found it necessary also to affirm that today's culture is bad and in need of reform. The question arose immediately: In a theory of cultural evolution, which identifies the "ought" with the historical "is," what meaning is there for saying that today's culture is bad and in need of reform? Within their theory this question has but one answer: The "is" for today is bad to the extent that it departs from tomorrow's "is." In other words, the ideal for today is tomorrow's actuality. But to make this answer meaningful as a basis for prescribing how today's culture is to be reformed, it is necessary to know today the character of tomorrow's "is." This is impossible unless there is a determinism such that knowing today's culture, one can deduce tomorrow's. Thus it happened that to the true doctrine that culture in the West evolves according to the dialectical logic of negation, Hegel and Marx added the false doctrine that this dialectical evolution of Western culture is deterministic.[6]

That dialectical evolution cannot be deterministic, the most elementary analysis will show. For if the philosophy specified by the thesis that defines the unity of today's culture is to generate deterministically by negation the antithetical philosophy which defines the unity of tomorrow's culture, it is necessary that the negation of a thesis give one and only one antithesis. This is not the case. Any thesis can be negated in more than one way. The philosophy of the Middle Ages can be negated by passing to the philosophy of Hume's British empiricism, of Locke's mental-material substance dualism, of Cartesian dualism, Spinoza's absolutism, Leibnizian monadology, Kantian idealism, Romanticism, Marxist Communism or in countless other ways. In short, if a cultural development is dialectical it cannot be deterministic. The attempt, therefore, to account for cultural dynamics by the dialectical determinism of either the idealist Hegel or the materialist Marx is a failure.

The attempt to do so by recourse to the logic of identity is an equal failure. The most rigorous effort in this direction is that of the sociological jurist Underhill Moore, described above. Using the deductively formulated behavioristic psychology of Clark Hull, Moore was able to put this approach upon an experimental basis. The use of Hull's behavioristic psychology is important for many reasons. First, it rests upon the work of the Russian Pavlov and hence should carry weight with contemporary Marxists. Second, the behavioristic concepts permit the determination of the present state of a cultural system to be given in objective terms with the same findings for different observers. This was not true of Hegel and Marx's approach to cultural facts. Third, Hull's behavioristic psychology is deductively formulated. The relevance of this is that Hume showed that induction gives no necessary connections. It follows, therefore, that if determinism is to hold over time for a given culture, only a deductively formulated scientific theory and method can find it.

It is because Newton's physics is deductively formulated that it is able to exhibit a deterministic relation of logical implication connecting the present state of a mechanical system in nature to its future state. Since the connecting relation is that of logical implication, the dynamic determinism of modern physics rests on the logic of identity. It was precisely this type of connection between the present and future state of a cultural system that Moore attempted to establish experimentally by recourse to Hull's deductively formulated behavioristic psychology.

The results, as Moore found, were negative. No possible selection of variables in the data enabled him to find a formula connecting the inner order of the system at one time to its inner order at a later time. Thus he concluded that the attempt to achieve a deterministic cultural dynamics by recourse to the logic of identity fails, just as does recourse to the dialectical logic of negation.

It follows that there is no evidence whatever for cultural or historical determinism. Both Lionel Robbins and the writer have shown that a cultural determinism obeying the logic of identity cannot be achieved within the introspective psychological theory of value of the Austrian school of economic science.[7] Moore's work shows similarly that a cultural determinism based on the logic of identity is impossible on the assumptions of a Pavlovian behavioristic psychology. A dialectical determinism is a self-contradictory theory, for to be dialectical is to relate the thesis defining an earlier state of cultural change to the antithesis defining its later state, by negation; yet the negation of a thesis does not give a unique antithesis, and without a unique antithesis there is no determinism.

As noted also in Chapter V, a deterministic cultural dynamics is self-defeating on other grounds. For, as Karl Popper has noted, if cultural evolution were deterministic, reform would be both impossible and unnecessary. For on the one hand man could then do nothing to reform present society, and on the other hand the reform would come quite automatically.

How then is one to conceive of cultural dynamics? Clearly it must be conceived as a process which is free. There is no determinism in cultural history.

On the other hand, cultural evolution is not completely chaotic. The philosophies of Descartes, Locke, Hume, Kant, etc., are not entirely unconnected with those of St. Thomas and St. Augustine. Can this relationship be specified in part? This at bottom is the heart of the problem of cultural dynamics.

One thing can be said with definiteness. Hegel and Marx are right in their thesis that cultural evolution in the West is by the logic of negation, not the logic of identity. From this fact it follows, however, that it is not deterministic.

Even so our philosophical theory of cultural unity can tell us something more about the shift from one philosophy of the unity of Western culture to a later antithetical philosophy of its unity. This shift depends at bottom upon at least two things. First, the appearance of novel facts in natural science causes informed rare minds to reject old theories for conceptualizing and integrating the raw data of experience. Second, the creative imagination of some man of genius, such as a Newton, a Locke, a Kant, or an Einstein, enables him and the people who learn from him to find a new natural philosophy for the integration of experience.

Always, however, through the jumps — for jumps rather than continuities characterize cultural change in the West — three factors remain constant. First, the new conceptual system negates some premises of the old conceptual system. For example, in the shift from the physics of Aristotle to that of Galilei and Newton, final causes were replaced by mechanical causes so far as ontology was concerned, and Aristotelian concepts by inductive abstraction were replaced by Democritean and Platonic constructs so far as epistemology was involved. These negations of old theories in natural science brought with them corresponding changes in the norms for culture. Second, true knowledge of any individual is always regarded as the specification of the universal laws which the particular individual satisfies. Normatively this means that moral man is, when scientifically understood, neither patriarchal family or tribal man nor class-of-the-proletariat man, but universal man. The third constant is that any knowledge presupposes the creative inventiveness of the freely inquiring human spirit. Without the creativity of Aristotle, St. Thomas, Galilei,

Newton, Locke, Kant, Marx and Whitehead and their like, there would be no cultural dynamics. Instead, culture would be dead, static and frozen, merely mumbling old normative unities.

There are reasons for believing that the dynamics of Far Eastern cultures uninfluenced by Western factors is not dialectical. This is why above we have restricted dialectical cultural development to Western civilization. The culture of China before the Western-inspired revolution of Sun Yat-sen in 1912 was governed by the same philosophy in 1900 as in the second century B.C., namely that of Confucius.[8]

We conclude, therefore, that it is only by finding the unity of a culture in the philosophy held in common by its people and by noting whether the philosophy changes with time that one has the key to cultural dynamics. If the philosophy stays constant, the culture does not evolve but merely works itself out according to the logic of identity, remaining relatively constant through time after the manner of Confucian Chinese society. If the philosophy is altered, being replaced by a new philosophy in which one of the premises negates a traditional premise, as occurs in the West, then evolution occurs and it is by definition dialectical but not deterministic in character.

X

European Political Experience
Since World War II

THE complexity of Great Britain's relation to the Continent has been exemplified since World War II by her behavior regarding the unification of Europe. This behavior has been paradoxical; yet the paradox becomes understandable and resolvable if contemporary politics is approached by the method of philosophical anthropology and note is taken of the cultural differences as well as the cultural identities between Great Britain and her Continental neighbors.

In 1946 at Zurich, Prime Minister Churchill issued a dramatic call to all Europeans to unite. On May 8, 1948 at The Hague he made a similar appeal to a large and distinguished gathering representing practically every European political party and nation outside the Iron Curtain. In this appeal he launched the organization known as the European Movement and urged everyone present to bring pressure upon their respective governments to create a United Europe. Shortly thereafter the European Movement was established as an active organization with four Honorary Presidents: Mr. Winston Churchill, then leader of His Majesty's Opposition; Prime Minister De Gasperi of Italy; Prime Minister Spaak of Belgium; and M. Blum, leader of the Socialist Party of France. Forthwith, through action of the member national governments, the Council of Europe was created at Strasbourg with high hopes that Great Britain and the Continental European nations would collaborate immediately to bring about a United States of Europe.

One sobering qualification had appeared, however, before the Council of Europe was established. The response of Great Britain's

Translated into French by M. Bouvier and published in *Comprendre, Revue de la Société Européenne* (1955).

Labour Party government to the creation of the Council of Europe was first negative and then lukewarm. The Council of Europe came into being more in spite of the British Labour Party government than because of it.

It was hoped and expected, however, by Continental Europeans, such as Prime Minister Spaak, that this lukewarm British attitude represented only the Labour Party and would disappear if the Conservative Party under Mr. Churchill's leadership came back to power. Events soon showed such expectations to be unfounded. In the British general election of October 1951, the Labour Party was defeated. Referring to these events afterwards, M. Spaak wrote as follows:

"When Churchill returned to power, it was generally felt that the situation would change. Yet a short moment of hopeful waiting was followed by a deep disappointment. From the very first days following the Conservative victory in Britain it was plain that if the Laborites were holding fast to their positions, the Conservatives had simply joined them." [1]

Mr. Churchill's admonitions in 1948 and Prime Minister Churchill's deeds in 1951 seemed to Continental Europeans to have little connection with one another. Such is the first paradox in Great Britain's relation to European Union.

As a consequence European Union received its first major setback and the Council of Europe split into two groups. One group, led by Great Britain, insisted upon restricting the Council of Europe to a merely consultative function. The other group, composed of Belgium, France, Italy, Luxembourg, the Netherlands and West Germany, demanded a real transfer of national sovereignty to the supranational European Community in the economic, military and political spheres.

Because of this division the lesser Continental European Union, composed of the latter six nations, was born and its High Authority for Coal and Steel became a political and economic reality. At the same time the foreign ministers of the six Continental European nations signed the European Defense Community Treaty, which would create a European army under a European general staff with its soldiers in a European rather than in their traditional national uniforms. On the same day, May 27, 1952, at Paris, a Protocol to the

NATO Treaty was signed which placed this European army under the command of NATO, which is led by the United States.

The EDC Treaty contained a statute authorizing the creation of a Continental European Political Community, having as its aim the bringing of German, French, Belgian, Dutch, Luxembourgian and Italian soldiers under the control, not merely of a supranational Continental European general staff, but also of a democratically elected supranational legislature. Again Great Britain remained aloof, associating herself with the High Authority for Coal and Steel at Luxembourg while refusing to become a member and making no commitments with respect to the EDC army or the Continental European Political Community.

In 1952 a general election took place in the United States. This election, quite apart from its issues, had the inevitable effect, arising from the NATO Treaty Protocol, of bringing the movement toward European Union to a standstill. Because the EDC Protocol to the NATO Treaty places the Continental European army under the direction of United States military commanders, and hence subject to the foreign policy of the United States, the French National Assembly and many other Continental Europeans would not vote on the EDC Treaty until the 1952 elections in the United States showed what the future United States foreign policy was to be. As has been shown elsewhere,[2] when the election campaign showed that this foreign policy was likely to shift from the "containment" of Communism to its "rollback" in Europe, European opinion and especially French opinion became increasingly anti-American and the French reversed their decision about the wisdom of rearming the Germans in an EDC Treaty which was tied to the foreign policy of the United States. On August 30, 1954, the French National Assembly repudiated the EDC Treaty.

At this point the unity and morale of Europe were at their lowest ebb since World War II. Paradoxically, it was Great Britain that saved the situation so far as it has been saved. Her Conservative Foreign Minister, Anthony Eden, came upon the idea that the French National Assembly might be willing to rearm the Germans, even under a German general staff, in a collaboration of European armies with British participation and under British rather than United States political leadership. This undoubtedly is why Foreign Minister Eden turned to the Brussels Treaty, in which the United States does not participate, as the basis for his desperate move to restore some semblance of unity in Western Europe. By keeping the United States as an associate on the outside rather than the decision-maker at the top, Great Britain attempted to allay French fears with respect to the use that would be made of the rearmed Germans. With reservations concerning the solution of the Saar problem and with many other misgivings, the French National Assembly in an uncomfortably close vote accepted Foreign Minister Eden's proposal on December 30, 1954.

For this partial success, Great Britain paid an unprecedented price. The price was the commitment of British troops on the Continent for fifty years and the placing of some British units under French military command. Great Britain refused to make commitments of much less than this in the early days of EDC. Had she done for MM. Schuman, Spaak, Adenauer and De Gasperi in early 1952 what she did for M. Mendes-France in late 1954, it is hard to believe that Continental European military and political, as well as economic, union would not have become a fact before the elections in the United States brought their unfortunate influence to bear. As *The Economist* of London wrote on October 9, 1954, "There cannot be any real doubt that EDC in 1952 would have been preferable to NATO–Brussels in 1954. If the same British offer that has now been made had been made two years ago, EDC might have been in working order by now." [3]

Why did Great Britain in 1954 give, in what *The Economist* has described as an *"ad hoc"* [4] way to "a new and flimsier venture," [5] what she had refused on principle to give in 1952 to a much more promising undertaking? This is the second paradox in Great Britain's relation to European Union.

Why this paradoxical character of Great Britain's relation to the Continent? *The Economist's* designation of Foreign Minister Eden's commitment to Premier Mendes-France as *"ad hoc"* suggests the answer. This *ad hoc* behavior illustrates a mentality that is characteristically British. It may be described more completely as the piecemeal approach to politics. Its negative counterpart is the British suspicion of written constitutions and of any over-all systematic approach to the solution of particular problems.

It was precisely this mentality which expressed itself in the neutral and negative attitude of the British toward the Schuman Plan, EDC and the Constitution of the Continental European Political Community in the earlier days of their construction. A supranational community created by draft treaty and written constitutions is too artificial to be practical, the British said. Instead, as M. Spaak has written, the British were for replacing the "constitutional" method by the "functional" method, which, "foregoing all idea of concerted action, consisted in solving single, isolated problems one at a time. . . ." [6] For example, France and Germany must first solve the Saar problem.

Viewed from the British standpoint, however, there was nothing paradoxical about her neutralism or her discouragement of Continental European Union at the time of its initiation and her attempt to salvage European unity in the hour following its worst defeat. Both deeds flowed from a single, consistent mentality and philosophy — the mentality which is suspicious of systematic, over-all constitutional solutions of particular problems and which prefers, instead, to attack them piecemeal and *ad hoc*. As the informed Sir Arthur L. Goodhart has noted in his *English Law and the Moral Law,* in writing of the mentality of a Lord Chancellor of the fourteenth century, not only was it "inevitable that the canon law, in which he was trained, must have played an important role," but it "is equally true that the whole tradition of English life and thought must have influenced him not to place too much emphasis on general principles, but to seek to answer each problem as it was presented to him on grounds of practical common sense." [7] This, he adds, is what the English law means by the "reasonable man." In other words, the "reason" of an Englishman is that of a nominalistic, radically empirical philosophy.

Sir Arthur's description of British mentality indicates two of its cultural sources. One is the canon law. The other is British empirical philosophy. The canon law of the later Church of England, at least, embraced rules adopted "by custom and common law." [8] The latter inductive, common law mentality made its spirit and practice differ from that of the more orthodox Continental Roman Catholic hierarchy. The mentality of the latter tends to be systematic, deductive and what the British would term philosophically doctrinaire, deriving from the theory of professional philosophers and theologians like St. Thomas. The canon law, at least in England, was influenced more by the local, living practices and beliefs of the native peoples with whom the parish priests were in daily and intimate contact. This made it more inductive, empirical and relative to place, particular problem and circumstance. In this respect it is nearer to the common law of the Anglo-American secular legal and political tradition than to the more deductive type of law of the Continental European codes, which derive more completely and directly from Stoic Rome.

A third factor determining the philosophical and cultural differences between the British and Continental European approaches to particular European problems is the predominantly Protestant religious faith of the majority of the British, as compared with the Roman Catholic faith of the majority on the Continent. Protestantism tends to be more inductive, locating the source of legal and political norms in the private conscience of the individual person. This results in making any Protestant, particularly any Nonconformist Protestant, hesitant about transferring political sovereignty from even the individual person to his own nation, to say nothing about transferring sovereignty from the nation to the supranational community. Protestantism also has many different theologies, rather than one major orthodox doctrine. Under these circumstances the over-all, deductive, theoretical approach to practical problems is difficult if not impossible and seems exceedingly artificial. Not only does Roman Catholic thinking have one major orthodoxy — that of St. Thomas — but this systematic doctrine, with its emphasis upon the final cause in all things and upon the formally and theoretically rational in man, is excessively teleological and logical in its content, paying attention, to be sure, to place and to circumstance, but believing nonetheless that no particular practical problem is solved unless overriding general philosophical principles are also applied to it.

This difference between British and Continental mentality shows in a comparison of the British Labour Party and the Continental liberal Socialist parties. The lack of interest of the British Labour Party in the Council of Europe and in the Continental European Community has been noted. The role in founding European Union that was played by the Continental liberal Socialists such as former Premiers Blum and Spaak has also been mentioned. The later support of the liberal Socialists Saragat and Spinelli in Italy and Guy Mollet of France has been equally unequivocal. In fact, apart from the Christian Democrats, the Continental liberal Socialists have been the most vigorous supporters of a European unification that entails a genuine transfer of national sovereignty to the supranational Western European community.

To this there is one exception: the liberal Socialist Party of West Germany. But West Germany is the one nation in the Continental European Community in which a slight majority of the people are Protestant. Moreover, the German liberal Socialist Party draws more heavily for its leadership upon north and central Germany and Berlin, which are predominantly Protestant and Prussian, than on Bavaria and the Rhineland, which are Roman Catholic. Lutheran Protestant Germany is by tradition the Germany of Bismarck and East Prussia. This Germany has always been excessively nationalistic and chauvinistic. Hence its religious and secular living law, unless reformed, is not such as to provide normative content in common with that of Luxembourg, France, Belgium, Italy and the Netherlands upon which a common, positive, Continental legal, political, economic and military community can be effectively built.

But the predominant living law of the Rhineland and South Germany is Latin and Roman in both its secular legal and its Catholic religious customs and practices. It is this component of the Old Germany which the Christian Democratic government of Chancellor Adenauer represents and which the division of the Old Germany between Communist East Germany and liberal democratic West Germany has made the majority living law of the latter nation. Moreover, the normative content of its living law is, with minor exceptions, like that of the other free nations in Continental European Union. Hence, to examine Western European politics since World War II from the standpoint of philosophical anthropology is to find the common living law which has made possible the creation of such effective positive legal and political institutions as the High Authority for Coal and Steel, the Atomic Pool, the Parliament of Little Europe and its various courts to which the legal institutions of the six member nations have surrendered specified portions of their previous jurisdiction.

Such a philosophically anthropological examination of the living law of the Old Germany makes it evident also that it was the Old Germany, rather than the recent West German-French legal, economic, political and military collaboration inside Continental European Union, which was the artificial legal system and national state. Certainly between (a) the living law of the Protestant Lutheran Germany of Bismarck's Prussia and (b) the living law of Latin secular and Roman Catholic religious Bavaria and the Rhineland there is normative conflict rather than agreement. Bismarck recognized this artificiality of his Prussian-dominated Germany when he laid down the political dictum to the effect that if one is confronted with division at home, one must create an enemy abroad.

The effect, consequently, of Continental European Union is to tie Southern and Western Germany to the culture to its west and northwest and in Italy, with which it has common living law familial, Latin legal and Catholic religious ties. For a further study of this fascinating and important development in contemporary international law and European politics, the reader is referred to the writer's *European Union and United States Foreign Policy*. It contains charts which specify the quantitative support of the six major qualitative norms of the common religious and secular political parties in the six nations in this supranational European community, after the manner of the method specified for philosophical anthropology in Chapters VII and VIII of this book.

For concrete evidence also of the way in which otherwise able scholars, such as Professor Crane Brinton, have fallen into grave error in their judgments of the practicality of Continental European Union, because of their neglect of the cultural aspects of the situation, the reader may find it relevant to read the review by Professor Brinton of the aforementioned book in the *New York Herald Tribune* of November 28, 1954 with reviews by the informed European reporter Drew Middleton in the *New York Times* for December 26, 1954 and by the reviewer for *The Economist* of London in its issue of February 12, 1955. Clearly one neglects the method of philosophical anthropology in one's historical, political, legal and ethical judgments at one's peril, as Professor Brinton's self-confident but nonetheless erroneous pronouncements from the vantage point of his armchair in the Widener Library of Harvard University pointedly demonstrate.

The success and effectiveness of the High Authority for Coal and Steel and the other new supranational legal and political institutions created on the Continent of Europe since World War II have far-reaching implications for the world generally and for international law in particular. The High Authority for Coal and Steel and the Atomic Pool demonstrate that effective new international legal and political institutions can be created where they did not exist before, provided living law customs and practices are taken advantage of to support the new positive legal rules. The fact that there was not, antecedent to the creation of Continental European Union, a de facto political sovereign stronger than any national sovereign in the Community was not fatal, as legal positivists maintain, to the creation of effective supranational positive law and positive political, economic and military institutions.

It would be an error to leave the impression that West Germany, Luxembourg, the Netherlands, Belgium, France and Italy, which have transferred portions of their legal jurisdiction and political sovereignty to the supranational institutions of the Continental European Community, agree only with respect to the norms of the Latin secular and Roman Catholic religious component of their respective cultures. The other major political parties in these six nations have common norms also. This is true even of the anti-clerical liberal Socialists, nothwithstanding the Protestant Lutheran Prussian element that is peculiar to a portion of this party in West Germany. This becomes clear if one compares the norms and living law background of the liberal Socialist parties, which represent labor for the most part in the six Continental European nations, with the politicies and living law background of the Labour Party in Great Britain.

The policies and philosophy of the Continental liberal parties are the work of professional social philosophers, such as Saint-Simon, Comte, Kant, Proudhon and Marx. For the most part their leaders have been doctors of philosophy or of law. This shows in the Continental liberal Socialist leaders such as Guy Mollet, Spaak, Blum and Ollenhauer. Thus their unconscious approach to particular problems is theoretical as well as empirical and systematic rather than piecemeal and *ad hoc*. The British Labour Party, on the other hand, arose more inductively out of the specific needs and demands of the British laborers in the trade unions. This shows in men like Herbert Morrison who have no doctor's degree or university background. Even when university graduates, such as Mr. Clement Attlee, assume the leadership of the British Labour Party, their approach likewise is more inductive, concerned with the social services, rather than doctrinairely prescribed by professional social philosophers.

Also the British Labour Party has been influenced greatly by the ethics of British Nonconformist Protestantism. The late Lord Lindsay of Birker, the recent Labour Government's first appointee to the House of Lords, has described this Protestant factor in his article, "The Philosophy of the British Labour Government." After pointing out that its "members have all been trained in trade-union branches or 'chapels,' in cooperative meetings, or in organizations like the Cooperative Women's Guild," he adds, "Where Nonconformity was strong trade unionism was strong, and where it was weak trade unionism was weak." [9] He then notes the very concrete, particular and localized experiences from which a significant part of its philosophy derives. "One of the things most bitterly felt about the long-continued unemployment from which we suffered in the 'thirties was that the unemployed found themselves suddenly cut out of society. They had no clothes in which they could decently go to chapel." [10] It was the feeling that there was something fundamentally un-Christian about such a social situation, which sent so many Nonconformist Protestant members of the middle class into the British Labour Party. This again is an empirical as well as a religious approach to politics and quite different from the mentality of the liberal party and socialist party leaders on the Continent, who tend because of Comte and Marx to be anti-clerical, if not atheistic, in their attitude toward religion.

This difference in attitude with respect to religion that distinguishes the labor and liberal parties of the Continent from those of Great Britain expresses a difference in their living law. Religiously Great Britain is, according to the religious statistics, overwhelmingly Protestant, whereas the statistics for the 165,000,000 Europeans in the six nations in Continental European Union is at least as overwhelmingly Roman Catholic.[11] Furthermore, whereas in Great Britain all the parties are secular, as in the United States, and religion is kept as far as possible out of political issues, the political parties on the Continent either bear religious names or if they do not are avowedly anti-clerical and at times even anti-religious. In French politics, for example, the words "right" and "left" mean pro-church or anti-clerical. They do not mean economically "right" or "left."

These notable differences with respect to the people's belief in the relation between religion and politics mean that if the British were to put themselves in the wider European Parliament which their Continental neighbors urge them to join, they would find themselves caught in Roman Catholic religious and anti-clerical religious and secular issues which are quite irrelevant to the people of the British Isles. The British would also find themselves outvoted by the ratio of 165,000,000 Continental Europeans to 51,000,000 Britishers in a political community none of whose major political parties or cultural groups have norms in common with those of the Conservative Party, the Labour Party or the Liberal Party in Great Britain. Clearly, to expect Great Britain to transfer part of its legal jurisdiction and its political sovereignty to a supranational European Community under such circumstances is to fail to note the differences between British and Continental European living law.

To look, therefore, at European politics since World War II from the standpoint of sociological jurisprudence and philosophical anthropology is to understand the following things: (1) Why the division at the end of World War II of Germany, which brings Roman religious, familial and legal Rhineland and South Germany into leadership socially and politically, provides living law norms and foreign policy decisions in common with those of the five other nations in the Schuman Plan, the Atomic Pool and the other effective though limited activities of Continental European Union. (2) Why Great Britain could not join any legal and political United States of Europe that was more than consultative. (3) Why the German Socialists, of whom Dr. Eric Ollenhauer is the leader and with whom the American "sociological jurist" Professor W. Friedmann has such emotive living law feeling, have, due to their anti-clericalism, and due to Dr. Ollenhauer's desire to capture Protestant Lutheran Prussian votes, attacked European Union. (4) Why the leaders of the liberal Socialist parties in the other five Continental European nations believe that were the liberal Socialists to come to power in West Germany they also would be for a common Continental European community. The reason for the latter judgment is that the norms of Dr. Ollenhauer's German Socialists are not provincially German norms but norms common to the liberal Socialists of the whole of Europe. Hence they also provide a common economic and political philosophical basis for a European rather than a chauvinistically Prussian community.

A fifth factor distinguishes British from Continental European mentality. The modern philosophy which has determined the legal, economic and political theory of modern Britain is British empiricism; that of the Continent is Continental rationalism. Needless to say, the former is inductive and nominalistic, critical, analytic and pragmatic rather than systematic, and fearful of over-all generalizations; the latter is deductive, systematic and rationalistic, demanding clear and distinct ideas and a logically specific and consistent policy.

A sixth factor differentiates British from Continental culture and mentality. Britain has an unwritten constitution. This custom undoubtedly expresses the aforementioned British suspicion of solving practical problems by recourse to written axioms or doctrines.

This does not mean, however, that there is nothing in Great Britain, corresponding to the Bill of Rights of the American Constitution, to outlaw parliamentary legislation if it violates certain norms. The British control of democratic legislation derives, however, not from a constitutional bill of rights of the law of contract, but from "the rules of the game" of unwritten tradition and its law of status, where status is aristocratic and hierarchical, placing each man in his proper station.[12] In Great Britain certain things simply are not done. Furthermore, condemnation comes, not in the decision of a judge, but when someone in a higher station raises his eyebrows while remaining silent. In its sanctions as well as its content, the British constitution is unwritten. The Englishman, T. D. Weldon, has expressed this philosophy most aptly in his book, *The Vocabulary of Politics,* where, after identifying ethical, political and legal norms with conventional rules of the game, he gives, as the sole justification for what they are, the reply, "Well, this is Great Britain, isn't it?" [13] Thus British living law outlaws legislation, without judicial review, by unwritten custom and status before the legislation is passed, rather than afterward through the action of a supreme court that appeals to the constitutionally prescribed bill of rights of a written constitution.

The frequent argument of the American legal positivists that British experience shows the Bill of Rights of the Constitution of the United States, when interpreted as law, to be unnecessary is invalid. The argument overlooks, as legal positivists are required by their philosophy to do, the difference between the living law of Great Britain and that of the United States.

At the same time, in Great Britain final political authority does not center in the Crown or in the House of Lords or even in the entire unwritten law of status and station with its aristocratic and ceremonial hierarchical norms, but in the House of Commons with its egalitarian democratic values. This British compromise and synthesis, by which an unwritten regal and hierarchical law of status, retained from the medieval past, is merged with the written statutes of a modern democratic legislature with primary political authority, bespeaks an important difference in the effects of modern democratic revolutions in the British Isles and on the Continent. In Great Britain democratic political institutions were obtained while also preserving traditional regal, hierarchical, aristocratic and Canterburian religious customs, with their emphasis upon quality rather than quantity, their subtle atmosphere of good form and good taste and their disapproval of overstatement or extremes in political debate, as in scholarly discourse.

On the Continent, with minor qualifications in the case of Belgium, the Netherlands and Luxembourg, the introduction of democracy in the political sphere tended to carry with it the destruction or depreciation of the old in every other sphere, with the consequence that most of the social order is placed under the written law of contract. These different modern democratic mentalities and ways prepare the Continental Europeans for a constitutionally constructed supranational Continental European Community to a degree that is not the case with the British.

To the British, the comparative stability and sobriety of their modern ways and institutions are an empirical confirmation of their empirical philosophy and its pragmatic, compromising and particularized approach to politics. The fragility and frequent shifts of French governments are to the British a similar proof that a French mentality which makes Cartesian clarity, distinctness and logical consistency, expressed in the Continental codified type of law and its declarations, the criterion for the practical solution of any political problem is a mentality which indulges in the artificial and the impractical. Clearly *for the British* the constitutionally constructed Continental European economic, military and political community would be in fact an artificial and impractical thing.

It does not follow, however, as the initial British neutralism and negativism toward Continental European Union assumed, that a contractually constructed supranational Continental European Community is artificial and impractical *for Continental Europeans* with their different legal and political mentality. All that follows is that such a community does not fit British mentality. It is the *non sequitur* involved in arguing from what is artificial and impractical for the British to what is artificial and impractical for Continental Europeans that constitutes the error in Britain's failure to encourage Continental European Union in its early days.

Even a common-sense, piecemeal approach to the Saar issue between France and Germany confirms this conclusion. It will be recalled that the British maintained that this and other similar particular problems must be solved in isolation by negotiation between the particular Continental nations involved, before there is any point in even thinking about a supranational Continental European Community. In concrete practice this would mean that France and Germany in such negotiations would have to assume that a supranational community does not exist and may not exist in the future. Under such circumstances each party must assume that it is in the old power-politics guided, nationalistic Europe in which force and war, rather than the legally established institutions of a supranational Continental Community, will be the final arbiter of a violation of any agreement which might be negotiated. In such a Europe neither France nor Germany can allow the other to have the Saar. Any government in either country which did so would fall. Thus even from the standpoint of common sense, the British piecemeal approach to the solution of the Saar issue between France and Germany is impractical.

Again the error becomes evident of taking the mentality and philosophy of politics which are vital and appropriate domestically for one's own people, with their particular philosophical and cultural traditions, as the criterion for judging what is practical for other people. What happens when this occurs, even when one's domestic mentality is empirical and realistic, is not that one is empirical and realistic with respect to the problems of other nations, but that one is judging their particular problems *a priori* in terms of one's own cultural tradition and presuppositions.

The Continental Europeans committed this error also when they assumed that a constitutionally constructed supranational community, appropriate for them because of their more rationalistic and deductive legal, political and religious mentality and because of their similar political parties, would be appropriate for the British also with their contrasting legal and political mentality and their quite different political parties. The leaders of the United States were guilty of the same error when they based their foreign policy with respect to EDC not upon the inner living beliefs, mentality and political parties of the Continental Europeans, but solely on domestic issues and desires in the United States with respect to Communist Russia.[14]

The foregoing considerations permit certain conclusions to be drawn with respect to practical international politics and legal and political philosophy. What any nation will do depends upon its essential properties. The essential properties of anything, given by its definition, must include the difference as well as its genus. The differentiating properties of British mentality and behavior contrast so sharply with those of the Continent, notwithstanding the generic factors common to both, that any British transfer of present national sovereign powers to a European supranational economic, military or political community in the foreseeable future is unlikely. Provided, however, that Great Britain and the other nations of the world do not discourage the Continental Europeans, by pursuing a foreign policy with respect to the Continent which judges what is practical for the Continent by a non-Continental political and legal mentality, an effective Continental European supranational community is possible and practical. This is the case, as suggested above and shown elsewhere,[15] because *so long as Latin and Roman Catholic Southern and Rhineland Germany* provides the leading party or, with the liberal Socialists, one of the two leading parties in West Germany, the six Continental European peoples have differential as well as generic European norms in common. They also have similar major political parties.

This does not mean that there can be no political unification whatever between the Continent and the non-Continental nations of Europe. Any such wider political European unification must, however, root itself in the principle of cultural and political sovereignty which is monistic with respect to the generic properties of Western peoples and which is pluralistic with respect to their differential traits. The latter requirement would prohibit the extension of the differential mentality and norms from one member to the entire community, as economic and complete political supranationalism requires, and would thus restrict the amount of sovereignty that could be transferred to the larger community. In short, European Union, which extends beyond the Continent, must face and respect not merely the underlying generic unity but also the rich diversity of Western civilization.

The first practical step toward this end might well take the form of revivifying the present Council of Europe by drawing up a new charter which is based unequivocally on the generic monistic and differential pluralistic principle of international sovereignty. A second step might consist of expanding such a Council of Europe into an Atlantic Assembly including Canada, the Latin American countries and the United States, as *The Economist* of London has suggested.[16] It is to be noted that all the latter nations derive their culture, in major part at least, from Europe. Such a generalization is necessary if Britain is to reconcile her duties to the Continent with her duties to Canada and her natural cultural affinity with the United States. It is equally necessary if the Continental Latin nations of Europe are to give similar expression to their cultural affinity with Latin America. A third practical step would be to include also Australia, New Zealand and any other nations in the British Commonwealth whose political forms and beliefs derive from Western civilization. Only if this is done will an instrument be at hand for reconciling Great Britain's cultural ties to the Continent with her obligations to the British Commonwealth of Nations and her cultural and philosophical affinity with the United States.

The new charter of such a restricted or generalized Council of Western Civilization might well require one specific, restricted transfer of national sovereignty to the supranational Western Community. The ground for this transfer would be the aforementioned generic monistic and differential pluralistic principle of international political sovereignty upon which the new charter rests. The aim of this transfer would be twofold: first, in the name of the generic monistic factor, to protect the unity of Western civilization and define the role of European internationalism; second, in the name of the differential pluralistic factor, to protect the rich cultural and spiritual diversity of Western civilization and define the role of Western nationalism. In other words, the aim of the transfer of national sovereignty would be not merely to protect Western cultural values in their unity but also to protect each member nation in its right to build its social institutions in the light of its own particular differentiation of that unity. The content of the sovereignty transferred would consist of two things: (1) the automatic acceptance of the verdict of the international community concerning when a violation of its aforementioned principle of international political sovereignty had occurred; and (2) the automatic acceptance by each member nation of the responsibility to contribute to any community-authorized policing of such a violation.

The basic consideration, however, is not this interconnected set of practical proposals, but the principle upon which they must rest and by which they must be guided and controlled if they are to be effective. The great Austro-Hungarian sociologist of law, Ehrlich, has shown that positive laws and institutions are not effective unless the normative principles upon which they rest conform to the underlying living beliefs, associations and customs of the peoples to whom they are applied.[17] Our brief comparative examination of British and Continental European mentality and customs has been sufficient to show that European mentality and culture is a heterogeneous rather than a homogeneous unity. The principle, therefore, upon which any European policy embracing Great Britain and the Continent or the other free Western nations must rest if it is to be effective and if later disappointment and disillusionment are not to result must be one which expresses and protects the heterogeneity as well as the unity. This is precisely what the generic monistic and differential pluralistic principle of international political sovereignty would do.

One final caution is to be noted. It does not follow, because a Council of Europe or a Western Assembly based on the latter principle is practical, that such an effective European or Western Union will come into being in fact. Nor does it follow, conversely, because of the defeat of the European Defense Community in the French Chamber of Deputies and the recent setbacks to a wider Atlantic Union, that, therefore, our conclusion that both are practical is fallacious, as some have inferred. Our conclusion is not that these positive international institutions are practical regardless of what statesmen in Great Britain, the United States or on the Continent have done or may do, or regardless of the principle upon which they are based. The conclusion, instead, is that the aforementioned specific, positive international institutions are practical provided statesmen will fit their national foreign policy for Europe to the de facto, richly diversified cultural resources of Europe and the remainder of the Free World.

XI

Philosophical Anthropology and International Law

INTERNATIONAL like domestic law must face the difficult question of norms. Without at least some common norms between *most* of the nations and the cultures of the world there can be no effective international law.

The word "most" in the preceding sentence is important. It reminds us, as noted in Chapter VII, that in no culture or nation do all the people live by common norms; only a statistically large number do. Hence, in order to settle disputes between nations by international legal processes and political institutions rather than by war in an atomic age, it is not necessary that every nation in the world have living philosophical beliefs and customary behavior in common; it is only necessary that most of them do.

Our analysis of Continental European Union in Chapter X shows also that even when every nation has basic living law beliefs and norms in common, it is not necessary that all their normative beliefs and behavior be similar in order to have an effective transfer of some legal and political jurisdiction and sovereignty from a present nation to a larger international legal community. It is merely necessary that their most basic naturalistic and cultural beliefs be similar. Then, providing the new positive international law assigns legal jurisdiction to the international court and political community only with respect to the more basic quantitative norms which *most* of the nations have in common, while at the same time reserving to national legal and

Reprinted by permission from the *Yale Law Journal*, published by Yale Law Journal Company, Inc. Copyright 1950 by the Yale Law Journal Company, Inc.

political jurisdiction those living philosophical beliefs and customary practices which differentiate them from one another, an international law which is effective because it expresses and is sustained by the living law is both obtainable and practicable.

Do such generic norms for *most* of the nations of the entire world as well as for most of the nations of Western civilization exist? Moreover, if so, what are they and where are they to be found?

Contemporary developments in the social sciences and in the philosophy of natural science indicate that there are two sources. One is in the norms common to the diverse cultures of the world. The other is in scientifically verified philosophy of nature. The former source happens to be intimately connected with the latter.

There are reasons for believing that the philosophy of nature as given content by the epistemologically analyzed, empirically verified theory of natural science can be used as a criterion of those living law norms which are universally valid and, hence, of the character required to undergird a more effective international law. It is the purpose of this chapter (1) to show that this is the method of ethical and legal science of the traditional Orient and of the classical West up to at least the time of Kant; (2) to specify in greater detail what the method requires and how it proceeds; and (3) to point out that a new contemporary positive international law rooted in such empirically verified, universally valid norms has a chance of being effective since it meets the crucial criterion of effective law of the great sociologist of law, Ehrlich.

By an empirically verified science and philosophy of nature we shall mean one whose basic assumptions are confirmed either (*a*) directly or (*b*) indirectly through their deductive consequences, by appeal to data given with immediacy. This inclusion of directly verified theory permits us, as the sequel will show, to regard Oriental philosophy as empirically verified scientific knowledge, even though it differs from the formally constructed, experimentally confirmed type of science and philosophy that arose with, and has grown in vitality since the time of, the ancient Greeks in the West, and which, as Albert Einstein and others have shown,[1] is only indirectly verified.

Verification of a scientific theory is indirect if its basic assumptions refer to entities such as electrons which cannot be directly observed and if consequently the theory can be tested empirically only indirectly by the way of theorems which are deduced from its basic assumptions. Then the logic of verification takes on the following form of the hypothetical syllogism: If A (the unobservable postulated scientific objects), then B (the deduced theorem or theorems). B is the case. Therefore A is the case.

As is well known, such an argument of the hypothetical syllogism commits the formal fallacy of affirming the consequent. What follows is not that a theory verified in this manner is false and should be rejected — quite the contrary, since the argument tells us that the implication of the theory has been confirmed. What follows instead is merely the warning that the uniqueness of the theory has not been established. In other words, from the fact that A implies B which is directly verified to be the case, it does not follow that A is the only theory from which can be deduced the directly and experimentally verified fact described by B. Hence, while indirect verification confirms what one would expect if the theory in question is true and, hence, warrants our retaining the theory, the presence of the fallacy of affirming the consequent involved in such a logic of verification tells us also that the theory must be held tentatively with the mind open to other theoretical possibilities and with a willingness to reject the theory the moment any empirical fact turns up which is contrary to any of its deduced theorems.

Verification of a theory is direct when its basic assumptions refer only to entities and relations which are immediately apprehensible, thereby permitting its postulates themselves rather than merely some of its deduced theorems to be empirically tested. Curiously enough, it is Oriental rather than Western science and philosophy which meets this more certain and stringent test for empirical verification. Thus, there is a sense in which Oriental philosophy is not merely as scientific as, but even more scientific than, that of the West. Certainly, no science or philosophy can be more scientific than one which insists upon direct verification of its basic assumptions.

The Ethical and Legal Method of the Orient

The most widely accepted belief of Hindu philosophy is its fundamental concept of the true self which is Brahman. Of Brahman, two things are asserted: (1) Brahman, which is the cosmical principle in nature, is identical with Atman, which is the psychical principle in the self. (2) Brahman is known by immediate apprehension. The first of these two assertions assures us that Brahman refers to nature and, hence, is a concept in the philosophy of nature. The second assertion guarantees that Brahman is verified directly and denotatively by immediate apprehension.

In all Buddhist philosophical systems, the major concept is Nirvana or Suchness or the Void. Again we are told that this important factor in knowledge embraces nature as well as man and is known only with immediacy. Hence, its verification is direct. In fact, Nirvana and Brahman alike embrace not merely nature and man as an object of knowledge in nature, but also man as the determinate particular subjective knower of nature.

In China the three major philosophies of indigenous origin are Taoism, Confucianism and Chan or Zen Buddhism. Although Buddhism arose in India, Chan or Zen Buddhism, as Professor D. T. Suzuki has emphasized, is a creation of the Chinese. That Chan Buddhism is equally naturalistic is shown by the setting of its monasteries in the mountains, the communion with nature of its practitioners, and its naturalistic intermixture with Taoism in Chinese landscape painting.[2] Only in the case of Confucianism might it seem that Chinese philosophy is an exception to the traditional rule that ethical and legal norms are to find their verification in nature. This exception is, however, a mere seeming. If the Confucian sages are asked why their particular norms for social and personal behavior are the true ones, the answer is that these norms put man in harmony with nature.[3]

This recursive reference of Confucian personal and legal ethical norms to one's directly verified knowledge of nature has been obscured by many students of Confucian ethics because they have neglected to reconstruct the very technical conception of nature referring to the directly sensed colors of the different seasons of the yearly cycle of nature and to the natural differences between types of men. The latter differences, like sensed sequences of colors designating spring, summer, fall and winter, are regarded as characteristics of groups of individuals who are quite independent of cultural beliefs or of culturally conditioned and relative norms, much after the manner of the different natural personality types and their role with respect to ethics in the studies of Charles W. Morris in our own time. Good personal and social conduct, according to the Confucian Chinese, is that behavior of individuals and that ordering of social relations which takes into account these directly sensed sequences of the seasons and the empirically evident natural diversities of human nature. As the neo-Confucianist Hu Yan Mung, quoting from the Confucianist Siun Tseu, said of a specific ethical and legal social norm, "This rule is called 'equality conformable to "natural" differentiation' or 'union without injury to "human" diversity.' " [4]

The connection between the ethical and legal ordering of people in society and empirically grounded conceptions of nature in Confucian Chinese culture is even more explicit. Granet has shown that when the early Chinese shifted from a two-fold conception of natural phenomena expressed in terms of *yin yang* to a four-fold conception of nature based on the four-sensed directions projecting out from the perceiver, their rules for the proper ethical ordering of people in man-directed society underwent a corresponding change. [5]

This naturalistic criterion for the validity of ethical norms in traditional Oriental philosophy and culture shows even more markedly when we look at the practical behavior which these norms prescribe. The Chinese painting which gives the greatest expression to Buddhist and Taoist religious and other human values is the naturalistic landscape painting. In this painting man is usually portrayed as either a relatively insignificant item in one corner of the picture or a sage sitting under a tree immediately apprehending the all-embracing immediacy of nature within which he is immersed. It is a commonplace that the Hindu of the morally highest caste, after establishing his family and training his son to succeed him, is required, as an ethical prescription by the norms of his philosophical and religious beliefs, to withdraw from cultural institutions and conventional family and social relations and return to the pristine relation to nature of a forest hermit and an itinerant seer, making a pilgrimage to the naturalistic freshness of the Himalayas. Even the Confucianist Chinese painter succeeds in conveying the values of his art only, he tells us, by becoming the naturalistic object which is bamboo.

For all these Orientals — Hindu, Buddhist, Taoist and Confucian — alike, humanistic and cultural values are good to the extent that they conform to nature and the naturalistic differences of men. Furthermore, man prevents even these cultural norms from becoming dead, mechanical rules devoid of the spirit which sustains them only by immediate apprehension of, communion with, and return to the all-embracing immediacy of nature which is their source. It is not an accident in the philosophical tradition of India that one of the earliest bodies of written treatises, upon which the later Upanishads and the even later philosophical systems are largely commentaries, is called Aranyakas or forest treatises. Only by returning from the man-made normative ethical and legal conventions of cultural and social organization to the non-man-made pristine freshness and absoluteness of the primeval forests and nature can man find the source in which the ethical norms and institutions find their objective validation and from which they derive their spiritual vitality.

The Rig-Veda is the oldest book of Aryan civilization, East or West. Professor N. G. D. Joardar, in his lectures in the Yale Law School on the nature and background of the traditional law of India, has pointed out that there are in this Rig-Veda twenty seers or sages who describe the nature of legal rules or norms and the source of their validation. The basic common thesis is that law, called *rita,* has its basis in, derives from, and in fact is the source of the cosmic order of nature. To be sure, for some of them this law is prior to the natural cosmic order. Even so, the law which is the true rule for men to use in ordering their man-made cultural institutions is derived from the order of non-man-made cosmic nature.

These early seers of the Rig-Veda go even further, distinguishing the normative law for society, called *vrata,* from natural law, called *rita,* and adding that *vrata* has its source and validation in *rita.* In fact, it is from *rita* that *vrata* or *dharma* and the later Sanskrit word for law derive. In his treatise on the Ancient and Medieval Religious and Civil Law of India, Pandurang Vaman Kane writes: "The idea of Dharma took the place of the very ancient conception of rita. In the Rig-Veda *rita* denotes the supreme transcendental law or the cosmic order by which the universe and even the gods are governed. . . ." [6] He then quotes with approval Berolzheimer's statement [7] that *vrata* and *dharma* are "derivatives" from *rita.*

The ancient seers of India made another distinction between *vrata* or *dharma* and *smritis* or *samaya.* The *smritis* express the positive law and commentaries of tradition; *samaya* refers to the more recent usage or conventions. Thus the *smritis* and *samaya* refer to the positive and living law of society as it is in fact. For this reason, while suggestive with respect to legal norms, they cannot be taken as authoritative; in fact, they may be evil because, being man-made, they may derive from a conception of nature and natural man which is false. Thus P. V. Kane writes: "The smritis are composed by human authors and so have no independent authority in matters of dharma, as a man may say what is either false or mistaken." [8] *Vrata*, on the other hand, because it derives from *rita*, which is verified against non-man-made nature, provides an ethical and legal "ought" against which the cultural "is" of sociological jurisprudence as described by *smritis* and *samaya* can be judged. In short, sociological jurisprudence, restricted as it is to the cultural "is," gives trustworthy norms only to the extent that it embodies a true or verified conception of nature and natural man.

The same naturalistic criterion for personal and legal norms appears after the Rig-Veda in the most important of all legal books in India, the book of Manu. Its conception and specification of personal domestic and legal norms still operate in the villages all over India. Although probably edited in its present form in the period between the second century B.C. and the second century A.D., it is continuous with the earlier tradition of the Rig-Veda. It does not surprise us, therefore, that the legal tradition of Manu begins with cosmology and the philosophy of nature and then refers all norms to this naturalistic source for their validation.[9]

The Ethical and Legal Method of the Classical West

It is well known that the technical terminology used even today in every law school in the Western world was created when Western law was made a science by those Roman jurists of whom the Scaevolas were the leaders. E. Vernon Arnold in his classic treatise, *Roman Stoicism*, has made it clear that most of the Romans who created Western legal science were Stoic philosophers. It is a commonplace of Stoic philosophy that the good is defined as conformity to the philosophy of the true for nature.

It is another commonplace of this scientifically formulated Roman law with its abstract technical legal concepts that the legal norms which it regarded as valid for all men were called the *jus gentium*. At the beginning of his *Institutes*, Gaius writes as follows: "Every hu-

man community that is regulated by laws and customs observes a rule
of conduct which in part is peculiar to itself, and in part is common
to mankind in general. The rule of conduct which a people has settled for its own observance, and which is peculiar to that people, is
termed the *jus civile*. Those principles which natural reason has
taught to all mankind, are equally observed by all, and collectively are
termed the *jus gentium*." [10]

It is to be noted that the criterion for distinguishing the local provincial legal rules of the *jus civile*, from the universal legal norms
valid for all men of the *jus gentium*, is "natural reason." Moreover,
natural reason was not regarded as *a priori*. As will be shown in the
sequel, it was defined by scientific methods which proceed from directly given data to deductively formulated scientific theory. In other
words, it is reason applied to the facts of nature which provides the
criterion for universally valid ethical and legal norms.

The point in part is that, whereas men live in different cultures
which generate the relative and often conflicting ethical and legal
norms of the differing instances of *jus civile*, all men in the different
cultures nonetheless live in the same nature. Consequently, whereas
the derivation of ethics from a philosophy grounded in the humanities of the differing cultures will lead to the pluralism and relativity of
ethical and legal norms of the *jus civile*, an ethics derived from a philosophy based on nature alone gives the ethical and legal norms universally valid for all men of the naturalistic *jus gentium*.

It is to be emphasized that the distinction between *jus civile* and
jus gentium, while necessary, is not a sufficient criterion of the universally normative. There is more than one *jus gentium*. It is only the
naturalistic *jus gentium* which gives ethical and legal codes that are
universally valid. As Arthur Nussbaum has pointed out in his *Concise History of the Law of Nations*,[11] there are two different meanings
of the *jus gentium* in Roman legal science. The one we shall call the
philosophy of culture or sociological *jus gentium*, the other the philosophy of nature or naturalistic *jus gentium*. The sociological *jus
gentium* of the Romans is determined by studying the de facto legal
rules and conventions of diverse societies and abstracting from them
those legal rules and conventions which all the de facto societies have
in common. By this standard slavery would be a normative good in
society since every society known in Roman times contained slaves.

There was, however, for Roman law another *jus gentium* derived not from that which is universal in the sociological "is" of different societies and cultures, but from the empirically verified science and philosophy of nature. It is only by the latter naturalistically grounded philosophical basis for ethical and legal norms that the Romans arrived at the theory that slavery, although universally present originally in every de facto society, is nonetheless evil. If status in nature rather than in the universal sociological "is" common to all de facto societies defines the good for men, then, since a slave is as genuine a creature of nature as is the head of an aristocratic family, status under the law must center in being a citizen of nature rather than a citizen of a proper aristocratic family and justice under such a law becomes the same for the slave as for the most aristocratic paterfamilias.

To be sure, this rule in ancient Roman times was followed more in principle than in fact, as is the case even today in the Dixiecratic portion of the United States. Nonetheless, even then, the norm against slavery was established as a principle, never again to lose its force as a norm in the Western world. Furthermore, an examination of the *Institutes* of Gaius will show that its codes make use of this naturalistic concept of legal status and citizenship to bring many people who were previously slaves under the protection of the law and into the legal status of free men in the Roman families.

These experiences of the Romans are illuminating with respect to certain contemporary suggestions for determining universally valid ethical and legal norms. Recent investigations by cultural anthropologists and sociologists have revealed the relativity and diversity of ethical and legal norms in the different nations and cultures of the contemporary world. The ideological conflict between the Soviet Russians and the traditional Western democracies underlines this fact. One suggestion offered by many contemporary social scientists for finding the universal common ethical and legal norms necessary to build an effective resolution of the international disputes by legal rather than by warful means is to seek out the common factors in the diverse national and cultural legal codes and social norms. Such an investigation would give us the kind of universal norms the Romans had in their sociological *jus gentium*.

Such a sociological *jus gentium* has two weaknesses, however, as a criterion of universal ethical and legal principles. The first weakness is that the common factor in the diverse norms of different nations and cultures is too weak to provide an effective norm for settling disputes. For example, the issue between Russian Communists and American New or Fair Dealers, which threatens the peace of the contemporary world, turns around the economic, political and other rules for human relations in society with respect to which the Americans and Russians differ, not around the norms which they have in common. The second weakness in the universal common norms of sociological jurisprudence is that the de facto legal norm common to all societies and cultures, even were it not weak, is not necessarily good. The universality of slavery in every legal system at the time of the Romans is a case in point.

The latter consideration indicates that an adequate ethical and legal science must have a *jus gentium* with its foundations outside the de facto ethical conventions and codes of the humanistic sociological *jus gentium;* otherwise there is no basis under any circumstances for judging the status quo sociological "is" to be bad. The only source for norms other than those of the sociological "is" of culture is nature. It was precisely for this reason that the Roman Stoic philosophers who created the Western science of law distinguished the sociological *jus gentium* from the philosophical naturalistic *jus gentium* and affirmed that only the latter *jus gentium* is the criterion of the good and the just. Hence, the well-known dictum of Roman legal science that *jus gentium* is grounded in *jus naturae.*

It appears, therefore, that the ethical and legal methods of the traditional Orient and the classical West are identical. Just as the Vedic and Upanishadic law, which forms the customs of India to the present moment through the persisting influence of the codes of Manu, distinguishes the sociological "is" of de facto custom, called *samaya,* from the normative "ought" of *vrata* and declares that *vrata,* which designates the normatively good and just derives from *rita,* the law of nature; so the Roman foundations of Western legal science distinguish the *jus civile* of local, relativistic de facto positive legal codes and customs from the *jus gentium,* and within the *jus gentium* distinguish the sociological *jus gentium* of those codes common to all de facto societies from the naturalistic philosophical *jus gentium* which alone specifies the criterion of the universally good and just because it is grounded in *jus naturae.*

In the classical West, it was not merely the Roman Stoic philosophers, who were the creators of the Western science of law, who used this method. E. Vernon Arnold has made it unequivocally clear that every school of Greek philosophy — Zenoian Stoics, Platonists, Aristotelians and Epicureans — used the same method.[12]

Of Zeno, the founder of the Greek Stoic School, Arnold writes: "The ideal state must embrace the whole world, so that a man no longer says, 'I am of Athens' or 'of Sideon,' but 'I am a citizen of the world.' Its laws must be those which are prescribed by nature, not by convention." [13] Arnold continues, "Zeno, after writing his *Republic*, . . . could not, perhaps, avoid noticing that the coming of his model Kingdom was hindered by the narrow-mindedness of the philosophers, their disagreement with one another, and their lack of clear proofs for their dogmas. He began to realize that the study of dialectics and physics was of more importance than his Cynic teachers would allow; . . . From this time he no longer restricted his outlook to force of character, but sought also for argumentative power and well ascertained knowledge. The foundations of his state must be surely laid, not upon the changing tide of opinion, but on the rock of knowledge." [14]

Platonists, Aristotelians and Epicureans used the same method. "It was," continues Arnold, "a common complaint of [the Aristotelians] that the Stoics had stolen their doctrines wholesale and had altered their names only." [15] Of the Epicureans and Stoics, Arnold adds: "Both founded, or conceived that they founded their ethical doctrine upon physical proofs; that is, both maintained that the end of life which they put forward was that prescribed by natural law. As a consequence, they agreed in removing the barrier which Socrates had set up against the pursuit of natural science." [16]

Apparently Socrates reached the same conclusion before he died. Otherwise it is difficult to believe that Plato in Book VII of the *Republic* would have put the following words into the mouth of his beloved Socrates: "But I must also remind you, that the power of dialectic alone can reveal this, [the idea of the good] and only to one who is a disciple of the previous sciences." [17] If one turns back a few pages in the *Republic*, where the description of these previous sciences appears, one will discover that every one of them is a mathematical natural science. This means that the later Socrates, if Plato's description of him can be trusted, believed that the ethical norms for human conduct and legal institutions must be verified against the experimentally verified theories of mathematical natural science when the latter theories are analyzed by the method of dialectic to bring out their epistemological assumptions and the attendant theory of natural man as a mind or knower which they entail.

Nor is it difficult to find the reason why Socrates changed his mind about the method of ethics in the later portion of his life. As E. Vernon Arnold has made clear, the attempt of the early Socrates to ignore the philosophy of nature and set up ethics as an independent subject, appealing to the facts of intuitively given conduct and of the intuitively given humanistic values of culture for its validation, led to the ethical relativism of the Sophists and the cultural relativism of the *jus civile*. It led also to the skepticism about the possibility of validating ethical norms that produced the Cynics. In short, Socrates, in the early portion of his life, tried out the non-naturalistic method for validating ethical norms, pursued by some modern philosophers since the time of Kant, and found it to end in failure.

The later Socrates, and all subsequent schools of Greek philosophy — the Zenoian Stoics, the Platonists, the Aristotelians and the Epicureans — brought physics and the philosophy of natural science back into ethics as basic. Forthwith for all schools of Greek and Roman philosophy, ethics is the philosophy of natural science applied. As H. Rackham writes in his Introduction to Cicero's *De Natura Deorum:* "In spite of the strong antagonism between the Epicureans and the Stoics, their doctrines had features in common which indeed characterized all the thought of the period. From Aristotle onward Greek philosophy became systematic; it fell into three recognized departments, Logic, Physics, and Ethics, answering the three fundamental questions of the human mind: (1) How do I know the world? (2) What is the nature of the world? (3) The world being what it is, how am I to live in it so as to secure happiness?" [18]

The character of logic as conceived by all these schools of Greek philosophy, which came to expression in Roman Stoicism, is described in detail by Arnold.[19] He makes it clear that logic — the first branch of philosophy — "is subdivided into 'dialectic,' which deals with reasoning, and 'rhetoric,' the art of speech." [20] Dialectic includes the specification of the epistemology of knowledge and the inductive methods by which the content of knowledge of nature in physics is obtained as well as the rules of syllogistic deductive reasoning. It is to be emphasized that reason is never conceived by any of these Greek or Roman schools as *a priori*. It starts, instead, with data given empirically through the senses. Of sensations, it is affirmed that they are always true. Only propositions, because they are constituted of ideas referring to "mind-pictures," are sometimes true, sometimes false.[21]

What is most interesting of all is that the definition of sin $(\alpha\mu\alpha\rho\tau\iota\alpha)$ appears at the very beginning of inductive logic before one arrives at deductively formulated scientific theory with which the later stages of epistemology, scientific method and dialectic are concerned. Sin is defined as assent to false propositions about inductively given data of natural science.[22] Assent is wrong when it is based merely on "mind pictures" alone rather than on "mind pictures" that are verified against inductively given knowledge. In other words, sin is assent to false propositions concerning the empirically verified factors of nature and the natural man or refusal to assent to such empirically verified propositions. This puts in very precise terms the thesis that the criterion of virtue and sin for culture and cultural man is the empirically verified criterion of the true and false for nature and natural man.

By nature and natural man is meant any and all facts concerning either which is not in part at least an effect of the beliefs of men. By culture and cultural man is meant any artifacts; that is, facts which are in part at least what they are because of behavior resulting from the beliefs of men. Natural facts, not being man-made, merely are; they are neither good nor bad any more than they are true or false. Only artifacts, because by definition they are man-made, deriving from beliefs of men which are true or false to natural facts, can be good or bad. Moreover, cultural facts are good or bad solely because the propositions concerning natural facts from which they derive are true or false.

This theory of ethical verification has the merit of providing a meaning for sin in the methodology and science of nature. Certainly any moralist wants to brand as sinful an untruthful report of facts by any natural scientist. This definition of the Greek and Roman philosophers accomplishes such a purpose.

Although a meaning for sin is provided by the Greek and Roman philosophers in the preliminary inductive methods of natural science, these methods do not provide a sufficient criterion of virtue. One can sin by falsely reporting a solitary inductively given fact. To have virtue, however, according to the Greek and Roman criterion, one must be truthful not merely about piecemeal facts in isolation, but also about all the intuitively given facts in their relations to one another and to the whole. For this reason, virtue requires the methods of deductively formulated scientific knowledge of the latter stages of scientific inquiry as well as inductive methods of the earlier stage.[23] One can sin by the false reporting of data given by inductive methods. One cannot, however, obtain virtue by purely inductive methods. To obtain virtue, one must have systematic knowledge taking all the inductively given facts concerning nature and human nature into account in a single consistent theory. This is the meaning of the dictum of all the schools of Greek and Roman philosophy that "virtue is knowledge *in the light of the whole.*" * [24]

Because dialectic includes epistemology as well as the specification of the successive inductive and deductive scientific methods for knowing natural facts, it is not the empirically verified deductively formulated scientific theory in the form in which it comes from the scientist that alone provides the criterion of the good. In addition, the method by which the theory is verified must be analyzed to bring out the relation between the technical concepts of the theory and directly inspectable data, thereby revealing its precise epistemological meaning. When this is done for any verified scientific theory of nature, an entailed theory of man as mind or knower is given. Thus, any scientifically verified theory of nature turns out under methodological and epistemological analysis to be as much a verified theory of the knower, his knowing, the meanings involved in his knowing, and, hence, of mind, as it is a verified theory of nature.

Nor should there be any surprise over this. For every successfully verified theory of nature is as much a verified instance of mental activity and human knowing as it is an instance of a verified theory of nature. Failure to note this is the major error of those who affirm that a philosophy of natural science and its ethics of natural law ignore human nature. But conversely, failure to realize that before scientifically verified theories of natural man and nature exhibit their impli-

---

* Italics mine.

cations for ethics, they must be analyzed to bring out their epistemological meaning with respect to the nature of man as a mind and
knower is the equally frequent error of many contemporary scientists
and philosophical naturalists when they turn to ethics.

It is scientifically verified theory of natural man and nature (1) in
the light of all the facts about both, not merely about some facts,
which is (2) analyzed methodologically and epistemologically to
bring out the type of mind, meanings and modes of knowing required
to arrive at its basic technical concepts, not merely the verified scientific theory unanalyzed, which is the criterion of the good and the just
for the artifacts which are culture and cultural man. It is because all
the facts, as far as it is humanly possible to obtain them in a single
theory at any stage of human history, not merely some facts, are required that the Greeks specified virtue to be not conduct in accord
with knowledge of one particular fact about nature and human nature, but knowledge *in the light of the whole*. It is because even systematically verified scientific theories which aim to include within
themselves all the facts must be analyzed methodologically and epistemologically to bring out the nature of natural man as a mind and as a
knower that the Greeks, with the later Socrates, added that the idea
of the good is to be found only *by applying dialectic* (methodological
and epistemological analysis) to the hypotheses of the verified natural
sciences.

A crucial question remains for consideration: If both traditional
Oriental and traditional Occidental philosophy have the same naturalistic method for verifying personal and legal norms, why is it that
the different traditional Oriental and Occidental philosophical systems produce different and often conflicting personal and legal normative prescriptions? This question has two answers, both of which
are rooted in the epistemology of natural knowledge. We can merely
state the answers here. Reasons for believing the answers to be correct will be found elsewhere.[25]

One reason for the difference in Oriental and Occidental living
law, notwithstanding the fact that both appeal to nature for their
verification, is that Oriental science and philosophy in their appeal to
nature tend, for the most part, to restrict knowledge of nature to entities and relations which are known by immediate apprehension
directly; whereas Western science and philosophy introduce inferred

theoretically designated entities and relations, the existence of which is verified empirically only indirectly by way of consequences deduced from the postulated unobservable system of entities. When ethics is interpreted as the philosophy of nature applied, it follows therefore, since nature as immediately apprehended and described after the manner of Oriental philosophy is different from nature as theoretically designated after the manner of Western science and philosophy, that customs and legal norms proceeding from these different philosophical conceptions will be different also.

In Chapter XII of *The Meeting of East and West* reasons have been given for holding that nature involves both of these factors and that the Oriental philosophical conception of nature is quite compatible with the Western philosophical conception. From this it follows, according to the aforementioned theory of ethical verification, that an adequate ethics not only can consistently, but must combine the ethical implications and applications of Oriental natural philosophy with those of Western philosophy. The fact, therefore, that there are differences in ethical values between Occidental and Oriental systems is an argument for rather than against this naturalistic method of ethical verification.

It follows also that the different scientifically philosophical beliefs and their religious, aesthetic, political and other cultural values of classical Oriental and classical Occidental civilization, each still vital and some twenty-odd centuries old, give compatible living law roots for an effective positive international law *providing we will take advantage of them* after the manner, noted in Chapter IX, in which the Continental European statesmen, within the few years since World War II, have used the previously untapped living law that is common to West Germany, France, Luxembourg, the Netherlands, Belgium and Italy to create the effective positive international legal institutions of the Continental European Economic, Atomic Pool, Military and Political Community.

Differences in the living law may, however, be of a different kind from what we find in either the Continental European Community or in classical Oriental and classical Occidental civilization. If, as is the case in Western science and its normative applications, nature as designated by its empirically verified theory cannot always be deduced from immediately apprehended data but must also be determined by trial and error, mathematically constructed theory which is merely indirectly verifiable by way of its deductive consequences, then quite reasonable scientific and philosophical students of nature may arrive, especially at different periods of history, at not merely different but also incompatibly different theories of nature and natural man and his normative conduct. It follows, then, that if ethics and the living law are but naturalistic philosophical theory applied, the respective cultural exemplifications of these incompatibly different natural philosophies will be incompatibly different also. Such is the case with: (1) the living practices and positive legal rules of the Communists which derive from the self-contradictory, naïvely realistic and materialistic-dialectically deterministic natural philosophy of Marx and Engels. (2) The living law of the Old South, which, as noted in Chapter II, derives by way of the Virginia Company, Sir Robert Filmer's patriarchal, theocratic, Christian, Canterburian England, Shakespeare, Queen Elizabeth I and Hooker's *Ecclesiastical Polity* from the law of status ethics and the natural history physics and metaphysics of Aristotle. (Roman Catholic Christian cultures and nations, when left to themselves, are similar, deriving from Aristotle's physics and metaphysics by way of St. Thomas rather than via Hooker, the Church of England and Sir Robert Filmer.) (3) The living and positive law of most of the people in the United States, their Declaration of Independence and the Federal Constitution with its legal Bill of Rights, all of which derive from cosmopolitan Stoic Roman law of contract and the mathematical philosophy of Bacon and Newton by way of Locke and Jefferson. The latter derivation of the Federal America which he wanted and which he and his colleagues created is what Jefferson meant when he wrote that in his opinion the three wisest men in the history of mankind were Bacon, Newton and Locke.

Needless to say, it is the incompatibility of the naturalistic philosophy and cultural norms of (1) and either (2) or (3) which is the naturalistic and normative meaning of the Cold War in the West. Similarly, it is the incompatibility between (1) and the naturalistic and normative beliefs and values of Confucian, Buddhist or Hindu peoples and nations which is now, at long last and let us hope before it is too late, being demonstrated to Asians by what has happened recently in Tibet. Likewise, the negative reaction of the elder political leaders of the Old South, who are still trying to live in seventeenth-century patriarchal law of status Christian England in the face of their own Jefferson and the unanimous decisions of the Supreme Court justices in the segregation cases, expresses the incompatibility of (2) in either its Roman Catholic or its Protestant versions and (3).

Clearly, contemporary domestic and national legal and political problems bring together incompatible as well as merely different natural and normative philosophies and living legal cultures and nations. The theoretical distinctions necessary to resolve such inescapable contemporary problems and the method for doing so will be our concern in the remaining chapters of this book.

Fortunately, however, we do not have to wait for the application of this method (which will be the writer's concern in a later book) in order to have an effective international law for the entire world community now. Never in any domestic community or nation, let it be repeated with emphasis, do *all* the people have common or compatible scientific beliefs and norms. It is only necessary that such is the case for *most* of them in order to bring the disputes between individuals or social groups to a settlement by due process of law rather than by recourse to fighting. The peoples and nations whose naturalistic beliefs and normative customs are those of either (a) Confucianism, Buddhism and Hinduism or of (b) Stoic Roman Western cosmopolitan law of contract in its modern declarations of independence versions comprise *most* of the nations and *most* of the people on the surface of this earth. Hence, since (a) and (b), though different, are compatible, a present positive international law and reformed United Nations which appeals to, expresses and is based upon such naturalistically normative foundations will generate the world community morale and draw unto themselves the instrumental police power and economic wealth necessary to be effective. To this end the compatible differences between (a) and (b) merit additional attention.

XII

Natural Law in China and the West

A RECENT study of natural law in China and the West has been made by Joseph Needham.[1] His little booklet of but thirty-nine printed pages packs within itself a prodigious amount of material of great importance to any student of the world's comparative philosophy or law. Its author, very erudite in natural science and linguistics as well as the philosophy of science and law, shows that in both the Far East and the West there is an essential connection between the theory of ethics and law and the scientific concepts of nature. In short, his studies of Taoist, Confucian, neo-Confucian, Hindu, and Buddhist Asian and classical Western cultures show that the ethical concepts of either personal conduct or social conduct in law simply do not have the primitive *a priori* and hence irreducible meaning and status which much recent Western ethical theory has assumed. Speaking of Hindu and Buddhist Indian doctrines as well as Chinese Taoism, neo-Confucianism and Buddhism, Dr. Needham concludes: "Human morality was still inextricably bound up with the phenomena of non-human Nature" (pp. 36–37). Dr. Needham shows also that it is quite erroneous to suppose that there is no science in Asia. Its philosophical, ethical and legal concepts go back to the facts of empirical experience and natural science just as do those of the West.

The difference is merely, as the writer has indicated elsewhere,[2] that Asian natural science is more of the purely natural history, inductive type, whereas Western science, in Dr. Needham's sense of "the Laws of Nature," goes on beyond the natural history stage, with

Reprinted from *Philosophy East and West*, Vol. 7, No. 1, April 1952 by permission of University of Hawaii Press.

its concepts by intuition, deriving their meanings from inductively given immediacy, to deductively formulated theory with its non-inductively given scientific objects and relations constructively designated by concepts by postulation. To be sure, Dr. Needham does not use this particular language, but this is in considerable part the purport of what he has to say.

He puts his finger upon the unique characteristic of the laws of nature in this Western sense of constructively designated, deductively formulated theory when, in describing Ulpian and the Stoics' concept of law, he writes: "For Ulpian (as for the Stoics) all things were 'citizens' subject to universal law" (p. 32). He puts his finger on the difference between this unique Western concept of natural science and natural law and the Far Eastern Asian one when in the same sentence he continues, "for Chu Hsi all things were elements of a universal pattern" (p. 32).

The heart of the Ulpian, Stoic, classically Western concept centers in the theory of the concept of the individual as a real rather than a nominalistic universal. This realistic concept arose in indirectly verified, deductively formulated Western mathematical physics with the schools of Democritus, Plato and Eudoxus, in which each and every scientific object was not inspected inductively as a particular but was known only theoretically and constitutively as an instance of the formally constructed determinate universal laws or postulates which it satisfies. These postulates are to be found in Books V and VII of Euclid's *Elements*. The only major omission in Dr. Needham's compact treatise is his failure to note the source of Ulpian and the Stoics' concept of good law in Greek mathematical physics by way of Greek philosophy.

The difference between this classically and contemporaneously Western concept of natural science and law and the Asian one illustrated in Dr. Needham's aforementioned statement concerning Chu Hsi becomes evident when Chu Hsi's "universal pattern" is made evident. A clue is given in Dr. Needham's quotation from the *Elegies* of Ch'ü, dating from about 170 B.C., which follows immediately upon Chu Hsi's statement. The two last sentences of this quotation are: "Now it runs together, now it disperses, sometimes moving and sometimes resting. But there is no fixed law, and in the thousand changes and the myriad transformations there is no definite norm" (p. 32). This is Chu Hsi's "universal pattern."

Clearly it is the pattern of nature as given inductively with its sensed objects "sometimes moving and sometimes resting," with its "thousand changes" and countless alterations. The meaning of this purely inductively given "universal pattern" of Asian natural science becomes the more clear if one centers attention upon the inductively observed cyclical sequence of differing colors and other qualities which are immediately sensed, such as fresh, cool spring; dry, hot summer; yellowish-brown fall; and black-white-gray winter. This is a universal pattern, but it is also a natural history, inductively given one. Dr. Needham is quite right, therefore, when he adds that Bruce, Henke, Warren and Bodde are not correct when they translate the neo-Confucian term for organization in Asian natural science, which Dr. Needham designates as Li^b (p. 31), as law, suggesting thereby "law" in the Western scientific and attendant moral meaning. He is quite right also when, in comparing Ulpian's concept with that of Asian natural science and ethics, he concludes: "But the profound difference is that while Ulpian had spoken quite uncompromisingly of *law*, Chu Hsi relies chiefly on a technical term the primary meaning of which is *pattern*" (p. 32). One should add inductively given, immediately apprehended pattern.

It is not an accident that Dr. Needham also finds much in common between Asian natural science and its attendant ethics and law and Whitehead's philosophy of natural science. Whitehead's initial philosophy of natural science is an attempt — as it turns out, an unsuccessful one — to derive all the concepts of contemporary Western mathematical physics by "extensive abstraction" from inductive immediacy. What one of necessity comes out with when this is done is the inductively given rhythms and patterns which Dr. Needham has found in Chinese philosophy as the basis of the Chinese concept of ethics and law. Recent analyses by Henry Margenau and the writer, among others, show, however, as Whitehead himself realized in part in the changes made in his philosophy of science in his later *Process and Reality*,[3] that an adequate theory of scientific objects cannot be achieved in this way. As Professors Einstein and Dirac among many others have emphasized, the basic concepts of contemporary mathematical physics are discovered only by an uninhibited leap of the intellectual imagination; they are not given in, nor can they be abstracted or deduced from, the inductively given rhythms, patterns and order of natural history science.

It is at this point that Dr. Needham's superb study needs one further inclusion. The philosophy of contemporary mathematical physics entails more than the philosophy of organism of Whitehead, which was foreseen in considerable part in the natural science of ancient Asia.

Dr. Needham also states only part of the truth when he asserts that all the laws of contemporary Western science deal only with probabilities, suggesting thereby only the inductively given probabilities of the *a posteriori* frequency theory. This is quite erroneous even for quantum mechanics, as Margenau and the writer have shown.[4] The probabilities of quantum mechanics are constitutively and theoretically constructed and designated, as the hypothetical *a priori* theory of probability asserts, as well as inductively and operationally given. Probability in both these senses occurs in each and every Western deductively formulated scientific theory. Only the latter meaning of probability can be derived from Asian science and philosophy.

Given the foregoing three additions, Dr. Needham's thirty-nine printed pages become well-nigh definitive. These three additions are: (1) the noting of the essential connection of Ulpian and the Stoics' doctrine of ethics and law and its thesis that justice is rendered only when an individual person or dispute is treated as an instance of a determinate universal rule or law with the discovery by Greek mathematical physicists that no fact in nature or man is ever accounted for until the universal determinate laws which it satisfies are discovered, formally constructed without recourse to images even of the imagination, and indirectly rather than directly verified; (2) the supplementation of Whitehead's and the Asian's philosophy of organism in the aforementioned specified manner; (3) the corresponding supplementation of the Asian and the British empirical frequency theory of probability with the hypothetical *a priori*, constitutively defined, indirectly verified theory.

XIII

The Relativity of Natural Law Theories

ONE of the most interesting developments in contemporary jurisprudence is the revival of interest in natural law. Volume V of the University of Notre Dame *Natural Law Institute Proceedings* adds something new.[1]

The novelty of this volume consists in its pursuit of the doctrine of natural law in cultures other than that of the Christian Western tradition. Following a foreword by the Reverend John J. Cavanaugh, former President of the University of Notre Dame, an editor's preface, and an introductory address by the Most Reverend J. Francis A. McIntyre, Archbishop of Los Angeles, five representative foreign scholars contribute chapters on natural law in the Jewish, Muslim, Hindu, Buddhist and Chinese traditions. The volume concludes with a summation by George E. Sokolsky, which is somewhat exaggerated in its enthusiasm, and a cautiously reserved epilogue by the Reverend Theodore M. Hesburgh, President of the University of Notre Dame.

The chapters by the five scholars from the non-Christian traditions make it clear that all the major cultures of the world have a classical natural law doctrine. In other words, they assert that at least part of the law of human culture is discovered by man rather than made by man.

This consideration reminds us that legal positivism, the dominant philosophy of law of the modern West in the recent past, is, so far as the history of Western civilization or the world as a whole is concerned, an exception to the general rule. To be exact, it is only since

Reprinted from *Northwestern University Law Review*, July-August 1953, Vol. 48, No. 3, by permission.

Kant's Second Critique that natural law has not been the accepted doctrine.

The situation with respect to Kant, so far as natural law is concerned, is indeed very complicated. To the positivistic legal thinkers who came after Kant, even the Kant of the Second Critique is regarded as a believer in the doctrine of natural law. Such usage does no harm provided one does not commit the frequent error of supposing that the Kantian doctrine of natural law is identical with the meaning of natural law in the Roman Catholic, Stoic Roman or Greek philosophical tradition.

The latter doctrine of natural law meant exactly what the name suggests. It stood for a doctrine of law which derived from nature and natural science rather than from the humanities and the cultural sciences. This is made clear in Aristotle when, after studying some one hundred different justices, he concludes nonetheless that there is an absolute justice measuring all these relative justices. This absolute justice, he tells us, is to be found in *physis;* that is, nature.[2] What this means is that the absolute or objective criterion for the just and good in law is to be found, not in the empirical order of man-made societies, but in the empirical and lawful order of God-made nature. In terms of human knowledge this means that the criterion of the objective and absolute good in law is to be found in the philosophy of empirically verified natural science.

This conception of natural law reveals itself in the Roman Catholic philosophical, theological and legal tradition, not merely in the fact that with St. Thomas this tradition formulates its doctrine in terms of the metaphysical and logical categories of Aristotle's philosophy of physics, but also in the fact that the Roman Catholic tradition argues directly from the empirical facts of nature by means of the teleological, causal and ontological arguments to the nature of God. Put more concretely, the traditional Roman Catholic doctrine of natural law rests upon the presupposition that empirical knowledge in natural science not merely validates the Aristotelian metaphysical and logical categories but also gives ontology. The Stoic philosophers who created Western legal science made the same point when they tell us that philosophy falls into three parts — Logic, Physics and Ethics or Law. By Logic they meant the scientific and epistemological methods with which one knows things; by Physics the knowledge of these things with the aforementioned methods of logic; and by Law the application of this scientifically determined knowledge of things to the ordering of human relations, to the end of human happiness. Once this conception of natural law in the classical tradition is grasped, it becomes evident that Kant, instead of representing the classical doctrine of natural law, is its very antithesis, for Kant stands for two things. The first is that the empirical knowledge of nature, either of common-sense, scientific or empirical philosophical inquiry, does not give ontological conclusions. This is why Kant repudiated all the traditional Roman Catholic arguments for the existence of God. Second, Kant, according to one interpretation of his *Critique of Practical Reason,* concluded that ethics and law cannot be grounded in the philosophy or methodology of nature and the natural sciences, but must instead be treated as autonomous subjects. This amounts to the rejection of the classical doctrine of natural law.

Why, then, have the legal positivists and other legal thinkers since the time of Kant identified his position with the doctrine of natural law? There seem to be at least two reasons. First, Kant agrees with the followers of the classical natural law doctrine in denying that ethical norms are relative, utilitarian, merely man-made, pragmatic social conventions. Second, his positive theory that the ought of ethics and of jurisprudence is an *a priori* presupposition of any person's moral or legal decisions is close to the classical natural law doctrine that human nature has within itself an absolute basis for moral judgment.

It is necessary to keep this Kantian and post-Kantian background in mind if legal thinkers not brought up in the Roman Catholic or the other classical cultural traditions are to understand and evaluate the aforementioned Notre Dame studies. All of these studies take the pre-Kantian doctrine of the roots of ethics and law in an ontologically known nature and reality for granted. None has faced the Kantian Critique, to say nothing about having met it. Each one of these classical traditions assumes also that a natural law jurisprudence gives absolute, universally valid, ethical and legal standards.

Because of the latter assumption it has become the fashion recently for Islamic and Asian leaders abroad, and for Roman Catholic thinkers at home, to attribute the contemporary relativity of ethical and legal standards, the conflict of ideologies and even the fascism of recent times to the modern Western belief in the secular, pragmatic and positivistic theories of ethics and law. The editor of this Notre Dame volume gives expression to this judgment when he writes:

> Secularism divorced Government from God. Pragmatism scorned "ethical absolutes" as criteria of human law. Positivism narrowed the "province of Jurisprudence" to the study of man-made law alone. The Relativist said "all concepts are relative." For Materialism there was "no significant difference between a man and a baboon or a grain of sand." In our own times, Nazis and Communists have erected legal systems with such "principles" as premises. They showed a shocked world only yesterday the inhuman but completely logical conclusions.[1]

The implication, of course, is that natural law jurisprudence escapes this relativity.

Is this the case? It is the light which they throw on this question that makes these Notre Dame studies exceedingly important.

One fact becomes clear immediately. Every major culture in the world in its classical tradition affirms a natural law jurisprudence. This fact alone, however, is not enough to establish the thesis that natural law jurisprudence escapes the relativity of ethical and legal norms. In addition it must be shown that the content of the natural law ethical and legal norms in the different cultural traditions treated in this volume is identical with the content of the ethical and legal norms of the Roman Catholic natural law jurisprudence.

Mr. Sokolsky, Professor Barrett and the Most Reverend J. Francis A. McIntyre suggest, or would like the reader to conclude, that this is the case.[1] Father Hesburgh, in his concluding pages of the volume, exercises more caution. He writes: "Our first reaction upon studying these papers was most optimistic. Perhaps, because of many first impressions of agreement that may be more semantic than real, we have been too sanguine." [1] Apparently he senses that the volume demonstrates slightly too much when it is used to prove that the Hebrew, Islamic, Hindu, Buddhist and Confucian traditions have a natural law with the same content as the natural law of the Roman Catholic tradition.

In order to prove the existence of a doctrine of natural law in their respective cultures, the representatives of the different traditions have

to become specific. The moment this happens the content of the natural law of each culture begins to show. The question then arises
whether it is to agreement or to disagreement with respect to moral
and legal rules that natural law jurisprudence leads one. When, for
example, Dr. Suzuki asserts that for the Buddhist tradition moral and
legal rules have nothing to do with God, since Buddhism denies such
a being, the difference between the content of the Roman Catholic
and the Buddhist doctrine of natural law becomes such that Father
Hesburgh is forced to conclude that "Dr. Suzuki presents a problem . . ." [1] A more detailed examination of the content of natural
law in the other cultural traditions will reveal similar "problems."

Nor is the relativity of ethical and legal norms in classical natural
law jurisprudence restricted to the content of natural law in different
cultural traditions. These Notre Dame studies show that even in a
single cultural tradition the content of the legal and moral rules of
its natural law are sometimes different for one sage or scholar from
what they are for another.

We have already noted this for the Christian West in the cases of
the Kantian and pre-Kantian doctrines of natural law. The Kantian
doctrine of natural law rests upon an idealistic epistemology and rejects an ontologically grounded natural law. The pre-Kantian doctrines of natural law rested upon a realistic epistemology and were
grounded in and assumed the validity of ontology. But even within
the pre-Kantian ontologically grounded doctrines of the Christian
Western cultural tradition, natural law was quite different in its content for John Locke from what it was for St. Thomas, or is for his contemporary Roman Catholic followers. This shows most dramatically
in the case of the Declaration of Independence. It opens with an affirmation of the doctrine of natural law, and the grounding of the independence of the colonies from Great Britain upon that doctrine. The
several authors of the introductions to this Notre Dame volume do
more than suggest that this proves that the philosophy of law upon
which the institutions of the United States rest is a natural law with
the Aristotelian, Thomistic content of the Roman Catholic tradition.
This quite overlooks the fact that the Declaration of Independence
was written in major part by Thomas Jefferson; that he tells us that
we have little to learn from Aristotle [3] and that the three members of

his trinity were Bacon, Newton and Locke.[4] In other words, the content of the natural law of the Declaration of Independence is Newtonian and Lockean rather than Aristotelian, Thomistic and Roman Catholic in content.

Writing of the Chinese tradition, Dr. Hu Shih notes that "The conception of the Way of Heaven or Nature as taught by Lao-tze and accepted by Confucius was too naturalistic and too radical to please the vast majority of the people who were followers of the traditional Sinitic religion, . . ." [1] And even with respect to Confucianism itself Dr. Hu Shih is of the opinion that at least two distinguished Western scholars have confused a purely man-made and priest-made set of social rules, which had very little popular following, with natural law when the true Confucian doctrine of natural law, if it is to be found anywhere, is of a different kind and content.[1] Similarly M. S. Sundaram in an excellent brief description of Hindu culture and law refers both to the Hindu law books and to Gandhi as expressions of the Hindu doctrine of natural law. Yet the ethical principles of these two components of the Hindu natural law tradition are quite incompatible. The Laws of Manu lay down rules of behavior for the Maharaja rulers which specify and take it for granted that war is ethically appropriate. Gandhi, on the other hand, found in the Bhagavadgita and the natural law tradition of the Hindu classics justification for an ethics which regards the use of war or of force under any circumstances as evil.

It appears, therefore, from these Notre Dame studies, that if the capacity to specify absolute, rather than relative legal and ethical, norms is the criterion of a correct and good jurisprudence, then the classical natural law jurisprudence is as incorrect and evil as are the recent modern Western theories of law which the followers of natural law jurisprudence so roundly condemn because of their failure to give the absolute in ethics and law. It would be interesting if the University of Notre Dame Natural Law Institute performed the experiment in a later session of asking the gentlemen who wrote the introduction and summation of its Volume V if they will accept not merely (*a*) the fact proved by this volume that each of the major cultural traditions of the world has a doctrine of natural law, but also (*b*) the special content which the natural law has in the Jewish, Muslim, Hindu, Buddhist, Chinese and, one may add, Kantian and

Lockean traditions. Until such an experiment is performed with an affirmative result, the caution, hinted at, but not pursued, by Father Hesburgh, about drawing any conclusions concerning either the absolute character or the world-wide universality of the University of Notre Dame's natural law jurisprudence must be taken very seriously.

Even so, it would be an error to conclude that natural law jurisprudence has no contribution to make to contemporary legal science. The fact, demonstrated by these Notre Dame studies, that it exists in every major traditional culture of the world shows that the burden of proof rests upon anyone who would affirm that it has no significance. If its importance is to be found, however, one cannot restrict oneself, as the Notre Dame volume does, to the bare fact that the major cultures of the world have a doctrine of natural law. One must go on to determine more in detail its specific content in each particular culture. Then one must go behind the specific content to the way of conceiving nature in the culture in question, at the time its specific ethical and legal norms were first formulated. This must be done in order to find the facts and empirically verified theory of nature which made the particular legal rules of the cultural tradition in question something that seemed to be confirmed by the facts of nature. In short, one must return to and apply the root meaning of natural law, which is that the philosophy exemplified in the ethical and legal norms of manmade traditional culture is to be measured against the philosophy implicit in the empirically verified theories of God-made — that is, nonman-made — nature.

Natural law jurisprudence in this, its root meaning, has yet to be pursued in the contemporary world. Such a pursuit will involve at least four major tasks: first, the determination of the respective philosophies of nature of the different natural law norms of the world's major modern, as well as ancient, cultural traditions; second, the analysis of the empirically verified theories of contemporary natural science to determine the epistemological and ontological philosophy involved; this will require the facing and meeting of Kant's critique of ontology; third, the measuring of the philosophies of the former against the philosophy of the latter; fourth, the specification of a philosophy of nature which has the capacity to account, within a single consistent set of assumptions, for all the facts which brought into existence the diverse culturally relative and limited theories of traditional natural law, such as the Hebrew, Thomistic Roman Catholic, Lockean, Kantian, Islamic and Oriental. Only when these things are done can the relativity of natural law to the content which it has in one's own religious and cultural tradition be escaped.

XIV

Linguistic Symbols and Legal Norms

UNDESCRIBED experience came first. Expressed experience, and hence language, came afterwards. Before one can express, there must be something to be expressed.

But one can give expression to experience in many modes. Language may refer not so much to experience itself as to the effect of experience upon the perceiver, as in the words "Ouch!" or "Damn it!" Because of its problematic character, experience may raise queries. Thus arises the interrogatory mode. In the present inquiry we shall restrict ourselves, however, to language in the indicative mode; that is, to the character which language takes on in its attempt to express experience itself, including the experiencer.

With respect to experience in the indicative mode, two components are to be noted. One component is experience in itself in its all-embracing entirety as given with immediacy. The other component is the factor in human knowledge which is inferred from, but not contained in, immediate experience. Elsewhere the writer has termed these two components the "aesthetic component" and the "theoretic component," respectively.[1]

These two components of experience in its indicative mode are important for any analysis of language, since the type of linguistic symbolism best suited to convey the one is quite different from that most appropriate for the other. Moreover, the type of ethical and legal norms of cultures handling experience in one or the other or both of these two different ways differ correspondingly. Hence the connection between linguistic symbols and ethical and legal norms.

Reprinted from Lyman Bryson, Louis Finkelstein, and others, eds., *Symbols and Society* (1955), by permission of Harper & Brothers.

To make the foregoing conclusions evident several things are necessary. It must be realized that we approach culture and symbolism at the end of a lengthy historical tradition which is the product of the converging of many cultures. This means that our symbolism is of necessity a mixed symbolism, even perhaps, as the sequel will suggest, a bastard symbolism, due to the fact that a given cultural language devised to convey experience in one indicative mode found itself forced, due to outside influences, to convey experience in the other indicative mode for which it was in many ways ill fitted.

It becomes necessary, therefore, if confusion and linguistic corruption of the diverse aesthetic and theoretic components of knowledge are to be avoided, to separate out from the complexity of our present linguistically expressed experience the immediately experienced factor — that is, the aesthetic component — from the theoretically inferred factor; that is, the theoretic component. Having done this, we should then be able to determine the two different types of linguistic symbols most appropiate for each.

To this end let us consider the following example. One directly senses within the all-embracing continuum of immediacy a specific, differentiated color. To this immediately experienced datum in the aesthetic component of knowledge, convention, in the English language, has assigned the word "blue." Consider with care precisely how "blue" in this sense gets its meaning. Clearly the entire meaning of the word is given by a datum in the all-embracing immediacy of experience, which itself is immediately experienced. Yellow, red, pain and pleasure are other examples of this type of symbol. Such a symbol we have called a concept by intuition, where by intuition is meant something not mediated to the knower through something else, but given immediately after the manner of a specific, particular, immediately sensed blue.

Consider now, by way of contrast, an electromagnetic wave traveling *in vacuo* with a speed of 186,000 miles a second and with a wave length of 4862 angstroms. To this wave with this specific wave length, the English language also assigns the word "blue." Clearly, however, "blue" in the latter sense has a fundamentally different meaning and designates a quite different object from "blue" in the former sense. Neither the wave with a speed of 186,000 miles per second nor its wave length is immediately experienced after the manner in which the sensed color in the all-embracing continuum of immediacy is directly inspected. In other words, "blue" in the sense of the electromagnetic wave is an object of knowledge inferred from but not contained in the all-embracing immediacy of experience. It is, in short, a factor in the theoretic component of knowledge.

But if the symbol "blue" in the sense of the concept of the electromagnetic wave refers to something which is not directly inspected in the all-embracing immediacy of experience, how, then, is this symbol given meaning in an unambiguous way? Clearly this concept cannot gain its meaning by the method of pointing or sensing or immediately apprehending after the manner in which the concept of "blue" which is a concept by intuition gains its meaning. The answer is that the concept of "blue" in the sense of the electromagnetic wave with a specific wave length obtains its meaning only through the construction by some scientist of an axiomatically constructed, deductively formulated theory in which the entity — that is, the wave with its specific wave length — functions as a variable, satisfying a certain type of formally defined order or relatedness. Because "blue" in the sense of the electromagnetic wave depends upon a set of deductively formulated postulates for its meaning, it is appropriate to call it, or any other concept knowable in whole or in part in this way, a concept by postulation.

One of the tragically unfortunate weaknesses of present education is that the same word "blue" is used in the conventional, commonsense English language for these two fundamentally different types of concepts, referring to radically different objects for their meanings, and that the reader is not made aware, nor is the English language appropriate or adequate to make him aware, of the radical difference in the method to be used to obtain the meaning of the one concept as compared with the meaning of the other. In fact, as the sequel will show, ordinary language, whether it be English, French, German, Sanskrit or Chinese, is ill fitted to convey the meaning of any concept by postulation.

Moreover — and this is the point of essential importance for the present inquiry — there is a fundamental difference between the relation of the object to the symbol in the case of a concept by intuition as compared with a concept by postulation. In the instance of "blue" in the sense of the ineffable sensed color, the symbol *qua* symbol says nothing. If one did not have with immediacy the experience of an instance of blue, the symbol "blue" would be a meaningless set of marks. Thus, in the case of this type of symbol one gets what it means when one throws the symbol away. In fact, what the symbol means cannot be said symbolically. The symbol instead is merely a conventional pointer which can be thrown away the minute the immediately experienced object of its pointing is found.

In the case of any symbol which is a concept by postulation, referring to inferred objects that cannot be directly inspected, such as an electromagnetic wave of a specified wave length, the relation of the symbol to its object is the exact converse of the relation of the symbol "blue," which is a concept by intuition to the sensed datum that is its object. Since electromagnetic waves traveling at 186,000 miles per second are not directly inspected, to throw away the symbol "blue," in the sense of the number for the electromagnetic wave length, is to be left with nothing. Without the language, this object cannot be known. In short, whereas the objective referents of symbols which are concepts by intuition cannot be said and can only be pointed at by their symbols, those of concepts by postulation can be said but cannot be pointed at symbolically.

Also, the sensed datum "blue" can be known in its full meaning quite apart from its sensed relations to other factors; the knowing of its relations to other things is not an essential part of the knowing of it. However, in the case of the wave length, or any other object of a concept by postulation, its relatedness to everything else is of the essence. An electromagnetic wave is only knowable through the specific systematically and postulationally constructed mathematical relatedness, with specified formal properties, which it alone satisfies. Consequently the language, the only exact language, for indicating such inferred objects within human experience is the language of mathematics and more particularly the symbolic logic of relations.

The ordinary prose of the ordinary languages, as studied by the traditional linguists, is quite inadequate to convey knowledge of inferred entities in the theoretic component of knowledge. In fact ordinary language, because of its two-termed, noun-verb grammar and subject-predicate way of thinking about everything, tends to corrupt this way of knowing experience in its indicative mode. Furthermore, Whitehead has given cogent reasons for believing that the ordinary languages of common-sense usage, upon which linguists have concentrated their attention, corrupt every dimension of experience — the aesthetic, the religious, the psychological, and the social — just as much as they distort and corrupt the knowledge of mathematical physics.[2] If the relatedness of experience, even of aesthetic experience, is a many-termed relatedness, this is the case. And if it be the case, our traditional linguistic habits have distorted and corrupted all our aesthetic, moral, religious, and social judgments. Again one sees the essential connection between language and ethical and legal norms.

This becomes evident in a concrete way when one compares the symbolism of mathematical physics with that of ordinary language with respect to the ethical implications of each. In mathematical physics individual entities are not regarded as truly known unless the universal laws — that is, the complex relations — which define their properties and which they satisfy are specified. This means that a truly known individual, even a truly known man, is always an entity which in its essential nature is an instance of a universal law. Directly experienced man is of a quite different character, as the ethics and the legal procedures of cultures which have never discovered the mathematical physicist's way of knowing clearly demonstrate. In all such cultures, where only the ordinary languages are used, moral man is always inductively observed, family and tribal man. Never, in the social norms for ordering human relations, is he conceived as universal man. Thus, the notion that color of skin or family connection or tribe has nothing to do with the norms of a moral society is in fact foreign to peoples and cultures which have not discovered the way of knowing individuals by means of the linguistic universalism of deductively formulated mathematical physics, a mode of knowing which occurred first with the ancient Greeks.

It was this way of knowing, passing over through Greek philosophy into Roman law, which gave rise to the Western law of contract and to the novel moral ideal that no rule for ordering personal or social conduct is truly moral unless any human being whatever can be substituted for an instance of the rule. Then, for the first time, moral and political man was broken loose from Roman, Greek, Hebrew, Arab, Hindu or Chinese family and tribal man. And even with the Romans, the break was made largely as an ideal and only in part in fact. The point to be noted, however, is that prior to the philosophers

of ancient Greek mathematical physics and the Stoic Romans the idea
of moral man being universal man had not been conceived even as an
ideal. In the case of Hinduism and its Laws of Manu, this is unequivocally clear. Different legal penalties are applied for identical
offenses according to the caste to which one belongs, and a higher
moral quality is assigned to the patriarchal families descended from
Manu than any other patriarchal families in the Hindu-Aryan community.

Sir Henry S. Maine has described this difference between (1) the
ethics and law throughout the entire world before the Stoic Romans
created Western legal science and (2) the ethics and law afterwards
as "a movement from status to contract." [3] The law of status is the
type of ethics and law that goes with a symbolism which restricts its
reference to experience in the indicative mode, to experience as conceived in terms of common-sense, substantial persons and things as
given in naïve common-sense observation in the ordinary man's language. Since such an excessively inductive and naïve way of knowing
restricts knowable reality to the status quo, the ethical and legal norms
of such a linguistic symbolism have nothing to which to refer but to
the status quo. In the status quo as immediately experienced, men are
not identical; they have different colors of skin. To treat them, therefore, as equal is to be untrue to their essential nature. It is not an
accident that the Sanskrit word for caste is the Sanskrit word for
color.

Moreover, even with respect to families with the same color of skin,
different families, as naïvely observed, have different ancestors. Thus
there are tribal differences as well as color differences. To act, there-
for, as if all tribes were equal is to act contrary to what is the case.
Moreover, one of the tribes must in fact lead. In Hindu-Aryan society this was the tribe of Manu. Hence its privileged position morally
and socially in Hindu Indian culture.

Even in societies, such as the Confucian Chinese, in which one
tribe did not enjoy ascendancy over all other tribes and families, the
law of status approach to human nature of a linguistic symbolism, restricting itself to naïve experience, reveals family ties to be given
with immediacy as stronger than other social ties. Hence people in
such societies concluded that to treat sons in other families under the
same legal or moral rules which one applies to sons in one's own fam-

ily is again to falsify human nature. In short, filial piety, or family loyalty, becomes the highest social morality, and nepotism, instead of being the vice it is in a society guided by the ethics of a law of contract, becomes instead the highest social virtue.

Historically the ethics of the law of status society, with its linguistic symbolism, which roots all symbolic meaning in experience as given in naïve observation, came first, and the law of contract society with its concept of moral man as universal man and its deductively formulated, mathematical symbolism, which finds its empirical meaning in the theoretical component of knowledge which is inferred from but not contained in immediate experience, arose afterwards. Moreover, it was discovered first by the ancient Greeks, who founded deductively formulated and indirectly verified mathematical physics. It is because this new way of arriving at symbolic meaning passed over through classical Greek philosophy to the Stoic Romans who created Western legal science that the ethics of the law of status with its moral attachment to family and to tribe was transformed into the ethics of the law of contract according to which moral man is universal man.

Seen from the linguistic point of view, this epoch-making ethical transformation centers in the shift from (1) the symbolism of common-sense language, which finds meanings for entities like a particular blue, a particular pain, a particular pleasure, a particular naïvely observed table or naïvely observed family apart from the relation of these entities to one another or to other entities, to (2) the more complex syntactical symbolism of mathematics in which the entities are meaningless by themselves and are meaningful only in terms of the formal properties of the postulationally constructed relations which they satisfy. In law and social morality, this permits the construction of utopias. It also permits the creation of non-empirically given legal entities such as the modern corporation. The ideal is freed from the actuality of the naïvely observed status quo. The moral and the ideal are released also from the restrictive emotional ties between parents and children and from the commonplace objects that are naïvely observed. At the same time the utopian constructions, expressed in the Western world's ideologies and political constitutions, express actuality — the actuality, however, of contractually and theoretically conceived rather than naïvely observed reality.

The exceedingly syntactical symbolism of mathematics and the revolutionary personal and social ethics of the law of contract, which it generates, have their limitations, however, as well as their unique assets. They cannot convey the syntactically inexpressible. This means that they cannot convey the elementary objects of immediate experience which have to be experienced to be known and which cannot be said. "Blue" in the sense of the experienced color is such a factor. Anything known with immediacy has this character of being inexpressible. The entire continuum of immediacy cannot be said. In its ineffability it has to be experienced to be known. This is why Oriental linguistic symbolism has to use words like "Om," "Nirvana," or "Suchness" to designate it. The point to note about such symbols is that they are devoid of syntax. They merely point, they do not relate, nor do they say. If you do not know, apart from them, what they mean, then such symbols are for you meaningless.

These considerations explain why the philosophy of traditional Western mathematical physics and the ethics of Western constitutional societies with their attention upon mathematical symbolism and upon abstract, dry and technical legally formulated constitutions, statutes and legal entities have tended to leave modern Western man starved emotionally with respect to aesthetic immediacy. For the latter type of experience — that component of indicative knowledge which is immediate — the early pictographical symbolisms of the Sind Valley or the Chinese civilizations with their lesser elements of syntax were the ideal symbolisms. Such a symbolism shows rather than says. This is why the Chinese symbolism, even with its additional syntactical elements going beyond the initial pictograms, and Chinese thought, expressing itself through Chinese symbolism, moves on the concrete aesthetic surface of things and, as Lin Yutang says, "always remains on the periphery of the visible world," and has a "dislike of abstract terms." [4] This does not mean that by sufficient additions and qualifications the Chinese symbolism cannot express syntactical ideas. The Japanese linguistic additions to the Chinese symbolism do exactly this. But they do it only by pointing to the syntactical meanings rather than embodying them exactly as English grammar points at and talks about the much more subtle syntactical meanings of mathematical language without actually embodying them.

By using enough ordinary English words and introducing sufficient definitions to give them precise meanings, other than their common-sense meanings, it is possible for a person who knows mathematical logic or mathematics to express the theories of mathematical physics with almost 100 per cent accuracy in ordinary English prose. But what such complex technical English prose does cumbersomely in an indirect and roundabout manner, thereby causing its superficial readers to criticize its writers as unnecessarily pedantic, mathematical symbolism can say directly and literally and elegantly with the utmost beauty and economy. As Wittgenstein has noted of the form of the perfect language of mathematics, the relatedness of the symbols is identical with the relatedness of the objects symbolized. Where the same thing is said by the circumlocutions of English prose, this isomorphism of symbols and symbolic objects is not present.[5]

We arrive, therefore, at the following important conclusion: For the factor in human knowledge in the indicative mode which is inferred from immediate experience but not immediately apprehended in it and which hence can be known only through linguistic expression, the symbolism of mathematics and mathematical logic is the ideal symbolism; whereas for that component of human knowledge which is knowable with immediacy, the pictograph symbolism with its lesser emphasis on syntax is the ideal form of expression and to each type of symbolism there is a corresponding ethics.

This conclusion has one important corollary. The present languages of the linguists and the humanists are bastard symbolisms corrupting both modes of knowing and both types of the good life. Ordinary language has too much grammar and syntax in it to convey aesthetic immediacy in all of its ineffable subtlety and richness, thereby leaving the warm-hearted mediational ethics of emotive aesthetic immediacy unexpressed, while at the same time not possessing sufficient syntactical complexity to convey the inferred theoretic component of man and nature. More than this, the partial syntax which ordinary language introduces, due to its subject-predicate form, actually falsifies the meager portion of the relatedness of things which it attempts to convey.

This is probably the reason why the morality of our humanists is so conventionally dull and so sterile and ineffective before the moral needs and demands of the contemporary world. This suggests that it is our humanists, owing to their worship and propagation of an inadequate symbolism unfitted for either mode of indicative knowing, who have let us down morally. In any event we must move away (1) by means of existential, scientific and philosophical thinking and by impressionistic art to aesthetic immediacy, on the one hand, and (2) by means of training in the logic of relations to an adequate syntactical symbolism, on the other hand, with the aim in the end of combining both in a harmonious synthesis. When this occurs, the humanists will measure up to their responsibilities, and mankind may bring its symbolically expressed values in accord with the richness of human experience in both modes of indicative knowledge.

XV

The Philosophy of Natural Science
and Comparative Law

THE diverse conclusions to which philosophical study leads inquiring minds are evident. But even the differences perhaps express a truth. This observation takes on more concrete significance when one notes that the diverse cultures of the world embody many of our different philosophical conclusions. Thus, the plurality of philosophical theories is in part at least paralleled by an empirical diversity of cultures which exemplify them. This suggests that even the disagreements of philosophers are less speculative and merely subjective in origin than might at first be supposed, and represent instead something in the experience of mankind which, in part at least, is empirical and objective in character.

It will help us in pursuing this suggestion further if we restrict our examination of both philosophy and culture to a single element in each. In considering different cultures, we shall, therefore, converge upon their law. In examining their respective philosophies, we shall attend to their theories of knowledge.

The restriction of culture to its legal factor has several advantages. Law is concerned with communal norms. Hence it draws attention immediately to the social ethos of a culture. Thereby ethics is brought into the heart of our inquiry. Also, law provides ethics with explicitly expressed content as formulated by the people themselves of a given culture.

Restriction to the law of a culture has a third advantage. Legal procedures and codes contain explicitly expressed content. Hence comparative law permits the problems of ethics to be examined in terms

Reprinted from *Proceedings and Addresses of the American Philosophical Association*, Vol. XXVI, by permission.

of the content of different types of specific ethical norms, after the manner in which the verified theories of natural science allow the nature of knowing to be determined by an analysis of different specific successful instances of knowing.

Finally, law provides ethics with operational definitions. Thereby the pragmatic differences of various ethical theories with respect to specific instances of ethical disagreement are exhibited. In law an ethical theory cannot protect itself from its weaknesses, as occurs in the ethical discussion of much contemporary philosophy, by remaining in an ivory tower restricting its attention to abstract nouns like "goodness," "duty," "emotive meaning" or "instrumental values which are at once means and ends." Of any ethical theory as proposed for law, the judge cannot avoid asking: What difference does it make with respect to my decision in this particular case?

The full role of law as the operational application of ethical theory does not become evident, however, until one examines the operational applications to similar disputes of different ethical theories in different cultures. The law of a single culture merely takes its particular ethical theory for granted and applies it to the settling of disputes in that culture. The full significance of comparative law appears, therefore, only when we find two or more cultures embodying different ethical theories and then examine the different legal operational consequences with respect to similar disputes in the two cultures.

Most if not all cultures have legal codes. There are, however, very important differences with respect to both the nature and the use of legal codes in different cultures. As a first approximation, the world's legal procedures and codes fall into three major groups. We shall call them (1) the intuitive mediational type, (2) the natural history type and (3) the abstract contractual type.

The Intuitive Mediational Type

This type of law predominates in any culture which is Confucian, Buddhist, Taoist, or non-Aryan Hindu. By non-Aryan Hindu is meant that portion of any Hindu culture which is not the contribution of the ancient Aryan conquerors of India. Gandhi's Hinduism is an example.

The procedure of this type of law is to push legal codes into the background, preferably dispensing with them altogether, and to bring the disputants into a warm give-and-take relationship, usually by way of a mediator, so that previously made demands can be modified gracefully, and a unique solution taking all the exceptional circumstances of the case into account is spontaneously accepted by both disputants. Codes there may be, but they are to be used only as a last resort, and even then recourse to them brings shame upon the disputants. The moral man, Confucius teaches, does not indulge in litigation. Gandhi's revulsion, during and after his South African period, to Western law and his use instead of the warm-hearted intuitive way of his beloved Bhagavadgita is an instance of the same ethical attitude. In Buddhist Bangkok in 1950 I found the Chief Justice of its Supreme Court and a former Chief Justice of its next highest court, the Court of Appeals, who ostensibly were applying that most abstract of Western law, the French Continental Code, assuring me that they refused often to hear the case and urged the disputants, if Thais, to settle their differences by themselves in the approved Buddhist manner. In one instance after two such refusals and two failures of the disputants to reach agreement by themselves, the judges declined a third time to proceed in the Western manner, with the result that the intuitive mediational way succeeded.

Note its distinguishing characteristic: Not only is there no resort to a legal rule; there is also no judge. Even the mediator refuses to give a decision. Instead, the dispute is properly settled when the disputants, using the mediator merely as an emissary, come to mutual agreement in the light of all the existential circumstances, past, present, and future.

The word "future" is used advisedly. In this type of ethics and law there is no irrelevant evidence; not even future possible evidence is neglected. For always the mediator or the adversaries themselves will remind any disputant that it is better to settle for a little less today and preserve tomorrow's goodwill than to obtain more today and lose tomorrow's goodwill.

Not the abstract universals of a legal code, but the existential particularity of the concrete problematic situation, in all its ramifications — familial, village, present, past and future — is the criterion of the just and the good in any culture in which this intuitive mediational type of law predominates. Evidently the first instrumental pragmatist, sensitive to the particular problematic situation in all its dimensions of experience, was not born in Vermont; nor did the first existentialist come to birth in Paris or even in Copenhagen.

Lest you suppose that this reference to Dewey, Kierkegaard and Sartre is strained let it be noted now, as the sequel will show, that behind this intuitive, mediational type of law in Asia there is a Confucian, Buddhist and pre-Aryan Hindu epistemology which affirms that full, direct and exact empirical knowledge of any individual, relation or event in nature reveals it to be unique, and from this observation infers that to treat any individual, such as a person, or any event, such as a dispute between persons, as an instance of a non-nominalistic class concept or a universal legal rule is to act contrary to fact and hence to falsify human nature.

Dewey's emphasis upon the unique character of each problematic situation and his identification of the good with that particular solution which results from a sensitivity to all its experienceable dimensions express the same theory of ethics. Note also that they entail that the good for ethics reduces to the true for empirically complete, direct and exact knowledge. Sartre expresses the same ethics and epistemology when he insists that one falsifies human nature and ethical decision when one exhausts the individual in the abstract universal, or in any number of such universals.

In Asia, as for Dewey here, this intuitive mediational type of ethics and law has been combined with another point of view. This brings us to the ethics of codified law. There are two kinds: the natural history type and the abstract contractual type.

The Natural History Type of Law

Its codes differ from those of our third type of law in two respects. First, they are expressed in the syntactical grammar of the language of common-sense objects and relations. Second, the codes describe the biologically conceived patriarchal or matriarchal familial and tribal kinship norms of the inductively and sensuously given status quo.

Those philosophers and lawyers known as the Legalists illustrate this natural history type of law for classical China. The Laws of Manu, which together with the syntactical Sanskrit language are the contribution to Hindu India of its ancient Aryan conquerors, exemplify it for classical India. Muhammadan legal codes, from the standpoint of which Allah, or his representative on earth, passes judgment, provide the Islamic example. In fact, as Sir Henry S. Maine has shown in his classic study of ancient law, all codified ancient law — Eastern, Middle Eastern or Western — before the time of the Stoic Romans was of this second type.[1] Not only were its codes expressed in common-sense terms, but they also merely described and thereby tended to freeze the norms of the traditional status quo. It was, in short, as he so aptly said, a law of status.[2]

It still lives in the contemporary world. Two years ago I was in Cairo, where Egyptians, who had received their legal education in Paris, apply the Stoic Roman and modern Western type of abstract contractual law modeled on the French Continental Code. After driving fifty miles west I entered a village where, through an interpreter, I questioned the village leader about the settling of local disputes. By a lucky circumstance our conversation was interrupted by a local villager. It seems that a neighbor's dog had killed some of his chickens. He had spoken to the neighbor about the matter but nothing had been done. Instantly the elder replied and, evidently satisfied, the villager withdrew. Meanwhile the interpreter translated the elder's reply. It was that he would speak to the neighbor, telling him to tie up the animal, and if he failed to do so he would have the dog shot.

Upon being asked how he could be sure that the one party to the dispute correctly portrayed the facts of the case, the reply was that he knew both parties well and that since there had been no previous ill will between them, there was no reason to think that the villager making the complaint had misrepresented the situation. This was as things would be in a Far Eastern village where the intuitive mediational type of law predominates.

There was, however, one important difference. The village elder had decided. He had sat in judgment and given a verdict. There was no mediation. This was the operational sign that in his Islamic village we were confronted with the second rather than the first type of law.

Furthermore, were the owner of the dog not to follow the common-sense rule, as applied by the village elder, the apparatus of the local and even the provincial police would come down upon him. The sanction for the decision is not, as with the intuitive mediational type of law, the mutually achieved and accepted agreement of the disputants, but instead the common-sense rule as applied by the duly constituted authority and backed with police power. The unique aspects of the dispute, the defendant or the problematic situation have nothing to do with the matter. Conduct is good if it corresponds to the common-sense code as applied by the appropriate authority; it is bad if it does not. Before this code all men are equal; they are instances of the same universals; their existential particularity is ethically irrelevant.

The Abstract Contractual Type of Law

This type of codified law differs from the natural history type in that it replaces common-sense language with a technical terminology. This has the very important consequence of freeing ethical and legal norms from the mere natural history biologically conceived description of the social status quo, thereby permitting the construction of legal and social entities and relations different from any which are observed in any traditional society. This type of law came into being for the first time with the Roman Stoic philosophers who created the Western science of law. The manner in which it differs from all previous codified law has been described by Sir Henry Maine, in his classic study, as "the shift from status to contract." [3]

We of the West are more cognizant of the differences between examples of this third type of law than of their identities. For the purposes of this paper, the identities constitute the really interesting and important factor.

The ethics to which this third type of law gives expression is radically different from that of either the mediational or the natural history type of law. It differs from the former in that it regards the initial recourse to codes as a good way to settle disputes. It differs from the latter in two very important ways. First, its identification of the ethical and the socially legal with abstractly and imaginatively constructed, rather than with inductively described, biologically conceived human norms and relations, such as primogeniture, makes possible ethical and legal reform. Both ethics and law are freed from the norms of the traditional status quo. Second, its norms have much greater generality. Instead of identifying the ethically good with inductively observed tribal, caste, class or color concepts, the good can be identified with all individuals who freely accept the postulates of the contractually constructed system. Thereby moral man becomes identified more and more with universal man. Put more exactly, what this means is that a contractually constructed norm cannot be regarded as ethical unless if it holds for any one individual it also holds for any other. The more concrete ethical implications of this type of law become evident when one notes that every culture in the world to which Western science and this type of law have penetrated is at the present moment undergoing a revolution in its ethical and legal norms.

Clearly, these three types of law express three different, and in part conflicting, conceptions of the ethically good. Is it possible to determine the factor upon which these ethical differences turn?

The Criterion of Ethical and Legal Norms

Consider first the difference with respect to the proper method to be used to settle disputes as conceived by the Confucianists and the Legalists in ancient China. The Confucian attitude has been described in detail by the Chinese lawyer and judge, S. F. Liu, and by the Confucian Chiang Monlin, former Chancellor of Peking National University, former member of President Chiang Kai-shek's National Yuan at Chunking and student of Professor Oversteet when he was at Berkeley and of Dewey here in New York.[4] Both Liu and Chiang agree that according to pre-Western Confucian Chinese theory and practice the resort to codes in the settling of disputes was regarded as morally evil, only to be indulged in as a last resort in the case of immoral and unwise men who do not accept the appropriate social norms and procedure. The appropriate way is that of warm fellow feeling, leisurely mediation through a third party and compromise reached by mutual agreement. The entire process proceeds informally, taking into account the whole lifetime and even ancestral family background of the disputants and all the unique circumstances of the case.

The Chinese Legalists, on the other hand, stood for the use of codes as the moral, legal and necessary way to order social relations and settle disputes. One of their arguments was that otherwise social organization over wider areas beyond the reach of warm person-to-person contact within the patriarchal joint family and between the joint families at the village level is not possible.

We begin to see the reason for the different ethical theories of the Confucian and Legalistic schools when we examine the epistemological theories which distinguish them. Epistemologically the issue between them turned around the question whether common-sense class concepts are nominalistic or real universals, where by a real universal is meant one in which the universality refers to something in the objects symbolized, and by a nominalistic universal is meant one in which the universality has its basis solely in the symbol, the objective reference of the symbol being comprised of nothing but particular individuals, each one of which is unique. The Chinese expressed this technical philosophical question in a very concrete way: When one is confronted by four individuals, is one faced with four things or with five? The Confucianists affirm the former alternative; the Legalists the latter, insisting that the class of the four individuals is the fifth factor.

The ethics of "the middle path" of Buddhist culture with its preference for and present persisting practice of the mediational, rather than the codified litigational method of settling disputes, notwithstanding Western influences to the contrary, derives also from a nominalistic epistemology. An examination of the Buddha's teaching and the training of his earliest priests shows that the basis of both was a testing of the meaning of abstract nouns against the immediately apprehended data of direct experience to reveal only nominalistic particulars, *esse est percipi* relativity and the transitoriness of any determinate thing including even the particular knowing ego. For the Buddha and his early priests, good conduct consisted in not being misled by words or, to put the matter positively, in being guided by the immediately given data from which all words in Buddhist knowledge derive their meanings.[5] Confucius expressed the same essential connection between ethics and epistemology when he said that ethics consists in "the rectification of names." [6] Apparently, the first semanticist was not born in the twentieth century.

During his South African period Gandhi developed a similar antipathy, from which he never recovered, to the Western legal methods of settling disputes by codes and litigation. He found the inspiration for the proper way, he tells us, in the Hindu Bhagavadgita and Upanishads.[7] Actually this Hindu tradition contains both the pacifistic mediational ethics common to Hinduism, Buddhism and Confucianism, which Gandhi singled out and espoused, and the codified litigational method with its use of law backed with force introduced into Hinduism by the ancient Aryan conquerors from the West. Gandhi conveniently overlooked this legalistic Aryan element in Hinduism when he read his Gita and other Hindu classics. The non-Aryan purely indigenously Asian component of Hinduism can be shown to rest also upon a nominalistic epistemology. Even the universal Brahman of non-dualistic Vedanta Hinduism is existential, and hence nominalistic, in character, as the Hindu philosophers Professors Chatterjee and Datta have pointed out.[8]

It appears, therefore, that the difference in the ethical norms of the Confucianists and the Legalists in classical China has its roots in a difference in their epistemology of natural knowledge. The epistemology of the ethics of the intuitive, mediational type of law which the Confucian illustrates is radical empiricism with its nominalistic theory of the class concept. The epistemology of the ethics of the natural history type of law which the Legalists affirmed is naïve realism with its theory of real as opposed to nominalistic universals.

Several facts support the latter thesis that there is an essential connection between the ethics of the natural history type of codified law and the epistemology of naïve realism. First, there is the aforementioned fact that the Chinese Legalists found the basis for their ethics of dispute settling by recourse to codes of the natural history type in the epistemological theory of real universals and fought the ethical issue with the Confucianists over this point. Second, an examination of the natural history type of code in any culture shows that such codes are clearly the product of a people who have conceptualized their empirical experience in terms of the objects, relations and observable tribal, caste, family and color groupings of naïve common sense and who believe that this way of thinking about things is basic to all ethical and legal relations and distinctions. Such a way of thinking is characteristic of anyone whose epistemological theory is solely that of naïve realism.

But what, it may be asked, does the epistemological issue of nominalistic versus real universals in the empirical knowledge of natural objects have to do with the ethical issue concerning whether legal codes are or are not good as the initial means for ordering social relations and settling disputes between men?

The answer seems to be as follows: If true knowledge of any individual entity or event in nature as determined by analyzing the empirically verified propositions of natural knowledge to bring out the character and sources of their meaning indicates that only existential, inductive particularity exists, then each person and dispute is unique and to treat either as an instance of a universal class concept is, as the Sartrean existentialists in our time affirm, to treat it falsely and hence to act immorally. If, on the other hand, as the epistemology of the Chinese Legalists affirms, true knowledge of individuals indicates that they instance a universal, common factor the same for all, then to treat them as measurable by the abstract nouns of universal propositions or codes which designate this common factor is the only way to treat them truly in terms of what they are, and therefore morally.

Note what the aforementioned connection between epistemology and ethics in Chinese, Buddhist and Hindu cultures signifies. It means that the word "good" is not, as the empiricist G. E. Moore or the idealist Urban affirmed, a primitive concept but is instead a defined concept — a concept defined in part at least in terms of the true with respect to the epistemology of empirical knowledge. It follows that ethical sentences are not merely emotive or hortatory; they are also cognitive. Or, to put the matter in another way, if epistemological propositions are cognitive rather than emotive, then ethical propositions are also.

This definition of the ethically good for dispute settling in terms of the empirically true for epistemology is not circular. Certainly no epistemologist would maintain that the empirical question of whether class concepts are nominalistic or real universals involves an ethical judgment.

It is to be noted also that the question of what we are knowing when we know an individual so far as his unique particularity or universality is concerned is quite independent of whether the individual be a human being or natural object or event. This means that the ethics of a culture is essentially connected not merely with epistemology but with the epistemology of the knowledge of natural objects and events, or in other words with its empirically verified philosophy of natural science. Certainly the empirical correctness of one epistemology rather than another can be determined by appeal to instances of individuals or events in nature which are the same for any culture. This has the important consequence of freeing ethics and law from cultural relativism.

But, it may be asked, if empirical evidence in nature, common to all cultures, decides the epistemology of any culture, which in turn determines its ethics, why then do different philosophers and different cultures facing approximately the same natural phenomena arrive at different epistemological and legal theories? Part of the answer to this question will become clear if we press one step further the analysis of the difference between the Confucian and Chinese Legalists' ethics for ordering social relations and settling disputes. What was there in the Chinese knowledge of nature which convinced the Chinese philosophers generally, and the people following them, of the correctness of the Confucian epistemology and ethics?

Chiang Monlin throws important light on this question when he tells us that the only method of knowing nature discovered by the Chinese was what he terms "naïve observation." [9] Such a method of knowing restricts the meaning of concepts to what is given purely empirically and directly with immediacy. To the philosophically uncritical such naïve direct observation seems to warrant the epistemology of naïve realism with its belief in gross public objects independent of perceivers, possessing the qualities and shapes which one actually senses. With time, however, in any culture a more exact examination of what radically empirical observation gives reveals this theory to be both false and self-contradictory. As Berkeley and Hume showed the modern West and as Confucian, Buddhist and Vedanta Hindu philosophers showed the classical Orient, every factor which naïve realism assumes to be the same for everybody and independent of the perceiver turns out to vary from perceiver to perceiver and hence to be relative to the perceiver. The assumption, therefore, that radically empirical or naïve observation gives objects independent of the perceiver with qualities the same for everyone breaks down. In fact the common-sense theory of naïve realism is self-contradictory since its realism asserts the belief in public objects with qualities the same for everybody independent of the perceiver and its naïve way of knowing gives only qualities and relations which vary from perceiver to perceiver and whose *esse est percipi*. Clearly a theory which defines subjects purporting to be independent of perceivers in terms of objects which vary from perceiver to perceiver is self-contradictory. The Confucianists had no difficulty, therefore, in showing that the very method of knowing nature used by Confucianists and Legalists alike, namely that of naïve observation, did not justify the Legalists' epistemology with its assumption of objective meanings the same for all individuals in a class and hence did not justify the Legalists' ethics for dispute settling.

The fact, therefore, that the scientists or sages of different cultures arrive at different epistemological theories of the meanings of the concepts they use to describe and coordinate the raw data of their experience, which in turn entail correspondingly different ethical and legal norms, does not mean that their conclusions are not objective in a sense which makes them valid for anybody in any culture. It may mean, as is the case with the Chinese Confucianists and Legalists, that one of the epistemological and ethical theories is erroneous in a sense which can be shown to be true for anybody in any culture. It may mean also, as Chiang Monlin has shown to be the case for classical Chinese culture and for the West, that one culture has found one empirically verified way of knowing nature with its particular epistemology and ethics and that the other culture has found a different empirically verified way and that both can be shown to be valid in a sense which can be confirmed by anyone anywhere.

The latter possibility brings us to our third type of law. Does it also derive from a particular scientific method and epistemology?

It was mentioned earlier that the intuitive, existential theory of ethics with its thesis that each ethical problem is unique, and hence not amenable to treatment by codes the same for all occasions, is supplemented with the belief in the resort to codes, not merely in the case of Asia, but also in the case of Dewey. Why in Dewey's case also?

The answer is that Dewey's procedure for resolving any problematic situation includes the methods of Western science, and, according to Western science, no individual or event is fully known when it is merely denotatively sensed as an existentially unique particular or even when it is described in terms of the common-sense objects and relations of natural history science; in addition, the hypothetically proposed and axiomatically formulated universal laws which it illustrates must be found and indirectly and operationally verified empirically.

The late Morris R. Cohen and his colleague Professor Drabkin tell us in their *Source Book in Greek Science* that this way of knowing individual entities, events and relations in nature was developed for the first time by the mathematical physicists of ancient Greece. They write that

> . . . all the evidence indicates that the ideal of rigorously deductive proof, the method of developing a subject by a chain of theorems based on definitions, axioms, and postulates, and the constant striving for complete generality and abstraction are the specific contributions of the Greeks to mathematics.[10]

Chiang Monlin tells us also in his *Tides from the West* that this way of knowing any individual or event in nature is foreign to traditional Chinese mentality and that he became acquainted with it for the first time when he came to the United States in the 1920's and was introduced to the natural philosophy of ancient Greece at the University of California at Berkeley by Professor Harry A. Overstreet, then beginning his teaching career there. Chiang Monlin notes also that this novel way of thinking arose in the abstract, deductively formulated mathematical physics of ancient Greece and entails a novel epistemology. Albert Einstein expresses the same fact when he tells us that the person who has not been thrilled by Euclid does not understand modern mathematical physics.[11]

Nor do the ethical implications of this novel epistemology of natural knowledge escape Chiang Monlin. For he concludes that there will be no effective introduction of modern Western technological, ethical and legal forms into China until his fellow countrymen are taught the epistemology of Western deductively formulated natural science. Otherwise the way of thinking about individual persons and the events that are their disputes, which is required to make modern Western ethical and legal values and forms meaningful and effective, will not be present.

This awareness on Chiang Monlin's part of an essential connection between the ethics of our third type of law and the epistemology of Western mathematical physics is not born of merely theoretical considerations. It has its basis also in his increasing awareness over many years, during his chancellorship of Peking National University, of the failure of modern Western ethical and political forms to take deep root in his country, and in his penetrating analysis of its cause.

Events in the West, following the mathematical physics of ancient Greece, support his conclusions. It is a significant historical fact that the abstract, contractual type of law appeared for the first time in history when this new scientific way of knowing individuals and events in nature passed over from the ancient Greek mathematical physicists through every school of Greek philosophy — Stoic, Platonic and Aristotelian — to Rome, where it modeled the action of the Scaevolas and other Roman Stoic philosophers who created the Western science of law. The idea of a truly known individual or event as a contractually constructed individual instancing deductively formulated universal laws had taken hold of their minds.

The novelty of this new way of knowing individuals and events has not received the attention which it deserves. It is as important for epistemology as it is for ethics.

For the first time in history it put a realistic epistemology upon a meaningfully consistent and empirically verifiable basis. This becomes clear if we compare the concepts of an atom in the deductively formulated mathematical physics of Democritus and in the theory of the Asian Charvakian materialists. An examination of the latter, or of any other Asian, realistic epistemology will show that in every instance its purportedly realistic common-sense or scientific objects were defined in terms of sensed objects, relations and qualities. For example, the atom of fire was defined as that which is sensed to be hot and dry. Clearly this is self-contradictory, as careful Asian epistemologists were soon to show and as we have previously indicated: Objects which are independent of perceivers clearly cannot be defined in terms of objects, relations or qualities every one of which have no existence apart from particular perceivers and perceptions.

Democritus and the other Greek mathematical physicists were aware of this and saw consequently that if scientific objects independent of perceivers are to be logically consistent and meaningful objects of scientific knowledge they cannot be defined in terms of objects and relations given through the senses. This is undoubtedly why he, and Plato following him, and Galilei and Newton following them, declared that sensed objects and relations are mere appearances and

designate nothing objective in nature independent of perceivers, but
are instead, as Galilei put the matter, "mere name[s]." [12] Put more
precisely what this means is that concepts referring for their entire
meaning to such individuals given through the senses are nominalistic rather than real universals. Their universality has its basis solely
in the name or symbol, not in what is symbolized.

But how, then, are scientific individuals and events independent
of perceivers to be defined if they cannot be defined in terms of factors given through the senses with radically empirical immediacy?
The answer of Democritus appears in Book VII of Euclid's Elements.
This is the portion of Greek mathematical physics that was the creation of the Democriteans. The answer is that a truly known scientific
object is an individual entity that satisfies or instances a formally
and postulationally constructed system of universal rules or laws
which have been experimentally verified. Or, to put the matter more
concretely, the scientific object which is a Democritean atom is, so
far as the realistic, non-*esse est percipi* component of its meaning is
concerned, any entity which satisfies the theorems and postulates of
Book VII of Euclid. Similarly the scientific object which is the electron of contemporary physics is any entity which satisfies certain
entity variables in the deductively formulated universal laws of either the electromagnetic theory of Lorentz or the theory of quantum
mechanics. What one means by an electron is quite different in these
two theories, since the postulates of the two theories are different.
Only the latter of the two theories, however, is confirmed in its deductive consequences. Thus the Lorentzian concept of the electron is
meaningful but not confirmed in all of its deductive consequences,
and the concept of the electron in quantum mechanics is both meaningful and verified.

The concepts of such scientific objects are real rather than merely
nominalistic universals. This follows because, by the very nature of
their scientific construction and designation, they are instances of universal laws. This, rather than sensed similarity, is the criterion of a
real, as opposed to a nominalistic, universal.

Sensed similarity fails as a criterion of real universals because
sensed similarity is as relative to perceivers as is any other item of
knowledge given through the senses. For example, I happen to be
color blind with respect to green. Thus, the colors which I sense as

similar are not those which other people sense as similar. Meanings the same for all minds, and in this sense universal, are not therefore given through the senses. Such universality is verbal rather than real, as Berkeley, and Galilei and Newton before him, emphasized, having its locus solely in the symbol and not in what is symbolized.

True universals are given only by formally or axiomatically designated individuals, since only such classes of individuals have, by virtue of the very nature of their scientific construction, the property of being instances of the same universal laws. Hence, only with classes of such individuals does the universality refer to something common to all the objects symbolized as well as to the character of the symbol. This, let it be remembered, is the difference between a real and a nominalistic universal.

Such individuals are universal also in a second sense. Being known as to their scientific properties only by the abstract formal method of axiomatic construction, no recourse to images is necessary for the knowledge of their theoretical scientific nature. This makes possible, to use the language of Socrates in Plato's *Republic*, "the dropping of all images," which in turn makes possible scientific objects whose meaning and existence is independent of their relation to perceivers.

Images have to be dropped if scientific objects of such a realistic epistemology are to be a logically self-consistent possibility, since all images, whether of the senses or of the imagination, are existential, denotative particulars, and all such items of knowledge, whether images of entities or relations, are relative to perceivers and not the same for all perceivers, and hence not such as to give, or to define, objects independent of, and the same for, all perceivers.

Axiomatically designated individuals may, and usually do, escape this relativity. This is the case because every elementary meaning going into their total theoretical meaning is a primitive in the logic of relations or of propositional functions or in some other branch of mathematical logic and all such meanings, when determined by the methods appropriate for knowing them, are the same for all men, having no relativity to any perceiver or to any act of perception.

It is necessary to say that such scientific objects and relations *may* and *usually do* escape such relativity, because it is possible by this axiomatic method of determining the nature of entities and events in nature to have a meaningful conception of nature in which certain entities and relations are the same for all perceivers, occasions and frames of reference and others exist only in such relativistic contexts. In fact, Einstein's special and general theories of relativity do exactly this.

Furthermore, it is doubtful if the distinction between the absolute and the relative in natural knowledge can be specified in any other way. Certainly it cannot be done by the epistemological method of radically empirical positivism since, as Asian epistemologists made evident long ago and as Berkeley and Hume have shown in modern times, all entities and relations known with empirical immediacy are relative to perceivers, as empirically known perceivers are relative to them; for all of them *esse est percipi*. This is another reason why classes made up of individuals that are sensed as similar do not give real universals.

Precisely because the entities and relations of deductively formulated natural science, whose meaning and existence are not such that *esse est percipi*, are not, and cannot be, identified with, or defined in terms of, sensed entities and relations, the verification of such individuals and relations has to be indirect by way of epistemic correlations joining them at some point with the relativistic, purely nominalistic classes of individuals and relations given through the senses, for which *esse est percipi*. For were axiomatically constructed natural objects and relations devoid of any specified relation to radically empirical immediacy, they would be theoretically meaningful but their existence as a highly probable actuality would not be verifiable. In other words, the epistemology of Western science is a correlation of two epistemologies: (1) critical realism with its indirect mode of verification, its scientific objects and relations for which *esse* is not *percipi* and its real universals; and (2) existentialism or radically empirical positivism with its direct mode of verification, its unique particular entities and relations for all of which *esse est percipi* and its nominalistic universals.

It is the former of these two epistemologies, first placed upon a consistent and empirically verifiable basis by the mathematical physicists of ancient Greece, that made possible and justified, in the minds and deeds of the Roman Stoic legal philosophers, the creation of the Western science of law with its technical terminology and its abstract contractual type of codes.

The Scaevolas and other Roman Stoic philosophers who created the novel Western abstract contractual science of law are explicit in saying that their ethics which this law embodies is the logic (that is, the scientific method and epistemology) of Greek physics applied to human institutions and conduct. In calling them Roman Stoics one must not commit the frequent error of supposing that they represented the view of only the followers of the Zenonian Greek Stoics. As shown in Chapter XI, the belief that ethics was essentially connected to the epistemology of physics was held in common in Stoic Rome by Zenonian Stoics, Platonists and Aristotelians alike, as E. Vernon Arnold makes clear in his classic study of Roman Stoicism and as H. Rackham notes on the first page of his Preface to his English translation of Cicero's *De Natura Deorum*.[13] In fact, Cicero, who held this theory of ethics, tells us that he was a Platonist.

In cultures whose sages or scientists have not discovered the deductively formulated, indirectly verified method of knowing individual entities, relations or events in nature, the ethics of our third type of law and the law itself does not exist, except as foreign influences have brought it in. In fact, the ethics of the law of contract in society is but the empirically verified epistemology of the law of constructs in natural science applied to the resolution of human disputes and the ordering of human relations.

We noted earlier that the three major types of law are operational applications of three different and in part at least conflicting conceptions of the ethically good. This caused us to ask whether it is possible to determine the issue upon which these differing conceptions of the ethically good turn. To this end we examined two things: first, the issue dividing the Chinese Confucianists, who affirm the ethics of the first type of law and condemn that of the second type, from the Legalists, who reverse the Confucian thesis. Second, we examined the factors which gave rise historically to the ethics of the third type of law. The result is as follows: The issue upon which the theories of the ethically good turn is epistemological rather than merely ethical in character. Moreover, the epistemological issue is resolved not by referring to ethical considerations or to cultural facts but by examining the epistemology of natural knowledge. In other words, the ethics regarded as good for resolving the disputes of men and ordering their social relations in any culture derives from its antecedent epistemology which is exemplified in, and hence found by analyzing, its empirically verified way of knowing individual entities, relations or events in nature.

If the analysis of empirically verified knowledge reveals only individuals and events and relations which are private to particular percipients and perceptions, then there are no meanings, the same for all men, and all the differing occasions which are their disputes, in terms of which codes applicable to all people and all disputes can be formulated. There only seem to be such meanings and rules due to a faulty semantics, or, to use Confucius' language, due to a failure to rectify names. Or, to say the same thing in still another way, if empirically verified knowledge of nature reveals any individual or event to be a unique particular, then it is simply false to people and the events which are their disputes to treat them, as the resort to codes the same for all men does, as if one individual or dispute were like others, and hence not unique.

If, on the other hand, empirically verified knowledge of any event or individual in nature exhibits the scientifically essential thing about anyone to be that it illustrates something in common with other individuals of a specifiable class, then there are meanings the same for all those individuals of that class in terms of which ethical codes for resolving their disputes can be formulated. Furthermore, if such is the nature of any empirically known event or individual in nature, then one does not treat individuals truly in terms of what they are unless one uses an ethics of codes for judging their moral behavior or resolving the dispute to which it gives rise.

The Confucianists seem to have won out over the Legalists in China on this issue because the Legalists' epistemological theory of natural knowledge was naïve realism and the Confucianists have no difficulty in showing that the radical empiricism of its naïve method of knowing gives only unique, denotative existential particulars each one of which is relative to perceivers and to perceptions. In other words, the only source of the meaning of words that the Legalists, like the Confucianists, had to point to was empirical immediacy as given in naïve observation, and this gives only nominalistic, not real, universals.

This is also probably the reason why in the dialectical and historical development of Buddhism the realistic Hinayana system gives way to the radical existentialism and empiricism of nihilistic Mahayana and that in the history of the philosophy of India the realistic Hindu philosophies give way, under analysis, to the similar radical empiricism and existentialism of unqualified non-dualistic Vedanta.

Furthermore, because cultures in the world that have not derived from the science and natural philosophy of the ancient Greeks seem never to have discovered the axiomatic constructional method of knowing individuals as instances of universal laws, which alone justifies a theory of real universals and a belief in objects and events with empirically verified essential scientific properties the same for all instances of the variables for which they are the material constants, and the same for all perceivers and perceptions, they do not have the ethics of the abstract contractual type of law. Instead, their codes are always of the natural history type and tend, because of their epistemology of naïve realism, to be regarded as the ethically inferior way to settle disputes due to the tendency of a naïve realistic epistemology to reveal its self-contradictory character and to go over under careful analysis into radical empiricism with its nominalistic theory of individuals that warrants only the intuitive mediational type of ethics of the Confucianists, the pacific Buddhists and Gandhi.

The conclusion seems to be that if we mean by ethics what we find it to mean as operationally applied in the major types of law of the world, then the assumption held since the time of Kant by most Western philosophers — idealists, realists and positivists alike — that ethics is an independent or autonomous science is false. Instead, ethics is essentially and antecedently connected to the rest of philosophy, and especially to the epistemology of empirically verified knowledge of individual entities, relations and events in nature. This means that the word "good" is not a primitive concept as G. E. Moore has suggested or a primitive *a priori* intellectual presupposition as Urban affirmed. Instead it is a defined concept, a concept defined in part at least in terms of the epistemologically true as determined by analyzing the verified theories of natural knowledge.

One implication with respect to the verification of ethical propositions remains to be noted. It becomes evident when we ask how they are verified.

Ethical Norms and Their Verification

It has been the custom until recently to answer this question by saying that the verification of a set of ethical norms is possible after the manner of the verification of an abstractly constructed set of natural laws in physical science; that is, by testing empirically their logical consequences. The pragmatic legal realists, who started out with this theory, have, however, after careful analysis and experimentation, come to reject it. The reason is clear and decisive. Ethical norms do not conform to empirically given cultural facts; they transform them. This is especially true of ethical norms of the contractual type, as we have already shown. On this point, Professor Stevenson is unquestionably right when he says that it is of the essence of ethical values to be emotionally persuasive rather than cognitively conformative to social and cultural facts.[14]

Nevertheless, ethical norms are empirically testable and therefore cognitive. The test is, however, not through their deductive or operational consequences with respect to society and culture but through their epistemological, and other philosophical, antecedents with respect to nature. It appears, therefore, that ethics and law neglect the rest of science and philosophy at their peril.

XVI

Comparative Ethics and Epistemological Theory

THERE is a unique factor common to the most influential Oriental philosophical systems. There are also doctrines which distinguish some Oriental systems from others. In comparing the methodology and epistemology of Oriental and Western philosophy, therefore, it is necessary to consider both the unique factor and the differentiating factors in Oriental philosophical systems. It will be assumed that the different Western philosophies are well known.

I

The unique factor common to the most influential Oriental systems is variously called "Nirvana," "Suchness," "Brahman" or "the Void" and has the following characteristics: (1) It is *immediately apprehended*, not given by thought or inference, hence known by acquaintance, and therefore denoted by a concept by intuition.* [1] (2) Although usually apprehended as in considerable part differentiated, it *in itself* is *indeterminate* and *undifferentiated*. Since language is designed to convey the determinate and the differentiated, it *in itself* is, therefore, indescribable. (3) It *embraces the equally immediate differentiations which come and go within it*. Hence, it is aptly described as a continuum. (4) Summary: it may be expressed in Western language, therefore, as "the undifferentiated aesthetic contin-

* A concept by intuition is a concept the complete meaning of which is given by something immediately apprehendable; see references in note 1.

Reprinted from Charles A. Moore, ed., *Essays in East-West Philosophy* (1951), by permission of University of Hawaii Press.

uum," where "aesthetic" is taken in its root meaning of immediacy but not (unless we refer solely to the differentiations) in its usual meaning of *sensed* immediacy. (5) Consequences: The undifferentiated aesthetic continuum is equivalent to a nominalistic unity of apperception which is known by acquaintance rather than by description or *a priori*. It is also a necessary assumption of any empirical naturalism which would keep the knower in nature and would regard ancient and contemporary knowers as abstractions from one empirical nature. Without the undifferentiated aesthetic continuum there is no purely empirical meaning for one nature or for a nature which embraces both the differentiated empirical knower and the differentiated empirical object.

I I

The factors which differentiate the many Oriental systems from one another rise from three sources: (1) different ways of arriving at immediate acquaintance with the undifferentiated aesthetic continuum; (2) different ways of using knowledge of the undifferentiated aesthetic continuum; (3) different views as to what else is valid knowledge in addition to the undifferentiated aesthetic continuum.

Different Approaches to the Undifferentiated Aesthetic Continuum

(1) By immediate apprehension, with the sensed and introspected differentiations neglected. (*a*) Zen and non-dualistic Vedanta concentration and intuition. (*b*) Yoga practices, which eliminate from immediacy all sensed, introspected and theoretically conceived factors, leaving only undifferentiated and hence non-dualistic immediacy.

(2) Indirect methods: Since the undifferentiated aesthetic continuum, being undifferentiated, cannot be positively described, systems using language must proceed negatively. This negative linguistic procedure takes at least three forms: (*a*) direct negation, as illustrated by the "It is not this, it is not this" (*Neti-neti*) method common to Hinduism, Buddhism and Taoism; (*b*) the dialectic of negation method, as illustrated in the Buddhistic transition from realistic

Hinayana through nihilistic Hinayana and ideational Mahayana to nihilistic Mahayana, where nothing remains but the Suchness or Void, which is the undifferentiated immediacy. In this dialectical negative method, the three earlier systems represent differing positive beliefs in addition to the belief in the immediacy of the undifferentiated Nirvana Suchness; (c) the paradoxical linguistic method, as illustrated in the Zen Buddhist statement, "I am not I; therefore, I am I." This *seems* to involve, as Mr. Burtt has noted,[2] a flouting of the law of contradiction and a "jeopardization of logical responsibility," which Western philosophy cannot tolerate. This is, however, a mere seeming. Logical irresponsibility would be present if the word "I" had the same meaning throughout the two aforementioned statements. The whole point, however, of the paradoxical formulation is to preserve logical responsibility and to use it to establish the point that there are two different selves — the indeterminate, non-dualistic self and the introspected, determinate, transitory self. It is because I (the indeterminate, undifferentiated, non-dualistic self) am not I (the introspected, determinate, transitory self) that I (the indeterminate, undifferentiated, non-dualistic self) am I (the indeterminate, undifferentiated, non-dualistic self).

Different Uses of the Undifferentiated Aesthetic Continuum

Since this source of the differences among Oriental systems has to do with application, it falls under ethics. It may be noted here, however, that this common factor (that is, the undifferentiated aesthetic continuum) may be pursued in and for itself. This pursuit leads to Zen mysticism, non-dualistic Vedanta absorption and Taoist nonaction. It may be used, on the other hand, to infuse social relations with a common *man-to-manness* * or fellow feeling for all creatures.

* See E. R. Hughes' meticulous commentary on the meaning and translation of *jen* in his *Chinese Philosophy in Classical Times,* Everyman's Library, p. xxxvii. Note also the definite rooting of *jen* and a "sense of honor" in the all-embracing indeterminate Tao, *ibid.,* p. 20. See also my chapter "Complementary Emphases of Oriental Intuitive and Western Scientific Philosophy," in *Philosophy — East and West,* Charles A. Moore, ed., Princeton University Press, 1944, for further evidence that Confucianism rests upon and derives its vitality and effectiveness from the common undifferentiated immediate man-to-manness, which is Tao, as much as does Taoism or Buddhism. It is merely pursuing this immediately experienced Tao with respect to its effectiveness in fostering warm family and social relations.

This gives rise to the *jen* of Confucianism and to Buddhist sympathy for the inescapable suffering of all determinate transitory creatures.

Factors in Addition to the Undifferentiated Aesthetic Continuum, Admitted as Valid Knowledge in Some Systems

Three such systems have already been noted in connection with the Buddhist dialectic of negation. Realistic Hinayana Buddhism, for example, admits the reality of external, determinate material objects in addition to Nirvana or the undifferentiated aesthetic continuum. However, even in Oriental systems such as these, in which factors in addition to the undifferentiated aesthetic continuum are admitted to be real, these factors are defined in terms of, and hence involve only, concepts by intuition. The crucial cases, seemingly to the contrary, are Charvakian materialism and Vaisesika Hinduism, because of their affirmation of physical atoms; realistic Hinayana Buddhism, because of its belief in external objects; and Mimamsa Hinduism, because of its admission of *arthapatti,* or what Professors Chatterjee and Datta called "postulation," as a method of knowledge.[3]

Examination of all these systems shows that the atomic, common-sense, and "postulated" objects of knowledge are not constructed or designated syntactically in terms of non-immediately apprehendable properties and relations as specified by an explicit set of postulates of a deductively formulated, indirectly verified theory, as must be the case if they are concepts by postulation in the meaning of my *The Meeting of East and West,*[4] but are defined instead in terms of qualities given through the seasons, such as hot, cold, sweet, sour, etc. Since sensed qualities are immediately apprehended, the concepts denoting them are concepts by intuition. Consequently, any objects defined in terms of such qualities, whether they be atoms, common-sense objects or "postulated" (in the sense of Professors Chatterjee and Datta) objects, entail only concepts by intuition.

A concept by postulation is one the meaning of which in whole or part is not derived from something immediately apprehendable but is constructed or proposed for it by the specific postulates of some deductively formulated theory.[5] Precisely because postulates formulated of such concepts designate factors in knowledge which are not at any time capable of direct inspection, verification of such theory must be

indirect by way of the deduced theorems, and even then only by recourse to two-termed epistemic correlations which connect the deduced concepts by postulation with directly inspectable data denoted by concepts by intuition.[6]

Once this is noted, confirming evidence that Oriental philosophical
systems, even those which admit factors in addition to the undifferentiated continuum, contain no concepts by postulation is to be found
in Mr. Datta's statement that Indian philosophy has no interest in
the hypothetical syllogism but always reasons syllogistically from
premises which are empirically true.[7] This can be the case only if all
the concepts in the premises are concepts by intuition and hence
such as to permit direct verification of the premises. In short, the deductive syllogistic reasoning when it occurs is always of the form:
A is immediately apprehended to be the case. If A, then B. Therefore,
B is the case.

A problem arises for Indian philosophy when the deductively inferred conclusion B is perceivable and hence completely describable
by concepts by intuition, but is actually unperceived; that is, the inferred concept by intuition meaning is not directly verified in the
case of the inference in question. A case in point is the example, used
by the Mimamsa school, of the man who "we find . . . does not eat
anything in the day, but increases in weight." [8] The problem is: Are
we entitled to admit as valid the inferred conclusion, "He must be
eating at night"? Professors Chatterjee and Datta inform us that
but "one school of the Mimamsa" of all the anti- and pro-Vedic
schools in Indian philosophy answers this question in the affirmative, calling the particular method of such knowledge *arthapatti*,
which Professors Chatterjee and Datta translate as "postulation." [9]

It is to be emphasized that the admission of "postulation" in this
meaning is no evidence whatever for the thesis that even this one of
the many systems of Vedic Indian philosophy uses concepts by postulation in the sense specified in my chapter in *Philosophy — East and
West* (Chapter VIII), in my *The Meeting of East and West* and in
my *The Logic of the Sciences and the Humanities*. A concept by postulation is one the meaning of which in whole or part is not given
inductively or by syllogistic deduction from the inductively given,
after the manner of the syllogistic conclusion "He must be eating at
night," illustrated by the Mimamsa meaning noted above. Instead, it

is a concept the meaning of which in whole or part is proposed for it syntactically and systematically by the determinate postulates of some specific deductively formulated theory. Only when concepts by postulation in this latter sense are used must verification be indirect, since what is postulated appears not in the conclusion, after the manner of the Mimamsa illustration above, but in the premises from which the testable conclusion is deduced. Since premises constructed of concepts by postulation refer to factors not directly perceived and hence not denoted by concepts by intuition, the verification of such deductive reasoning cannot be by the verification of the premises. Verification must consequently have the form of the hypothetical rather than the categorical syllogism, as follows: If A as specified by the postulates, then B; B is the case; therefore, A is confirmed. The Mimamsa case is, therefore, not an exception to the general rule that Oriental philosophy uses only concepts by intuition and reasons deductively only from such concepts, whereas the novel factor in Western civilization is that, beginning with deductively formulated Greek science, Western science and philosophy introduced and, except in its positivistic periods, has reasoned deductively from concepts by postulation.

This conclusion is confirmed by two characteristics of *arthapatti* ("postulation") in Mimamsa. First, the postulation refers to the conclusion of the inference rather than to its initial premises. Where concepts by postulation in the unique Western meaning and usage are present, the premises, not merely the conclusion, designate what is postulated, as has been noted above. Second, the syllogistic conclusion, "He must be eating at night," which the one school of Mimamsa admits as valid, denotes what is perceivable even though actually at the time of the deduction it is unperceived. But for the proposition to refer to the perceivable, its concepts must denote what is knowable by immediate apprehension. Such concepts are by definition concepts by intuition. Thus, even in the rare Mimamsa example, the meaning of the *arthapatti* knowledge is not "postulated" in the sense of a concept by postulation which is formally constructed, without recourse to images, by postulational technique in a specific deductively formulated theory. It is only the verification of the deduced concept by intuition meaning which has to be "postulated" in the Mimamsa example, due to the circumstance that, while both perceivable and reasonably inferable from what is perceived, its immediate presence at the time of the inference is not perceived.

I I I

The method of knowing unique to Western science and philosophy is by concepts by postulation, which are given formally constructed, imageless meanings by postulational technique in an explicit set of postulates which are verified indirectly through their rigorously proved theorems or deductive consequences. These postulates are checked indirectly by way of their deduced theorems against local, rigorously controlled observational or experimental data. As E. A. Burtt has said, "Experimental manipulation of nature is rare in India and China." [10] Even when it occurs it is piecemeal — not envisaged as the testing of a deductively formulated theory.

Furthermore, a Democritean atom has little in common with the atoms of Charvakian materialism or Vaisesika, since the Democritean atom is not defined in terms of sensed qualities. It is, instead, an entity satisfying the theorems and assumed axioms of Book Seven of Euclid and of the deductively formulated mathematical acoustics of Democritus and Archytus. Similarly, a Platonic atomic triangle or regular solid is not the image given to the sensuous imagination, nor is it defined by any property given through the senses. It is, instead, an entity satisfying the proved theorems and assumed postulates of Books Five and Thirteen of Euclid. Likewise a physical object for Newton is not the concept by intuition object which is the association of sensed qualities relative to the perceiver given through the senses; it is, instead, an entity satisfying the postulates of Newton's deductively formulated physics as specified in his *Principia*. In short, the atoms of Charvakian materialism and Vaisesika Hinduism, being defined in terms of sensed qualities or introspected images which are relative to perceivers, are *esse est percipi*, concept by intuition objects, whereas the veridical scientific objects of Democritus, Plato and Newton are *non esse est percipi*, concept by postulation objects.

This distinction is precisely what Leibniz had in mind when he wrote in the *New Essays:* "That we have the angles of the triangle in the imagination does not mean that we, therefore, have clear ideas of them [that is, that we have the concept by intuition meaning of the symbol does not mean that we, therefore, have the concept by postulation meaning] . . . thus this idea [of angle in Western mathematical physics] does not consist in the images, and it is not as easy as one might think fundamentally to understand the angles of the triangle." [11] The point is that to carry through the deductions of mathematical physics, which involve the use of the concept of angle and which make its tremendous predictive power and quantitative verification possible, the concept by intuition angle given with immediacy is quite incapable of providing the meaning sufficient to permit the deductive proof of the experimentally verified theorems. Before a concept of angle sufficient for mathematical physics is achieved, postulates concerning the character of the lines in geometry going far beyond anything given in sensuous experience or the operations of measuring must be specified. One of these postulates must prescribe whether parallel lines, if extended without limit, intersect or not. Such postulates going far beyond the data of sense awareness are as necessary for the physical objects of physics as for the angles of geometry, since the very formulation of the laws of physics entails all the concepts of some specific deductively formulated geometry or chrono-geometry.

This existence of concepts by postulation in Western science is as important for Western philosophy as it is for Western mathematical physics. Leibniz' *New Essays* was written as a result of his reading of Locke's famous *Essay Concerning Human Understanding*. Leibniz agreed with Locke's emphasis upon those concepts in human knowledge which are concepts by intuition deriving their meaning from what can be known with immediacy through the senses. It was precisely, however, because of the concepts by postulation which Leibniz knew to be present also in mathematical physics that Leibniz affirmed there are concepts which are universals in addition to the nominalistic concept by intuition ideas of Locke's epistemology. In fact, it has been by means of these concepts by postulation discovered first by Greek science that Western science, philosophy, ethics, law and theology have escaped the predominant Oriental thesis that all determinate things, including the determinate perceiver, are transitory.

Certainly this predominant Oriental thesis is correct for all determinate things known with immediacy. As Locke and Hume emphasized, immediately apprehended introspected and sensed data are "perpetually perishing," and, as St. Paul said long before Locke and Hume, "The things that are seen are temporal." If knowledge is restricted after the manner of the Orient and of radical Western empiricism to what is immediately apprehended, then only one bit of knowledge is non-transitory, the same for all men, holding under all circumstances, namely the all-embracing otherwise indeterminate, undifferentiated and hence non-dualistic immediacy within which the transitory determinate differentiations come and go.

To this predominant Oriental philosophical thesis that all determinate things are transitory, the Greek scientists, who created the concepts by postulation, which are the universals of subsequent Western philosophy, had an answer: There is a way of knowing other than direct intuition or immediate apprehension with its nominalistic concepts by intuition. There is also an indirect way of knowing which makes use of postulationally and theoretically constructed primitive or basic meanings designating factors in nature and man not immediately apprehended and hence not defined in terms of transitory, perpetually perishing *esse est percipi* sensed qualities.

Moreover, this indirect way of knowing, with its postulationally constructed basic concepts, gives knowledge of determinate factors in man and nature, such as Democritus' timeless mathematically designated atoms and Eudoxus' mathematically designated determinate astronomical principles, which escape the *esse est percipi* relativity and perpetual perishing of immediately apprehended determinate things. Furthermore, by deducing theorems from the postulationally constructed meanings designating determinate factors in man and nature which obey conservative laws and hence are invariant and timeless, and by relating epistemically these deduced concept by postulation consequences of the theoretically constructed basic meanings to directly inspectable concept by intuition data, the existence or nonexistence of the postulationally and solely theoretically designated determinate factors in man and nature can be verified indirectly.

Hence, notwithstanding the fact that this novel concept by postulation way of knowing designates determinate factors in, and principles applying to, man and nature which are not directly apprehendable, it nonetheless gives determinate knowledge valid for all men which is verifiable by anyone. In fact, unless the deduced consequences of the postulationally constructed theory are such that they refer to directly inspectable data which anyone who takes the trouble can find and verify, the criteria of truth for this way of knowing are not satisfied.

These postulationally constructed basic concepts of Western science and philosophy differ from the concepts of Oriental philosophy not only because they do not refer to what is directly apprehendable but also because they are non-nominalistic universals rather than nominalistic particulars. Concepts by postulation are universals because the postulates which they satisfy are universal propositions. To be an atom in the Democritean or Newtonian sense of the word "atom" is not to be a denotatively known particular, since Democritean and Newtonian atoms have no sensuous properties and hence cannot even be thought of in sensuous terms, to say nothing about being sensed; instead, Democritean or Newtonian atoms are entities satisfying certain universal mathematical laws; in other words, they are individual entities, the essential nature (that is, the scientific definition) of which is to be an instance of a determinate universal law.

It is from this concept by postulation universal derived from Greek science that Zeno, Cicero and the Roman Stoics, who created Western ethics and Western law with its theoretically constructed technical terminology, arrived at their concept of a moral and just man as an individual who is an instance of a determinate universal law. It is from this same source also that the great Roman Catholic theologians like St. Augustine and St. Thomas acquired the concept of the determinate universal necessary to put the Christian faith in a theistic religious object which is immortal and determinate on a philosophically meaningful and verifiable basis. Such a morality, law or religion rooted in the concept by postulation meaning of the moral, legal and religious person as an instance of universal determinate laws or principles is something poles apart from the concept by intuition moral, legal and religious person of the Orient, who, restricted in his knowledge of man and nature to the immediately apprehended, finds nothing universal, the same for all men and all circumstances, except the pushing aside of relativistic, perpetually perishing introspections and sensations to achieve the indeterminate, undifferentiated and hence indescribable non-dualistic immediacy which is Brahman, Atman, Nirvana and Tao and the source of *jen* with its mediational method for settling disputes.

To be sure, as noted above, there are Oriental systems such as realistic Hinayana Buddhism and Vaisesika or Mimamsa Hinduism which affirm external objects to be real (that is, existent apart from the perceiver, or in other words *non esse est percipi*), as there are Hindu systems which *affirm* the existence of a theistic (that is, with determinate properties) religious object. The point is, however, that because these purportedly real determinate objects were defined in terms of directly inspected qualities (that is, concepts by intuition) for which by their very nature *esse est percipi,* other more careful Oriental thinkers had no difficulty in showing such theories to be self-contradictory. For certainly a determinate object for which *esse est non percipi* cannot be defined consistently in terms of determinate properties for which *esse est percipi.*

Not having concepts by postulation, by which alone determinate common-sense, scientific or theistic religious objects can be given consistent *non esse est percipi* meaning, epistemological realism and religious theism were not able to be established even as meaningful (that is, self-consistent) theoretical possibilities, and Oriental philosophy and religion when developed self-critically and consistently were left with nothing but an indeterminate real epistemological and religious object, as occurs in nihilistic Mahayana Buddhism and in non-dualistic Vedanta. This is the reason undoubtedly why the dialectic of negation in Buddhism and the development of Hindu thought culminate in these two systems.

When the sensed properties, whether primary or secondary, which define the common-sense objects of a naïve realistic epistemology, are found to be relative both to the observer and to the moment of perception and when formally and axiomatically constructed image-less concepts by postulation have not been discovered, as was the case in classical Asia, nothing remains to provide a cognitively meaningful standard for settling their disputes but the indeterminate formlessness of the all-embracing continuum of conscious immediacy, within which the relativistic, perishing particulars come and go. Morally and legally, this has the consequence, as the previous chapter showed, of supplementing the "second-best" method of dispute settling of a biologically conceived family and tribally centered law of status ethics which goes with a naïve realistic conception of truly known man and nature with the "first-best" method of dispute settling of a radically empirical, nominalistic epistemology and its mediational type of law. When, on the other hand, as in the classical West, the Greek mathematical physicists discovered formally constructed imageless cognitive concepts for which *esse est non percipi* and this way of thinking passed over through Greek philosophy to the Roman Stoic lawyers, such as the Scaevolas who taught Cicero, then the constructs which make Western law unique were created and the ethics of the law of contract came into being. Thus it is that whereas the development of man's moral ways and legal institutions in non-Westernized cultures may best be described as the supplementation of the ethics of the codified law of status with the "first-best" ethics of mediation, the development in the West has been succinctly described by Sir Henry S. Maine as the "shift from status to contract." [12]

XVII

Common Law, Roman Law
and the Civil Law

THE Cold War has made it evident that the fate of any people depends as much upon international as domestic factors. This means that any lawyer who would be effective in governmental service, either as a legislator, a civil servant or a secretary of state, must know something about the cultural and legal mentalities of other nations. In short, comparative cultural philosophy and comparative law are becoming more and more necessary in legal education.

This is already recognized in the case of Soviet law. The introduction of Western political and legal forms into Asian and Islamic societies makes comparative studies of the modern Western and the classical Asian and Mohammedan cultural and legal mentalities equally important. Recent misunderstandings between the British and Continental statesmen with respect to political and legal collaboration in a European Union at Strasbourg and between American and French statesmen with respect to the European Defense Community demonstrate an equal need for a comparative understanding of the identities and differences between Anglo-American common law and Continental European civil law. The latter consideration gives practical as well as theoretical significance to the recently published Fifth Series of Thomas M. Cooley Lectures at the University of Michigan Law School. This series is by the Professor of Comparative Law of Oxford University and bears the title, A Common Lawyer Looks at the Civil Law.[1]

Professor F. H. Lawson's comparative study has special significance for judges and lawyers in the United States. The civil law, as

Reprinted from Michigan Law Review, Vol. 54, No. 7, May 1956, by permission.

Professor Lawson shows, has unique formal scientific properties which derive from Roman law. When one relates these formal properties, as described by Professor Lawson, to Stoic Roman philosophy and to the Greek philosophy and mathematical physics by way of the Scaevolas and the later Roman and Byzantine jurists, it appears that the formal scientific properties which distinguish Roman and civil law from the common law depend upon a particular legal philosophy which affirms the thesis that moral and legal man is universal man. The effect of this Greek and Stoic Roman natural law philosophy upon Roman law was, through the idea of the *jus gentium,* to break moral and legal man free from the various family-centered and tribally-centered men of each particular *jus civile,* to identify the morally and the legally good with any man whatever regardless of his family and tribal status as determined by his color of skin. This legal philosophy, given modern content by Newton and the early John Locke of the *Lectures on Natural Law, The Letter Concerning Toleration* and the treatise *Of Civil Government,* went into the Declaration of Independence through the mind and pen of Jefferson and into the Bill of Rights of the written Constitution of the United States due to the initial insistence of Jefferson. It is from this natural law philosophy of Jefferson, the early John Locke and the Stoic Romans that the legal tradition for the judicial review of majority legislation in the light of the Bill of Rights derives. In fact it is very difficult to see how the recent unanimous decision of the Supreme Court of the United States with respect to segregation in education can be justified except by appeal to this natural law theory.

The analytical proof of this conclusion is as follows: The thesis that moral and legal man is universal man is the assertion that for anything to be good or just it must hold for any person whatever. Expressed symbolically, this gives:

$(p) : x$ is just $= (p) x$, where $(p) x$ means that x holds for any person.

Substituting "The public educational system of any state in the United States" for x in the foregoing expression gives:

$(p) :$ The public educational system of any state in the United States is just $=$ This educational system must hold for any person.

It appears, therefore, that if contemporary judges and lawyers in the United States are to understand their own legal system and justify some, at least, of its contemporary Supreme Court decisions, they must understand Roman law as well as the common law. In fact, the early legal system of the United States and at least part of its present constitutional law have a content which is that of a theory of justice appearing first in Stoic Roman law and a form which is that of the common law.

In what do the differences between the form of the common law and that of the civil law and Roman law consist? The major importance of Professor Lawson's book is that it provides an answer to this question.

His first general specification of the difference between the common law and the civil law is that the former is largely the creation of practical lawyers and judges in their handling and settling of disputes, whereas the latter, since the time of the Scaevolas, is largely the work of jurists; that is, of legal scientists and professors rather than of merely practical dispute settlers.[2] This does not mean that the common law does not have theorists and theory or that the civil law and later Roman law did not have practicing lawyers and judges. What it does mean, however, is that in the common law, because of the primary role of the lawyers and judges in its creation, the cases tend to be at the focus of attention and to predominate over the generated and generalized principles, whereas in the civil law the reverse tends to be true. This difference shows in the fact that in the common law there are always cases for which no satisfactory principles are at hand and always principles for deciding certain cases which do not lie down comfortably with the principles used for deciding other cases. In the civil law, on the other hand, the theory, as in certain portions of mathematical physics, tends to outrun the cases or the facts, enabling one to construct and predict certain possible facts and cases which have never appeared in court.

The difference between the legal positivism of Austin and that of the Continentally trained Kelsen comes to the writer's mind in this connection. For Kelsen, the fundamental thing in the legal system is the *grundnorm*. This fits in with the mathematical physicist's deductively formulated conception of scientific method in which all the facts of a given subject matter are brought under a single set of minimum basic assumptions. British legal positivists, in the common law tradition, however, are very critical and suspicious of a single *grundnorm*. This shows even in the British-trained Italian defender of natural law philosophy, Professor A. P. d'Entrèves of Oxford.[3]

The conception of scientific method of British legal positivists and of lawyers in the common law tradition, apart from the late Underhill Moore, is the more piecemeal, purely inductive natural history method of the traditional biological and descriptive natural history sciences. These sciences obtain principles, to be sure, and thus have theory, but the theories tend to be as complex in their basic concepts and generalizations as are the inductive data. Furthermore, the concepts and principles do not reduce to a small number of elementary notions and primitive postulates. Hence the British legal positivist's and the common lawyer's suspicion of a single *grundnorm* or the norms of the First Constitution.

Professor Lawson points out, however, that there are exceptions in the common law world to this general conclusion. It is not, he adds, until we put the small number of precise legal concepts of Hohfeld under the analytical jurisprudence of *Williston on Contracts* that we obtain the type of legal thinking in Anglo-American common law that is comparable to the legal mentality of the later Roman jurists and the modern civilians. This type of legal thinking comes very late in the common law tradition.

This distinction between the different conceptions of scientific method in the common law and the civil and Roman law traditions has considerable historical and philosophical importance. It means that the conceptual generalization in the *jus gentium* of Roman law and the eventual triumph of the concepts of the *jus gentium* over those of the *jus civile* in the Digest of Justinian did not have its origin solely in the practical needs of the Romans to carry on trade with non-Romans, as some legally positivistically minded students of Roman law would like to suggest. It finds its basis instead in a novel scientific way of thinking about these and all other practical transactions and disputes.

For this and other reasons, Professor Lawson affirms that it is necessary to put oneself inside the content of Roman law to understand either it or the civil law. A mere viewing of Roman law from the outside, from the standpoint of British common law, legal positivism, German *historismus,* Ihering's psychological theory of interests or any other modern mentality, will not do. Nor will dictionary renderings of words in the Latin text suffice. Commenting upon the suggestion of Dean Roscoe Pound that the "essential difference between the civil law and the common law is one not of substance but of method," Professor Lawson says, "I think it is time for English and American comparative lawyers to shed this preoccupation and study more closely the chief components of the substantive civil law." [4] Nor does Professor Lawson believe that codification is the key to the difference between the common law and the modern civil law or Roman law, since "a code is not a necessary mark of a civil law system nor the absence of one a mark of a common law system . . ." [5] What is important, instead, with respect to codification as it bears on this question is the "type of mind" of the civil law system which, while more "favorable to codification," is also "more important than codes." [6]

Turning to the substantive content of the Roman law of contract of the Institutes of Gaius and Justinian, Professor Lawson notes that contracts are of four types: (1) real, (2) verbal, (3) literal and (4) consensual, together with a miscellaneous "innominate" group.

A contract is real when one party hands over a thing to the other party. A "verbal contract" was called by the Romans a "stipulation" and took a question-and-answer form. It contained two elements: form and agreement. The form required that the same principle verb be used in the question put by the questioner and in the answer given that sealed the commitments of the agreement as expressed in the question. The stipulation or verbal contract had two important implications quite apart from the verbal constancy of its form. First, it placed the burden of specifying the contract upon the questioner. Second, it required the agreement of the person who answered. This has the consequence in civil law societies of making all donations devoid of legal validity unless there is a verbal acceptance from the recipient of the donation by the donee. Because of this requirement, Professor Lawson notes that in Quebec some lawyers have rejected trusts for unborn persons on the ground that a trust to be legal requires the acceptance by the actual person who receives it. The key, however, to the mentality of Roman law and civil law shows in another characteristic of the stipulation, which Professor Lawson describes as follows:

"If we consider the content of the stipulation, we shall see at once that it must have been infinitely variable. The stipulation was not a contract but a contractual form, a mould for contracts." [7]

Expressed in terms of mathematical logic, this means that the stipulation in Roman law entailed two technical concepts: (1) the concept of the variable, designated in modern mathematical and logical notation by the symbol x and meaning "any one" as opposed to the proper name of a specific one, on the one hand, and to the class concept of all the sensuously similar ones on the other hand; (2) the concept of the matrix, or propositional form, in which the material common-sense concepts, called by modern logicians "material constants," are replaced with variables. The scientific importance of these two logical concepts is that they break scientific statements loose from specific material examples of the formal properties of the statements. This is precisely what the stipulation did with respect to the rigid codes with their specific law of status content of the pre-Stoic Roman Twelve Tables. Anything whatever could be contracted regardless of its common-sense material content provided that the form by which the content was specified possessed certain formal properties. The second scientific importance of the notion of the variable is that it enables one to achieve generality for more than one individual or instance while at the same time preserving the fact that one is dealing with one particular individual and one particular instance. Thereby justice is done to the individuality of the case as well as to its generality. In short, the concept of the variable brings both the concept of universal formal lawfulness and the notion of equity into Roman legal science. This occurred in the stipulation.

The third type of Roman contract, the literal contract, need not concern us since it disappeared very soon. The fourth type, the consensual contract, is exceedingly important. It arose, Professor Lawson suggests, because the stipulation, due to its infinite variability, was ideal for dealing with "odds and ends," but lacked the standardization for the easy handling of transactions which constantly occurred. The consensual contracts met this deficiency of the stipulation. They covered four species — sale, hire, partnership and mandate. They were

called "consensual" because "they were quite informal and . . .
were binding from the moment of agreement. . . ." [8]

The consensual contracts were distinguished from stipulation in
one other respect. As previously noted, the stipulation had to specify
in the question all that was legally valid and enforceable. The consensual agreements, on the other hand, even though informal, entailed legally what was "naturally implied" as well as what was literally said. How, in the case of the consensual contracts, is the naturally
implied to be determined?

We are prepared for the Roman's answer to this question if we
note a logical property of the literal character of the stipulation. Professor Lawson expresses this logical attribute as follows, using the
words of a judge: "But you are asking us to interpret something
which can have only the specific shape which you give to it by your
formal act." [9] The point here is that, in the stipulation, one is enter-
ing not into a standardized familiar transaction but into an agreement which is unusual and exceptional, or what Professor Lawson
has described as "odds and ends." Hence, the judge can only interpret what one entered into if one specifies what it was. This specification, the stipulation requires. In other words, the law has, in the
case of the stipulation, "the specific shape which you give to it by
your formal act." [10]

But how, then, could Roman law make so much use of the consensual contract with its "naturally implied," as well as explicitly
stipulated, meanings? Again the answer of the Roman jurists is a
formal logical answer rather than an intuitive, material and merely
inductive one. "The consensual contracts," Professor Lawson writes,
"were not so much contracts as what have been called contractual
figures . . ." [11] They were standardized forms with formal relations
and implications quite independent of any stipulated material content which may illustrate them, after the manner of the four figures
of the Aristotelian syllogism. These four contractual figures were, let
it be recalled, sale, hire, partnership and mandate. But they were
these four standardized transactions in their formal properties, not
in their merely concrete, inductively given material content. In short,
the consensual form of Roman contract is formalized legal knowledge
rather than merely the material content of that knowledge. Being thus
formalized, each of the four species of the Roman consensual type of

contract had its formal logical implications. The pursuit of these formal logical implications specified the method to be used by the judge in determining what was "naturally implied" in the standard contractual figure in question in any legal case.

Professor Lawson suggests also how the formal properties of the four contractual figures which define the possible consensual contracts were determined. These contractual figures were not merely four different, inductively observed classes of transactions frequently entered into by men in an informal way, they were also internally related due to the fact that they were the products of a deeper analysis of the subject matter of law. As Professor Lawson writes,

> The consensual contracts were not so much contracts as what have been called contractual figures [which were] the products derived from an analysis of movement in the legal world. . . . It is as if the Roman jurists of about 100 B.C. had said Go where you will, you will find that almost everything can be reduced to four processes: (1) shifting goods permanently from one man's estate to another for a money price; (2) placing one person's property or services temporarily at the disposal of another for a consideration usually in money; (3) the pooling of property, skill, or experience by several persons for a common purpose; and (4) the gratuitous performance of a task by one person on the instructions of another.[12]

One is reminded of the derivation of the four figures of the Aristotelian syllogism as products from the four A, E, I and O propositional forms in which any syllogistic argument on any material subject matter whatever must be expressed. In this connection it is to be noted that the most important Roman jurist "of about 100 B.C." was Scaevola, the first systematic formulator of Roman law, who died in 95 B.C. Scaevola and his colleagues were primarily jurists rather than merely practicing lawyers and judges. They were also dominated in their thinking by Stoic philosophy.[13] The latter philosophy was permeated with the logical categories and formalism of Aristotle. These Stoic philosophers and legal thinkers also affirmed that their theory of ethics and law derived from their logic and from their physics.[14] Their physics was Greek. Greek physics was dominated by mathematics. In short, it exemplified the logically and mathematically formalized, the universally quantified use of variables, and the deductive formulation in terms of a minimum set of basic assumptions.

Although Professor Lawson does not go outside his description of the formal, logical and analytic character of the substantive content of the Roman law into Roman Stoic philosophy and Greek mathematical physics, it is not irrelevant to note that ethical and legal thinkers like the Scaevolas and their Roman and Byzantine successors, who referred to Greek physics as the source of their theory of ethics and law,[15] must have been aware of the greatest achievement of Greek mathematical physics. This achievement was the solution of the problem produced by the discovery of arithmetically incommensurable geometrical magnitudes. The solution was achieved in Eudoxus' definition of the equality of ratios for any magnitudes whatever which has come down to us in Definition V of Book V of Euclid's *Elements*. The importance of this definition is that for the first time in the history of science the notion of the universally quantified variable (x) is used to define a technical scientific concept. This is precisely what occurs with the Greek and Stoic Roman philosophers and lawyers when they use the universally quantified variable (p), where p is a person, to define the ethically and legally good, thereby arriving at the notion that moral and legal man is not the old family and tribal man of the law of status of the Twelve Tables, but is instead any tribe, and, even more, any man whatever. It is this use of the universally quantified free variable to define the words "good" and "just" which gives the aforementioned formula:

(p) x : x is good or just $=$ (p) x, where if x confers specific rights or obligations on a particular p, any one person whatever must be substitutable for p.

Furthermore it is this formula which enables the Roman Empire, when the tribe of Rome conquers the tribes of other city-states, to put the *jus civile* of any other tribe and state on the same footing of equality under Roman law as is enjoyed by the *jus civile* of the local law of Rome. Furthermore, it is the universal quantification of the individual as well as the tribe which eventually in the *jus gentium* begins to break down the *patria potestas* of any law of status *jus civile* whatever to inaugurate the lengthy effort, which the recent Supreme Court decision in the United States on segregation in education is attempting to complete, in which not merely all families, but also any individual regardless of his family or tribe of birth has an equal right before the law to any public education or any other public thing if that thing is to be publicly good, or just.

Need one wonder, therefore, that Professor Lawson concludes his chapter on "The Form and Sources of the Civil Law" as follows:

> I must end this chapter by describing the way in which the Roman instinct for sharpness of outline, intensified in its operation by the natural lawyers, marked off the Civil Law itself from all other parts of their law. . . . The Civil Law was essentially a law between equals. That is why the *patria potestas,* the absolute power of the father over all his descendents in the male line, interested the jurists only incidentally, as something by getting out of which one became the equal of other citizens and as affording the *paterfamilias* useful ways of doing business through others, often with limited liability.[16]

Similarly, in the chapter on "The Contribution of Roman Law," Professor Lawson speaks of its "universal tendency." The *jus civile* of the citizens of Rome became restricted largely to family law and the law of succession with respect to family property. As the Empire expanded, such laws, Professor Lawson notes, "were no concern of the Roman state or its courts; but the greater part of the law of contract was universal, and so were in substance the whole of the law of tort and of property." [17] By the time of the Edict of Caracalla in 2 1 2 A.D.,

> almost all the free inhabitants of the Empire were Roman citizens, and by a parallel process the more formal and less rational elements of Roman Law disappeared, leaving the universal elements, which were also the more rational, to stand alone. There is little or nothing that is purely national in the Roman Law contained in Justinian's *Corpus Juris.*[18]

Clearly, Professor Lawson has established his general conclusion that civil and Roman law are to be distinguished from the common law due to a difference in their form and that this difference in form has its source in a difference in the legal mentalities that created the two systems. When we place his findings concerning the formal properties of the substantive Roman law of contract in the historical contexts of its creators, *vis-à-vis* Stoic Roman philosophy, Aristotelian logic and Greek mathematical physics, we are able to describe the mentality of Roman and civilian lawyers with more precision. It is the mentality of men who have taken deductively formalized Greek mathematical physics as their criterion of scientific method and its concept of the universally quantified variable as their definition of the morally good and the legally just.

Our more precise specification of the legal mentality behind the civil law, so far as it derives from the Roman law of the jurists, requires a qualification to be placed upon one conclusion of Professor Lawson. He questions the well-known thesis that the difference between the civil law and the common law is that between deduction and induction, pointing to the fact that the common lawyer has generalizations going beyond the inductive cases, from which he reasons deductively, just as does the civilian. This, of course, is true. Nevertheless, there is a more important sense in which the civilian is deductive in a technical scientific sense in which the traditional common lawyer is not. The common lawyer, as previously noted, has principles to which he appeals, as well as his cases. But his principles are mere piecemeal inductions from a natural history type of scientist's description of his particular facts and cases. He does not have theory in the sense of the logically and mathematically formalized, deductively formulated theory of mathematical physics. Nor does he take this type of scientific theory and method as his model for legal science. It is in this latter sense of the word "deduction" that the mentality of the civil lawyer is deductive and that of the common lawyer is not.

After his emphasis upon the universalizing tendency of Roman law, Professor Lawson stresses that it has another "remarkable characteristic"; it is a "law of movement." By this he means that Roman law is not "concerned to describe what *is*"; instead it asks the question concerning how "a particular legal situation come[s] into existence and how [it will] disappear." [19] An example occurs in the law of property, where "the Roman bias is for studying the acquisition rather than the transfer of property. The Romans never discuss the nature of ownership or possession." [20] Expressed more formally, this means that Roman law finds the key to law in verbs rather than in nouns. Recall how the stipulation requires the questioner and answerer to use the same form of the verb. It means also that the formal properties of the law refer to relations or operations, after the manner of the functions of mathematics, rather than to things. Things are thrown, as in mathematics, into the realm of the material constants. It is the formal properties of the relations or functional operations with respect to the quantified variables that matter.

Is it not precisely at this point that Roman law and the civil law, following it, receive their theoretical unity? Relations or functional operations, considered in their formal properties, have a range of application far wider than that of inductively given and classified things. Thus, by concentrating attention on the formal properties of functional relations, Roman legal science appears to have found, or to have come near to finding, the primitive concepts of its axiomatically or contractually constructed deductive theory. This way of thinking had two consequences. One appeared immediately. In any axiomatically constructed theory, the primitive operations or relations are, by definition, ultimate; they are never regarded as abstractions from a wider context. In natural history deductive science, on the other hand, because of its use of sensed material qualities in the definitions of its objects and classes, any relation is always an abstraction from a wider context. This difference shows in Roman law. Professor Lawson describes it as the "isolation of the relation between the parties from its surrounding circumstances and problems . . ." [21] He describes this as "artificial." It is only artificial for the natural history descriptive, more purely inductive type of science. For axiomatically constructed theory, and particularly for the primitive operations of such theory, it is the only non-artificial scientific procedure.

The second consequence of basing law upon the operations rather than the objects in legal transactions was to set the specification of a few elementary ideas, from which everything else is derived deductively, as the ultimate goal of legal science. Professor Lawson makes it clear that Roman law realized this ideal only in part, not having a "general law of contract," and that this process of generalization went on with the modern civilian, reaching its most perfect expression in the German civil code of the late nineteenth century.

The application of the Roman legal ideal and way of thinking to the modern national states brought with it certain conflicts and complexities. There were the local living laws of the different peoples to be reckoned with. Even in France today, the living law of its southern portion differs from that of the north. The old law of status familial ways still carry on. In fact, as Professor Lawson notes, the French democratic reformers used the French Revolution to wipe out the political control of the aristocracy and to preserve in considerable part the law of status of the peasants. Consequently the move toward a single, unified, analytically axiomatized and deductive theory of law did not go as far in France as it did in Germany. These considerations, put into perspective by Professor Lawson's lectures, show that the contemporary legal institutions of the Western world become intelligible only if one pays attention to the Roman factor in positive civil law as well as to the positive common law and relates the positive law in each case to the local living law of sociological jurisprudence.

In this connection, it is of interest to note that the predominant religious living law of most common law nations today is Protestant, whereas that of most civil law communities is Roman Catholic. With the fall of the Roman Empire the mentality of Greek mathematical physics and philosophy and of Stoic Roman law passed into Roman Catholic and Greek Orthodox Christianity. One of the consequences of the Protestant Reformation was that, in throwing off Rome in religion, it tended also to throw away the ethical, legal and scientific mentality of ancient Greece and Stoic Rome in law and politics. Also Rome, even in the days of its Empire, never dominated Britain to the extent, or for the length of time, that it commanded the people of the Western portion of the Continent. It is likely also that it was the strength of the diverse living laws of Angles, Saxons, Jutes and Celts in Britain that enabled Roman legal terminology and the Roman substitution of the law of contract for the law of status to pass into English law in the Roman period without its Greek scientific and Stoic Roman formalism going there also.

Also, with the modern scientific and philosophical revolution, led by Galilei, Descartes, Newton and Locke, modern British philosophy, following Locke, took the form of British empiricism with its final insistence upon the nominalistic and more purely inductive source of all conceptual meaning, whereas the modern philosophy of the Continental peoples, originating in Descartes, was the creation of the mathematical physicists Descartes, Leibniz and Kant and took the form of Continental rationalism with its emphasis on the *a priori* and the deductively formal rather than upon the merely nominalistic and more purely inductive factor in scientific method and knowledge. Thus the religious living law, the success of the Counter Reformation and their particular modern philosophy reinforce the Roman legal mentality in the civil law peoples, whereas the lesser influence of the

Roman Empire, the success of the Protestant Reformation and the excessively nominalistic and more inductively empirical form of modern British philosophy probably account for the difference between the common law in England and the civil law elsewhere notwithstanding the shift from status to contract and the technical Latin legal terminology which is common to both systems.

In the case of England there is one important thinker, noted by Professor Lawson, whose mentality is an exception. His name is Newton. To read his *Principia* is to be confronted with something like Euclid's *Elements*. His is the concept of scientific method of the Greek mathematical physicists and philosophers and the Stoic Roman and civilian lawyers. The mentality of the early Locke, who was a friend of Newton and who lectured on natural law at Oxford and wrote the aforementioned *Letter on Toleration* and treatise *Of Civil Government,* was undoubtedly similar. It was to the mentality of Newton and this early Locke and a Bacon undoubtedly conceived in harmony with them that Jefferson referred when he said that his three gods were Bacon, Newton and Locke.[22] Hence it is this mentality of the mathematical physicist's concept of scientific method and of universally quantified natural law, going through Jefferson into the Declaration of Independence and the Bill of Rights, only to be submerged with the triumph of the nominalism of the later Locke's *Essay Concerning Human Understanding* and its attendant psychological theory of ethics of Hume and positivistic theory of law of Austin, that reappears again in the recent Supreme Court decision on segregation in education to give the comparative study of the common law, civil law and Roman law its peculiar significance for everyone in the United States today.

XVIII

Concerning the Sociology of Knowledge

I T is not easy to overestimate the importance of the sociology of knowledge. Its implications are far-reaching, touching not merely the social sciences and philosophy, but also the practical problem of war and peace and even the fate of our civilization.

Its problem is that of the relation between the facts of social existence and the ideas making up human knowledge. That social scientists and philosophers have taken positions upon this question is evident. That statesmen making important decisions with respect to international policy affecting the peace of the world have taken similar positions is equally obvious.

Again and again we hear it said by social scientists, historians, philosophers, statesmen and laymen that the solution of the problems of peace and the causes of war center in economic factors. Laymen and social scientists often assert that the ideas of men are but afterthoughts, merely rationalizing — in the derogatory sense of the word "rationalize" — the group interests, the class aims or the forces of power politics which supposedly determine the beliefs and the behavior of men, both as individuals and as groups.

Suppose this popular opinion rests on error or is only partially true. It is easy then to appreciate the implications for social science and the concrete political decisions of statesmen which such a conclusion would entail.

Conversely, suppose that the aforementioned scholars and laymen are right. Then, clearly, much that is being done at present in carry-

Reprinted from *The Sociology of Knowledge* by Jacques J. Maquet (1951) by permission of The Beacon Press.

ing on the traditional practices in education with their emphasis upon cognitive rather than merely hortatory meanings should be changed. Also, many present efforts to set up international organizations and to seek for a truly international law which require for their success social principles and beliefs going beyond local, provincial class interests and the present socio-cultural premises and existential facts of our world should be branded as misguided and a waste of time. Men attempting to ameliorate or resolve the problems of our world by constructing new economic, political and legal norms different from those of the present or the past should also be discouraged and branded as misguided, scientifically uninformed folk who are attempting the impossible. This follows because, according to the foregoing conception of scholars and humanists, the ideas of men but reflect the facts or forces of the culture in which they are immersed or those of a unique future which will succeed the present culture in an inevitable manner.

Clearly, an inquiry which deals with these matters afresh and which in part at least reaches conclusions which are somewhat more informed and subtle than the traditional answers is important. Such is the nature of the study of the sociology of knowledge by the Belgian cultural anthropologist Dr. Jacques J. Maquet.[1]

Dr. Maquet indicates that the problem, as traditionally understood under the Continental European name of the *sociology of knowledge,* involves three factors: (1) the conditioning social facts; (2) the ideas making up human knowledge which are conditioned; and (3) the relation joining the former factor to the latter.

The investigation of the problem therefore involves asking of any given sociological theory three main questions: (1) What, specifically, are the conditioning social factors? More concretely: Are they purely economic? Are they physical circumstances such as climate or natural resources? Are they the military establishments of the groups in question, etc.? (2) What are the ideas conditioned? Is every idea in human knowledge conditioned by socio-cultural facts or are merely some? And, if merely some, which ones? To put the matter in more detail: Are all ideas and theories of the humanities and the social sciences thus conditioned, whereas, as Mannheim notes, the concepts of mathematics and mathematical physics are not? Is even one's philosophical theory of knowledge thus conditioned, in which instance even this thesis itself becomes not a cognitive proposition but a purely emotive and instrumental one? (3) What is the precise nature of the relation by means of which the facts of social existence determine the ideas of human knowledge? Is it a completely deterministic relation, such as that of rigorous cause and effect between the states of physical systems at different times in mathematical physics, or such as the formal relation of logical implication? Or is it the weaker form of the causal relation as designated by Mill's methods, which give merely observed, repeated sequences and rather weak empirical correlations? Or is it something even weaker than this, a mere compatibility or harmony, such as Dr. Maquet reveals to be the case in certain instances, as for example, Mannheim's position when it is carefully analyzed?

Furthermore, in answering all these questions, what method is to be used? Is one to use nothing but the purely inductive method of the historian, noting merely temporal sequences? Also, if the historian's method is used, what guarantee is there that, in the inevitable selection from the infinite number of facts in history, all those relevant to the inquiry have been examined? Or is some more powerful method of analysis to be applied to the inductive data? It is at this point that Dr. Maquet's choice of Professor Sorokin as well as Mannheim for consideration is a happy one. For Professor Sorokin brings much more powerful methods of inquiry, more like those of the natural scientists, to the discussion than does Mannheim.

Dr. Maquet's book forces its readers to ask an even more important question: Is the frequently asserted determination of human knowledge by social existence a determination which operates only in one direction? Put more technically, is this relation of determination insymmetrical? Is it the case that the facts of social existence determine ideas, and that ideas never determine the facts of social existence? Again, Dr. Maquet's study of the sociology of Professor Sorokin as well as that of Mannheim is fortunate.

The full force of Professor Sorokin's findings must not be missed. They reveal that a scientific study of any culture leads one to a connected set of basic predominant premises from which all the different predominant factors of that culture follow, exactly in the manner in which a scientific study of nature by the mathematical physicists leads to a connected set of theoretical principles from which the facts of nature and the instruments of technology derive. It is not an accident that the difference in the conclusions of Mannheim and Professor Sorokin are accompanied thus by a corresponding difference in their methods of inquiry. Nor is it an accident that the correspondingly more powerful conclusions of Professor Sorokin are achieved by the correspondingly more powerful methods analogous to those of the mathematical physicists. The historian's methods, excessively inductive, purely empirical and descriptive, seem to be as weak and insufficient, even though necessary, in social science as they have proved to be in the natural sciences.

A further thesis of Professor Sorokin's sociology must also be noted. Not only does a specific culture obtain its definition and its unity from an underlying set of premises, but these premises turn out also to be philosophical in character. One of the most notable developments of our time in the field of the cultural sciences is the independent demonstration of this conclusion by a large number of investigators who have approached the subject from quite different starting points. Professor Sorokin's sociology is one example. Recent study in the philosophy of the world's cultures such as my *The Meeting of East and West,* as noted in previous chapters, is another instance. The investigations of the cultural anthropologists, such as Professor Clyde Kluckhohn, have demonstrated that even the behavior and objective institutions of so-called primitive people such as the Navaho Indians cannot be understood until their philosophy is determined.[2]

One additional point first emphasized by Professor Sorokin is becoming increasingly clear. Values turn out not to be objective irreducible data appearing as common factors through different cultures. Instead, one's philosophical theory of the ultimate nature of reality and of man as a factor in reality defines one's values. Thus, the word "good" is not an idea within the total set of ideas making up one's ultimate philosophy. It is, instead, but a shorthand name for one's ultimate philosophy. This is the real point of Socrates' dictum "Know thyself" and of Plato's thesis that there will not be good government until philosophers are kings. The point of the latter thesis is not that Plato wanted philosophers in political positions. It is, instead, that one's philosophical theory of what is primary or ultimate in experience is one's criterion of the good. Hence, only those who have a true philosophical theory of experience can be good statesmen. Hence,

Professor Sorokin's findings, which show that cultures resting on different philosophical conceptions have radically different aims and values.

Dr. Maquet's analysis makes it clear also that one must watch the different definitions of the sociology of knowledge. One definition conceives it as "the study of the relationship between society and mental productions." Another defines it as the consideration of "mental productions in so far as they are influenced by social factors." It is to be noted that the first of these two definitions leaves the question open as to whether the relation of determination between social facts and human ideas operates only in one direction, whereas the second formulation does not. It appears that Mannheim's definition is the second one, whereas Professor Sorokin's is the former of the two.

One is, of course, free to define the sociology of knowledge in any way that one chooses. It is also probably the case that its original definition was the second or more restricted one. Nevertheless, it is not to be overlooked that if one takes the more restricted, traditional definition, then one can draw from it only very restricted and partial conclusions concerning the implications of the sociology of knowledge for the philosophical theory of knowledge. Clearly, if one has defined the sociology of knowledge as an inquiry into the determination of human ideas by social existence, then all that one can possibly conclude, so far as general philosophical epistemology is concerned, is that sometimes social existence determines ideas. It does not seem to be a misrepresentation to say that those who have defined the sociology of knowledge in the restricted sense have not restricted themselves to the limited conclusions so far as philosophical epistemology is concerned which such a restricted definition entails.

A consideration of the definition of culture is most relevant in this connection. Sociologists are well aware, as biological scientists frequently are not, that there is a fundamental difference between the biological organization of society and its cultural or social organization. Biological social organization and behavior are the organization and behavior which result solely from the genetical inheritance of the material bodies of the people in society and the effect upon these bodies of external stimuli. The cultural and social organization of society, on the other hand, is built on top of this. The fundamental differentiating factor is symbols and learned behavior in response to social symbols. This appears in the definition of culture as socially learned behavior. This is the key also to Professor Sorokin's emphasis upon cultural social behavior as meaningful.

This inescapable presence of symbols which are stimuli, often continuous, standing for factors other than themselves and hence having an intentional character or, in other words, a meaning, has implications not always noted. Since culture is learned behavior toward symbols and since learned behavior conditioned to a symbol always involves a stimulus taken as an idea referring to something other than the stimulus itself, it follows that culture is learned ideas embodied in individual behavior. From this it follows that the restricted thesis of the sociology of knowledge to the effect that cultural or social existence determines ideas is merely the tautology that a learned idea entails the idea that is learned. Thus, when one pays attention to the definition of culture used by those who define the sociology of knowledge as the conditioning of ideas by cultural existence, it turns out that the thesis rests upon a definition of culture which makes cultural existence the effect rather than the cause of ideas — the effect because culture, as opposed to merely biological society, is by definition the product of an idea or symbol to which one's behavior has become conditioned.

There is now experimental evidence combined by Drs. Warren McCulloch and Walter Pitts with the appropriate theoretical analysis which demonstrates the manner in which particular existences become turned into universals by the human nervous system, due to reverberating neural nets in the central nervous system, and how such universals can through their particular embodiments fire motor neurons, thereby determining human behavior and through human behavior social existence.[3] It appears, therefore, that Dr. Maquet's analysis, making more precise the traditional possibilities and opening up new possibilities of conceiving of the relation between social existence and human knowledge, especially when supplemented with the latter considerations, results in novel and very important conclusions.

One explicit result of Dr. Maquet's inquiry into the relation between social existence and human knowledge merits special attention. His examination of Mannheim's findings leads to the verdict that social conditioning means little more than coherence, correlation or harmony. This mitigates the limitation of Mannheim's definition of the sociology of knowledge which identifies its subject matter with a study of the way in which social existence determines ideas. For to find that this determination is mere correlation or harmony is practically to assert that the relation is symmetrical rather than insymmetrical.

Dr. Maquet's study escapes from the error of begging the latter question in another respect. He suggests that the definition of "the existential determination of knowledge" as mere correspondence or harmony may mean that "ontologically" ideas and social existence come from a common factor.

There is historical evidence in support of this conclusion in the case of the relation between Roman law and existential Roman society. An investigation of this topic recently by the lawyer Mr. Gray L. Dorsey [4] has brought out that any correspondence or correlation between the universal principle in later Roman law and existential Roman society is due to the fact that the ideas of Stoic philosophy not merely went into Roman law as it was finally codified by lawyers (practically all of whom were Stoic philosophers), but also went independently, through the ethical teaching and conditioning of children in the family, directly into Roman society. When to this is added the fact that existential family life and Roman law, by way of the common Stoic philosophy, were regarded as cognitively valid in their common ethical and legal norms because these norms reflected the law of nature as derived by the Stoics from Greek science and natural philosophy, it becomes clear that the basis of the validation of human knowledge and its cultural norms may be in existential nature rather than in social existence. In this connection, Mannheim's observation that human knowledge in mathematics and mathematical physics escapes relativity to cultural facts for its existential source and validation takes on a new importance.

Such a theory of the existential source of human knowledge and its non-culturally relative cultural norms must, however, face the crucial question put by Dr. Maquet in his study.

> Let us suppose [he writes] that we have shown that the principle of causality, a fundamental category of our logic, does not exist in Chinese thought and that what is closest to it is a sort of principle of

harmony. The question of validity with regard to these two categories claims our attention in these terms: Are there in the reality relations of causality or rather of harmony? How could the philosopher who would discuss this subsumability of the real in these two categories, reject as irrelevant the fact that his own mind has been formed by a tradition in which people are accustomed to see the world in terms either of causality relationships or of harmony relationships?

The answer to this question is that Mr. Gray L. Dorsey, in his aforementioned study of the source of universal ethical and legal principles in both Chinese and Roman law, finds that in both instances the ideas involved in these principles were grounded for their verification and cognitive meaning in the existence of nature rather than in cultural social existence. He has pointed out also that in my *The Meeting of East and West* it was shown that for the Chinese and the Orient generally, nature was known primarily, if not solely, by the intuitive method of immediate apprehension of pure empiricism, whereas in the West, nature has been known not merely in this way but primarily by means of theoretically designated, indirectly verified, deductively formulated theory. Now, it can be shown, as Hume made clear, that empirically known reality gives only the notion of temporal succession or correlation, or harmony, just as the Chinese maintain. It has been demonstrated similarly by Kant and more recently by Henry Margenau [5] and the present writer,[6] that causality, as applied to the states of systems in nature by Western mathematical physics, can be known only by the Western methods of knowing nature in terms of indirectly verified, deductively formulated theory. Thus one is not driven, in order to explain the difference between the Chinese intuitive notion of harmony and the Western technical concept of causality, to cultural existence for the cognitive source and validation of these different theories. They have their basis instead in two different scientific ways of knowing nature, each of which is correct for the component of nature which it grasps — both components of nature being real.

These are some of the crucial contemporary questions upon which Dr. Maquet's analysis focuses and which it illuminates. It is clear that they are important. It is becoming clear also that man through knowledge can be something more than a loudspeaker for the particular class or the provincial culture in which circumstances happen to place him. Nature exists one and the same for all men, as well as the many classes and cultures. Hence there is another source for the existential validation of philosophical knowledge and its ethical and legal norms than either class or culture.

XIX

The Theory of Types and the Verification
of Ethical Theory

As has been noted in previous chapters, one of the major errors of
the social and political philosophy of Hegel and of Marx and of
much contemporary social science is the identification of the "ought"
for society and personal human conduct with the "is." Elsewhere we
have called this error the "culturalistic fallacy." [1] This fallacy occurs
in social science when one attempts to determine the normative social theory which "ought to be" by applying the empirical methods of
natural science to social and cultural facts. This procedure gives
very important scientific social theory, but it is factual social theory
of what is the case or of the descriptive living law norms which are
the case; it is not normative social theory of what ought to be the case.

As Professor Lon L. Fuller has seen, actual legal experience is that
of a "law in quest of itself"; a law, namely, which is not merely what
it is but also something more than what it is, in the sense first of
trying to formulate what ought to be, and then of trying to be that
substantively specific "ought" which ever beckons us, thereby making
real differences in the law, but which, nevertheless, ever, in its com-
pleteness, eludes us. The same can be said of moral as distinct from
legal experience. But how to determine this "ought to be" is the
question.

Even social scientists and social philosophers such as Marx and
Hegel, who identify the "ought" for culture with the empirical, historical "is" of actual culture, recognize, however, that the culturalistic
fallacy occurs if the "ought" is identified with the "is" of present cul-

Reprinted from Charles A. Moore, ed., *Essays in East-West
Philosophy* (1951), by permission of University of Hawaii Press.

tural and social facts. The normative ideal for judging today's human behavior and cultural institutions cannot be the de facto "is" of that human behavior and those social institutions; otherwise the status quo would be perfect and reform and reconstruction would be unnecessary. The Hegelians and Marxists see that this is clearly wrong; otherwise there would not be the need for the criticisms of the social status quo in which they indulge and the need for radical and even revolutionary reconstruction of contemporary social and cultural institutions upon which the dialectical Marxists in particular insist. The Hegelians and Marxists believe, however, that the fallacy of identifying the historical "ought" for culture with its historical "is" is avoided if one identifies the "ought" with tomorrow's historical "is" instead of with today's. Historical jurisprudence and the humanistic historians commit the reverse temporal version of the culturalistic fallacy when they suggest that one can resolve normative questions concerning goal values by the historical method; that is, by identifying the "ought" for judging today's historical "is" with yesterday's historical "is."

The error which is present in the culturalistic fallacy does not arise merely because human behavior and human cultural institutions imperfectly realize the personal and social norms which they are attempting to actualize. The error of the culturalistic fallacy would be present even if a given culture realized its ideal perfectly in fact. The reason for this is that the correctness of the normative ideal itself is always open to question, as the existence of ideological conflicts with respect to goal values clearly demonstrates. This is shown by the fact that the normative personal and social ideals in the living law of one culture are very often regarded as evil from the standpoint of the ideals of another culture. Even if the Kremlin realized its normative theory perfectly, the Vatican would not approve of it. Similarly, even if the Vatican realized its Thomistic Christian normative ideal perfectly, not merely the Communists but also at least some Protestant Christians and naturalistic liberals would regard the result as the intensification of evil rather than the realization of good. Professor Y. P. Mei has indicated that the introduction of Western ethical, political, legal and other normative social theories into China had the effect of weakening the Confucian ethics and customs rather than of harmonizing with them.[2] Nor is this difficult to understand when Western normative social theories place dedication to specific, determinate law of contract economic and political principles above the warm feeling of patriarchal filial piety for one's parents and one's ancestors. Nor are Western Christian religious doctrines less in conflict with Confucian values than are Western secular, legal and political principles. Certainly a religion whose Savior said that he came to put father against son and husband against wife is hardly a religion whose goal values will sustain rather than disrupt Confucian filial piety and the classical Confucian patriarchal joint family.

The foregoing considerations make one fact evident which has not received the attention which it deserves. This fact is that there are within the West and between the East and West some normative theories which are not merely different but mutually incompatible. The one cannot be believed without the other being rejected.

This conflict of goal values is not restricted to the values of people in different cultures. It also occurs in certain instances with respect to the differing values of the same people at different stages of their cultural history. The traditional Tsarist Greek Orthodox Christian ideology, now superseded in the case of Russian social policy by the Marxist communistic ideology, is an instance. Conversely, a norm which a given people at a given stage of their cultural history may damn as unorthodox and evil may be regarded by them later as a true measure of the divine and the good. The Aristotelian formulation of Roman Catholic Christianity, which was branded by William of Champeau as heresy when it was first proposed by Abelard and which since the canonization of St. Thomas early in the fourteenth century has been used by the Vatican as the criterion of the orthodox and the good, is a case in point. In fact, the main characteristic of the contemporary domestic politics of any people or culture is the conflict of ideologies, normative social theories and values which it exhibits.

Each one of these differing and conflicting sets of values is in significant part the humanistic operational consequence of a specific philosophy. A philosophy is a set of propositions. Since the differing sets of propositions of the different philosophies with their respective operationally different overt values are in some cases at least not merely different but mutually contradictory, it follows that the given values or norms of any specific culture cannot be taken as valid on either *a priori* rationalistic or *a posteriori* empirical grounds. When any two philosophies or ideologies are mutually contradictory, both cannot be true. This entails that the prevalent ethical notion expressed by the proposition "There are facts and there are values," where by "are values" is meant "values given empirically as data the same for everybody," must be rejected.

Values are not facts given as data which are the same for everybody, against which the propositions of ethics can be verified after the manner in which the propositions of natural science are verified against its data. Instead, values reflect rather than define or verify the philosophical premises from which one's normative theory is derived. To accept non-dualistic Vedanta is to take the intuitive achievement of Brahman as the ultimate value. To accept Thomistic Roman Catholicism is to regard the actualization in society of a rationalistically determined natural law as the social good, and to regard discursive determinate reason as the criterion of perfection in both man and God. To embrace Communism is to use the principles of Marxist philosophy as the criterion of the good. As Edward Hallett Carr has written in his *Soviet Impact on the Western World*,[3] "A true revolution is never content merely to expose the abuses of the existing order, the cases in which its practice falls short of its precept, but attacks at their root the values on which the moral authority of the existing order is based." In short, a new philosophy which is accepted does not conform to given values the same for all men independent of philosophical beliefs; instead it repudiates the given values and puts new values in their place. This suggests that ethics is but philosophy applied. Hence when the philosophy changes, the norms and values change.

To use Socrates' language as expressed by Plato, values are not objective things, the same for everybody, out of which one's moral philosophy and normative social theory can be constructed and against which it can be verified; values, instead, are "shadows on the wall of the cave," reflecting one's philosophy or the philosophy of one's culture.[4] To mistake shadows (that is, cultural institutions and culturally conditioned introspective values) for objective things has been the error of most recent modern moral theory and social science.

Since specific values reflect a specific philosophy, it is fallacious, because it is circular and question-begging, to test any normative theory or philosophy against the denotatively given values of any given culture or against the historical institutions of culture. This is the real error in the culturalistic fallacy of attempting to derive the "ought" for culture from its "is."

But if a given cultural philosophy creates values rather than adjusts itself to values, and if a given philosophy therefore cannot be verified by appeal to values, either those of the present or those of the future or the past, how can the propositions or postulates of a particular philosophy of culture be tested? Unless one assumes that ethical propositions are non-cognitive and accepts the consequence that one culture and its philosophy with its particular values is as valid as any other, there is but one answer to this question: Nature rather than culture must be the source of verification.

This was the answer given by the Chinese philosophers of the Orient when they said that good conduct is conduct in harmony with one's conception of nature when that conception of nature is determined not *a priori* but "by an investigation of things." As noted in Chapter XI, E. Vernon Arnold, in his classical work *Roman Stoicism,*[5] makes it clear that for the Roman Stoics and for every school of Greek philosophy after the time of the early Socrates, philosophy was conceived as composed of three parts: logic, physics and ethics, where logic is the science which studies the methods with which one knows things, physics is the science which specifies the nature of things as known by the methods of logic, and ethics is the application of this knowledge of things to human conduct. As Arnold makes clear, even sin is defined as assent to false propositions about things.[6] In short, for the Greek philosophers and Roman Stoics, ethics is applied philosophy verified by the logical methods of science against nature and natural man.* In fact, this is the point of the basic dictum of Roman law that even the *jus gentium,* the humanistic law which is universally the case for all men, is tested by appeal to *jus naturae.*

This means that the normative theory of the good for personal behavior and cultural institutions is one's philosophical theory of the true for nature and natural man as verified by scientific methods, or by what the Chinese sages and the Greek and Roman philosophers

---

* By "natural man" is meant those characteristics of human nature which are not the effect of the beliefs of men.

termed "an investigation of things." There are in any non-question-begging philosophy not two philosophies, the one a moral philosophy defining values with its particular assumptions and the other a natural philosophy verified against the facts of nature and natural man with its different assumptions; there is in any cognitive philosophy but one philosophy, namely the philosophy of the true for nature and the natural man. Ethics is merely true (that is, empirically verified) natural philosophy applied to human conduct and relations. When the empirically verified philosophy of the true for natural man is pursued with respect to what man must do to fulfill what it indicates the full and true nature of natural man to be, then the philosophy of the true for nature and natural man becomes the idea or measure of the good for culture, cultural man and the humanities.

It is to be emphasized, however, that it is not the facts of nature that define the good for man, but one's scientific theory of the facts in their interrelations as a whole when this scientifically verified theory has been analyzed to bring out its epistemological and its substantive ontological assumptions, if any. A scientific theory is not a body of natural facts; it is, instead, a set of propositions verified by appeal to such facts. Hence, facts *qua* facts are neither good nor bad. Goodness and badness are predicates applying not to facts but to propositions which refer to facts for the criterion of their truth or falsity. This is the point of the ethical dictum common to all systems of Greek and Roman philosophy, that virtue is true knowledge in the light of the whole.

Furthermore, propositions are not good or bad because of any primitive ethical quality of goodness or badness which resides in them. The only properties which propositions possess, aside from their meaningful content, are properties such as truth or falsity. From this it follows that not only are facts *qua* facts neither good nor bad but also that propositions *qua* propositions are neither good nor bad. It is only their truth value relations to facts which make propositions good or bad. In short, a proposition is not good or bad because either it or the facts to which it purports to refer are good or bad; a proposition is bad because it is false to the facts to which it purports to refer; a proposition is good because it is true to the facts to which it purports to refer.

Those acquainted with issues in modern logic which were debated throughout the first decades of this century will recall that at one time the psychological act of judging was regarded as true or false. It is now generally agreed that no psychological acts are true or false. A psychological act, being a fact, merely is; it is not true or false. Instead, only propositions are true or false.

The analysis of this paper applies the same type of reasoning to ethics. The psychological act of assenting, *qua* fact, is neither good nor bad since facts merely are. Facts are not good or bad any more than they are true or false. Only propositions are good or bad, and even then only because of their truth value relation to the facts to which they purport to refer.

It does seem to make sense, however, to say that a murderer's behavior is bad or that Hitler's conduct was bad. Now, clearly Hitler's past conduct is a fact; the behavior of actual murderers is also a fact. How, then, can we reconcile this conclusion with the foregoing conclusion that only propositions, because of their truth values, are good or bad?

It is at this point that the theory of types becomes important for ethics. Facts can be good or bad if they are facts which are, in part at least, the consequence of man's assent to propositions which are true or false. Only the facts of culture and of culturally conditioned man can be of this character, since only the facts of culture are what they are, in part at least, because of the propositions believed in by men. The facts of nature and the natural man are by definition those facts about man and nature which are not man-made.

Making use of the theory of types, let us call natural facts, facts of a type of the first order. Such facts are antecedent to scientifically verified philosophical theory. Such facts are also neither good nor bad. Let us, on the other hand, call cultural facts, facts of a type of the second order. Facts of this type can be designated as good or bad. They achieve their goodness or badness, however, not because they are facts, but because they are facts which derive their character and existence in part at least from human behavior based upon beliefs in scientifically verifiable propositions about nature and natural man which are true or false.

This use of the theory of types enables us to assert that the factual conduct of Hitler was bad because this conduct was the consequence, in part at least, of philosophical beliefs about natural man which scientific method can demonstrate to be false. This distinction between the second-order facts of culture and cultural man and the first-order facts of nature and natural man permits us to obtain verifiable philosophical theory which, when applied, gives its particular norm for culture and cultural man, while at the same time preventing us from falling into the culturalistic fallacy of identifying the "ought" for culture with the "is" for culture. By making the first-order facts of nature and natural man the source of the verification of the philosophical theory, conformity to which in human conduct defines the good for culture and cultural man, one obtains a philosophically grounded norm for culture different from the "is" of culture, which is nonetheless verifiable.

XX

Ethical Relativism in the Light of Recent Legal Theory

ANTHROPOLOGY and sociological jurisprudence have extended the study of ethics and law to the cultures of the entire world. Two things result: (1) the relativity of ethics and philosophy to culture, and (2) the relativity of culture to philosophy. The distinctions necessary to clarify these two conclusions are the concern of this paper.

Its approach is through three developments in American legal science. They are (1) legal positivism, (2) sociological jurisprudence and (3) natural law jurisprudence.

Legal Positivism

Legal positivism received its fullest American expression in Thayer, Langdell and Ames. It is exemplified today in Mr. Justice Frankfurter and Judge Emeritus Learned Hand. Philosophically it derives secondarily from Wright, Peirce and James [1] and primarily from Austin, Bentham and Hume, supplemented with Hobbes. From Hobbes it takes its criterion of the effectiveness and sanction of law — namely in the power of the sovereign. From Hume, Bentham and James it receives its psychological ethics and its positivism.

Its positivism means that one need study only the positive law to make correct judicial decisions or to practice properly. By positive law is meant the statutes and judicial decisions. The positive law being declared, ethics is foreign to the judge's judgment. His duty is to ac-

Reprinted from *The Journal of Philosophy*, November, 1955, Vol. LII, No. 23, by permission.

cept the ethical content of the positive law, not questioning why. Ethics is assigned consequently to the theory of legislation.

This assignment of ethics to the private citizen, expressing himself through legislation, derives from the subjectivism of any psychological ethics, such as that of Hume, Austin, James and Learned Hand.[2] Its only meaning for the "social good" is the pooling of the private "goods" in the legislative market place. Were the judge, therefore, to introduce his ethical judgment into his legal decision, he would be guilty of confusing private with public justice.[3]

This leaves no basis for the judicial review of legislation. Judge Learned Hand draws this conclusion, interpreting the Bill of Rights merely as "counsels of moderation" to the legislature.[4] Justices Douglas and Black and Mr. Chief Justice Warren, however, in accord with Locke, Jefferson and Marshall, interpret the Bill of Rights in civil liberty cases as positive law which the judge must use to measure both the executive and the legislature.[5] This is to affirm a meaning of "socially good" other than the pooling of private goods in the legislature and to reject both ethical subjectivism and legal positivism.

But where is this trans-legislative meaning of "socially good" to be found? An obvious answer is: In an empirical study of the norms of social behavior. In short, the basis of law is not introspective psychology but empirical social science. This is the point of the legal philosophy of Savigny, Ehrlich,[6] Roscoe Pound [7] and Underhill Moore [8] and of the Yale Law School's policy, initiated in the 1920's when Mr. (now Justice) Douglas was a Professor there, of calling non-legally trained social scientists * and even a philosopher of culture to its faculty. Thus legal positivism gave way to sociological jurisprudence.

Sociological Jurisprudence

Its thesis is that positive law cannot be understood apart from the social norms of the "living law." Ehrlich defined the latter as "the inner order of the associations of human beings" [9] and described it as "the law which dominates life itself even though it has not been posited in legal propositions [that is, the positive law]." [10] Ehrlich's "inner order of associations" is equivalent to what the anthropolo-

* The economist Walton Hamilton and the sociologist Harold D. Lasswell.

gists call "the pattern of a culture." [11] Thus Ehrlich's theory might equally appropriately be called anthropological jurisprudence.[12]

For both the sociological jurist and the anthropologist, the inner order or pattern, which is the living law, is empirically and inescapably ethical. Thus in summarizing an appraisal of their science by some fifty anthropologists, Professor Kroeber writes: "Values evidently are intimately associated with the most basic and implicit patterning of the phenomena of culture." [13] Similarly, Ehrlich speaks of the "social norms" of the "inner order" of society, which provide the sanction for and determine the effectiveness of the positive law.[14]

Note that Hobbes is dropped. The sanction for positive law and the criterion of its effectiveness is not power, but the correspondence between its ethical content and that of the living law. When, as with the Prohibition Amendment or Chiang Kai-shek's Western constitution applied to Confucian China,[15] the norms of the positive law fail to correspond to those of the living law, the positive law fails even though plenty of power is at hand. Thus instead of positive law deriving its sanction from something ethically neutral, such as power, both power and positive law derive their sanction and effectiveness from the ethical content of the living law.

Sociological jurisprudence also provides a standard for judging legislation, thereby validating judicial review of majority legislation. Ethics is not consigned to the theory of legislation which is outside the judge's province.

Furthermore, the "social good" that measures majority legislation is neither vacuously abstract, after the manner of the neo-Kantians, nor subjectively arbitrary. Instead, it is given by the anthropologist's or sociologist's objective determination of the norms embodied in the inner order of associations or pattern of the culture in question. Hence, social ethics is a cognitive science. The sentences describing the normative "is" of the living law which sociological jurisprudence uses to judge the goodness or badness of the positive law, being empirically testable, are not hortatory.

Sociological jurisprudence also shows the prevalent assertion that the "good" cannot be derived from the "is" to be meaningless unless the context is specified. Law as conceived by the legal positivist provides a context in which the assertion is true. Clearly, one cannot obtain the standard for judging the "is" of a given subject matter, such as the positive law, from the "is" of that subject matter itself. It does not follow, however, as sociological jurisprudence clearly shows, that the "good" or standard for judging the "is" of one subject matter, such as the positive law, cannot be found in the "is" of some other subject matter, such as the living law. When this is possible, the statement, "It is impossible to derive the 'good' from an 'is,' " is false.

The sociological jurist's way of using the "is" of the living law as the standard for measuring the goodness or badness of the positive law is as follows: According to his theory, today's positive law is the deposit of yesterday's living law. But whereas the former tends to remain static, due to the principle of *stare decisis*, the living law may change. Then the positive law becomes bad, in the sense of the word "bad" as defined by sociological jurisprudence, and is in need of reform. The specific ethical content of the reform is determined by an empirical study of the normative inner order of today's living law. This is then used to define the positive legal statutes that correspond to it. These statutes specify the respect in which the traditional positive law is to be reformed.

But if this method of using the "is" of the living law, as the standard for measuring the goodness or badness, and attendant reform, of the positive law, is not to be circular and question-begging, the method of determining the living law must not appeal to the positive law. It was the great merit of my predecessor, the late Professor Underhill Moore, (1) to have noted that the traditional sociological jurisprudence did not meet this requirement and (2) to have devised a method which does meet it. He showed that so long as introspective psychological terms were used in describing the living law, different empirical observers gave quite different reports concerning its supposedly objective character. This led Moore to use the spatio-temporal concepts of Hull's behavioristic psychology to describe the living law.[16] It then became defined as the high-frequency, spatio-temporal behavior of the people in question.

Certainly this method gives objectivity. As noted in previous chapters, it is practicable, however, only for societies containing a small number of persons. Also, it is not clear that the spatio-temporal differences in the observable behavior of Hindus and Muslims in British India would be subtle enough to distinguish the living law norms of the two groups. Yet these norms were so different that the people found it necessary to divide into Pakistan and Free India. Some other method is required.

Cultural anthropology and the comparative philosophy of cultures reveal this way. Both disciplines have shown that the spatio-temporal social habits and ordering of people in any culture and its objective buildings, art forms and positive legal procedures for settling disputes are the deposit of an implicit or explicit common set of meanings for describing, integrating and anticipating the raw data of human experience. As Professor Kluckhohn has written:

> The publication of Paul Radin's *Primitive Man as a Philosopher* did much toward destroying the myth that a cognitive orientation toward experience was a peculiarity of literate societies. . . . Every people has its characteristic set of "primitive postulates." As Bateson has said: "The human individual is endlessly simplifying and generalizing his own view of his environment; he constantly imposes . . . his own constructions and meanings; these constructions and meanings are characteristic of one culture as opposed to another." [17]

When these primitive postulates or meanings were discovered or learned by a people initially in the distant past, the anthropologists call that philosophy implicit; when the philosophy is discovered or brought to consciousness in the present, they call it explicit.[18]

The method of anthropological jurisprudence for determining the norms of the living law without appeal to the positive law is that, therefore, of specifying the implicit or explicit philosophy, or complex of philosophies, of the society whose positive law is being judged. Professor Kluckhohn has shown how this is done in a homogeneous culture where the philosophy is implicit.[19] The writer has indicated how it is to be done in a heterogeneous culture, such as contemporary Western Continental Europe, whose living law is a complex deposit of several diverse and even conflicting, explicitly recorded philosophies.[20] The latter study shows that in such cases the method must be both qualitative and quantitative. Qualitatively it must specify the philosophy, including religious, economic and cultural assumptions, of each major association of individuals. Quantitatively it must determine the number of adherents which each qualitative philosophy enjoys.[21]

When one approaches the living law of the entire world in this manner, one fact becomes clear: It is heterogeneous and pluralistic in its normative content. The living law norms of one people are not those of another. This fact has important implications.

First, it reveals, as Chapters X and XI have shown, why traditional positive international law is so weak. The reason is not, as the legal positivists asserted, because there is no de facto supranational power. The reason instead is that, being modeled on the homogeneous living law of late medieval Europe, its norms failed to correspond sufficiently to the changing and pluralistic living law of the world, to draw unto itself the ethical vitality and power necessary to be effective. Conversely, this means that a more effective positive international law is possible providing we so formulate its normative content that it draws upon the ethical homogeneity and heterogeneity and pluralism of the entire world's living law.[22]

The latter fact also points up the sense in which each philosophy and its particular ethics is culture-bound. Why are there so few, if any, non-dualistic Vedanta philosophers in the American Philosophical Association and so many in its Indian counterpart? Is it not because the Indians have been born in Hindu culture and we in Anglo-American culture? To many Mexicans, viewing us from their culture with its Spanish philosophy of individualistic uncompromising passion and its Roman Catholic religious and Continental rationalistic secular tradition, most Anglo-American culture seems simple-minded, mediocre ethically and devoid of seriousness, spiritual subtlety and depth — all the consequence of the unfortunate accident of having been born in a culture whose living law was formed by the rather poverty-stricken set of meanings provided by nominalistic British empirical philosophy. If we answer that such Mexican judgments are the accident of the culture of their birth, we may answer truthfully, but in doing so are we not like the pot that calls the kettle black?

Is there any way out of this predicament? This question brings us to the third development in contemporary legal science.

Natural Law Ethics and Jurisprudence

What forces us to take this development seriously is not merely that legal scientists of Roman Catholic religious faith and Latin European legal training, such as Professor A. P. d'Entrèves of Oxford, are ably defending it,[23] but also that those of Protestant or Jewish religious background, trained in law schools teaching only legal positivism or sociological jurisprudence, are turning toward or to it — men such as Professor Lon L. Fuller and Dean Emeritus Roscoe Pound of the Harvard Law School,[24] Professor Friedrich Kessler [25] and Dean Emeritus Robert Hutchins of the Yale Law School, Dr. Mortimer Adler [26] of Columbia and the University of Chicago Law School and Sir Arthur L. Goodhart, Regius Professor of Jurisprudence Emeritus at the University of Oxford, who initially was a staunch Austinian legal positivist.[27]

The major reason is clear. One must judge the living as well as the positive law. The living law of Hitler's Germany forced us to do this; that of Communist Russia is now requiring it again. In fact everywhere, especially in Asia and Africa, people are reforming their domestic living law as well as their traditional positive law. Any theory of ethics and law which cannot provide a measure or standard for judging and reforming the living law is, therefore, inadequate. Is there such a standard? Clearly sociological jurisprudence alone cannot give the answer, since one cannot find the standard for measuring the "is" of the living law in the "is" of the living law itself.

Yet, judge the living law we must. The urgent question, therefore, arises: Is there any standard, objectively determinable, and hence an "is," other than the positive and the living law, against which the goodness and badness of the living law can be measured, after the manner in which the "is" of the living law measures the goodness or badness of the positive law? Natural law ethics and jurisprudence is the thesis that there is such a standard.

The clue to it is already implicit in the aforementioned method of sociological jurisprudence. This method consists in making explicit the meanings or concepts held in common by the people of a given society for conceiving, remembering, integrating and anticipating the raw data of their experience and ordering their social associations and behavior. In short, the living law of a given society is the deposit in cultural artifacts and in social human habits of a specific way of conceptualizing the raw unconceptualized data of anybody's experience. This conclusion has two components. Attention to the first generates sociological jurisprudence and the relativity to culture of each philosophy and its particular ethical and legal norms. Attention to the second generates natural law jurisprudence and the relativity of culture to natural philosophy.

The former factor shows itself in the philosophical pluralism embodied in the many living laws of the world. All of us are members of a culture which is the deposit of a particular composite of traditional philosophies. Hence, in so far as any person, or group of persons, without deeper philosophical analysis and criticism, allows the traditional philosophy of his culture and its particular ethic and law to determine his evaluations, his professional judgments are culturally relative and the doctrine of the sociology of knowledge holds.[28] The likelihood of this occurring should make one slightly suspicious about the number of British empiricists at Oxford and Cambridge and in the American Philosophical Association today.

But to stop here is to overlook the second factor in the living law of sociological jurisprudence: Any set of primitive assumptions which a people use to describe, remember, order and anticipate the raw data of their experience and to guide their social behavior refers to those raw data for its validity. In this sense man's empirically validated philosophy and its particular ethic makes culture and the living law norms of culture.

It becomes necessary, therefore, in order to specify (1) the sense in which culture is relative to philosophy and (2) the different sense in which philosophy is relative to culture to distinguish two types of fact, which in the previous chapter were called "first-order facts" and "second-order facts."[29] First-order facts are the introspected or sensed raw data, antecedent to all theory and all cultures, given in anyone's experience in any culture. Second-order facts are cultural artifacts; that is, they are the result in part at least of human theory of first-order facts. Nature and natural law are the names for all first-order facts and their relations. Culture and living law are the names for all second-order facts and their inner order. To the extent, therefore, that any philosophy or legal system appeals to second-order facts for its meaning and verification, it and its ethic are relative to culture. To the extent that any philosophy (1) derives its meaning and verification from first-order facts and (2) guides human behavior to create second-order facts, culture is relative to philosophy and to its ethic.

Conditions (1) and (2) above entail a clear distinction between science and art. The discipline for discovering and verifying theory of first-order facts is natural science. The discipline by which men, given an assumed theory of first-order facts, use this theory as the standard for guiding their behavior in the creation of second-order artifacts is called art or practical wisdom. Where the initial theories of first-order facts differ, there are different artifacts and hence different living laws and cultures. The discipline by which men discover and verify the theory of second-order facts is social science. It presupposes both art, or practical wisdom, and natural science, when it does not commit the error of confusing second-order with first-order facts. The opinion that *all* philosophical and ethical judgments are culturally relative is the result of the latter error.

Stated more precisely, therefore, natural law jurisprudence is the thesis that scientifically verified theory of the "is" of first-order facts provides the cognitive standard for measuring the goodness or badness of second-order artifacts. Thus just as sociological jurisprudence uses the scientifically verified theory of the "is" of the living law to judge both legislation and the cases of positive law, so natural law jurisprudence uses the empirically verified theory of the "is" of first-order facts to judge the goodness or badness of the living law.

Natural law jurisprudence recognizes, with sociological jurisprudence, that contemporary man observes the second-order facts of culture as well as the first-order facts of nature. It affirms, however, that it is possible and necessary, if a cognitive standard for judging and reforming the living law is to be found, to push the artifacts of culture aside and to use only first-order facts of nature and natural man in formulating and verifying a set of basic assumptions, which, since they do not derive from the "is" of the living law, can be used to judge and reform the living law.

Such a procedure is possible for two reasons. First, there was a time before human beings and, hence, before any culture. This would be impossible were there only cultural facts or were all facts culturally conditioned. Second, all science involves specialization. Specialization means neglecting certain facts to concentrate on others. Natural philosophy and its ethic are, therefore, both possible and scientific.

Additional distinctions are necessary if certain misconceptions are to be avoided. Natural law ethics is frequently described as the thesis that conduct and its fruits are good when they express "man's essential nature." Put this way, a difficulty arises. Since man's essential nature is what it is, how can man or anything else avoid expressing its essential nature? Clearly, unless one distinguishes two different senses of the "essential nature" of anything, there is no answer to this question. Not having made such a distinction, many critics have concluded that natural law ethics entails a *reductio ad absurdum*: Were it true, men would be good automatically and there would be no possibility, and hence no problem, of good or evil. We would be like the initial Adam and Eve in the Garden of Eden, entirely innocent of either good or evil in our natural behavior.

To meet this misconception, many defenders of natural law have fallen into the second misconception of supposing that this theory entails a teleological physics and metaphysics of becoming in which potential entities are being modified by their ideal final causes. Were this so, natural law philosophers, such as Hobbes and Locke, who do not affirm such a physics and metaphysics could not have an ethics. This is clearly false.

Both of these misconceptions evaporate when two additional distinctions are made: (1) between the essential nature of first-order facts *qua* fact and their essential nature *qua* theory, and (2) between (*a*) those natural entities whose behavior is completely the expression of their essential nature *qua* fact and (*b*) those natural entities whose judgments and behavior are in part at least the expression of what they think all first-order facts are *qua* theory. Stones are examples of natural entities whose behavior is completely the expression of their essential nature *qua* fact. This is the case because they do not have the capacity to frame theories of what they and other first-order facts are *qua* theory. Human beings are natural entities which have an essential nature both *qua* fact and *qua* theory. This is the case because they have the capacity to frame theories of their essential nature *qua* theory. This they do, when they proceed in a non-question-begging manner, by appeal to first-order facts alone.

The thesis of natural law ethics and jurisprudence, therefore, is not that any first-order natural entity is good if it expresses its essential nature *qua* fact. It is, instead, the thesis (1) that there are certain natural entities, namely human beings, whose judgments and behavior are in part at least the expression of what they think all first-order facts are *qua* theory,[30] and (2) that such judgments and behavior are good when the theory in question is true as tested empirically by reference solely to first-order facts *qua* fact.

Concretely what this means is that any person, confronted with the countless first-order facts from within and from without himself, selects, probably with hypothetical trial and error, certain facts as elementary and the key to the defining, remembering, ordering and anticipating of all the others. Then the explicit or implicit set of symbols or ideas, designating the totality of human knowledge as thus understood, constitutes that person's, or people's, system of meanings. To look at all the first-order facts which are taken thus as elementary and fundamental is to evaluate in the manner of natural law ethics. Consequently its evaluations are good or bad to the extent that its implicit or explicit set of meanings is true or false.

It is to be emphasized that the symbols can obtain their meaning by pointing to existential, intuitive factors such as a particular pain or passion as well as by axiomatically expressing formal, rationalistic relations. The contention that natural law theory is excessively rationalistic is, therefore, erroneous.

The question, also, whether first-order facts *qua* human theory entail a particular physics and metaphysics, or any metaphysics at all, is an empirical question for natural science to decide. In the days of Aristotle it seemed to do so. There is nothing, however, in the method of natural law ethics to require such a conclusion. Moreover, there is considerable evidence in contemporary mathematical physics to the contrary. All that natural law ethics requires or assumes in its method is that there is an empirically verified theory of first-order facts with some specific content.

The importance of the distinction between the essential nature of first-order facts *qua* fact and their essential nature *qua* theory is that, whereas first-order facts *qua* fact merely are and can be neither true or false nor good or bad, *theories* of first-order facts are true or false and hence may be in error. Consequently behavior which is in part at least the consequence of primitive assumptions concerning first-order facts *qua* theory may be in error also. This is why Adam and Eve had to eat of the tree of human knowledge and guide their behavior, in creating second-order artifacts, by this knowledge before there was any meaning for them to be, or know, good or evil. This meaning is that the second-order artifacts of human behavior are good or bad if the human theory guiding this behavior is true or false as tested empirically by appeal to the first-order facts of anyone's experience. Of three natural law theories with different theoretical content that one is the "best" which accounts for (1) all the first-order facts accounted for by the other two, and (2) additional first-order facts as well.

This definition of the "best" theory of first-order facts prescribes the two methods of natural law ethics. One proceeds through cultural anthropology and the comparative philosophy of the world's cultures and consists (a) in making explicit the implicit philosophy, or complex of philosophies, of each culture; (b) in seeking, in each culture, the first-order facts in anyone's experience which led its initial sages or scientists, and the people generally following their sages, to regard their particular philosophy as empirically verified; and (c) in specifying a single consistent set of assumptions which accounts for all the first-order facts at the basis of the traditional cultural philosophies. Procedure (b) rests on the assumption that no philosophy, or its ethic, ever captured a vast body of people unless it seemed to be required by specific first-order facts in their experience; that is, unless it was a natural law theory.[31] Procedure (b) may also guide one to first-order facts in one's own experience which our Western theories of natural science and philosophy have missed or neglected.[32]

The second method of natural law jurisprudence proceeds through the verified theory of first-order facts of contemporary natural science. Such theory is "best," in the sense defined above, because it takes into account facts never faced, and probably unexplained, by any previous philosophy of culture or nature. The procedure consists in making explicit, by philosophical analysis, the implicit theory of meanings and of mind which the verified theory contains. Any verified theory of first-order facts, even of introspected ones, focuses attention, as it comes from the natural scientist, on the object of knowledge. Nevertheless, any first-order theory, even Einstein's theory of the motion of a stone, tells us implicitly that the human mind is such that it can discover, construct and verify the type of conceptual and propositional meanings which the theory explicitly illustrates and contains. Consequently, the frequent assertion that the theory of natural science takes care of the object of knowledge to the neglect of the subject, its meanings and mind, is erroneous, provided, by philosophical analysis, its implicit theory of ideas and of mind is made explicit.

By combining the results of these two methods of natural law jurisprudence it should be possible to specify an empirically verified theory of first-order facts, including mind, which is scientifically truer than any traditional natural philosophy, in the sense that it (a) accounts for any first-order facts accounted for by any traditional theory and (b) is the only theory accounting for the first-order facts of all theories, including those of contemporary mathematical physics. This, to be sure, is a difficult, though not an impossible, undertaking. But one should not expect an easy solution of the problem of the cultural relativity of ethical values.

Such an approach through the comparative philosophy of culture and the philosophy of contemporary natural science is essential for two additional reasons. We are children of culture as well as nature. Second-order facts and their meanings not merely impress us daily, but are also built into our habits and personality structure. As sociological jurisprudence shows, to act as if tradition does not exist is to fail. Also the major influence transforming today's living law, the world over, is scientific technology. This transformation is as much a living law fact as is the traditional living law itself. Technology derives from the primitive concepts and the mentality of mathematical physics. Hence only by combining the explicitly stated philosophical assumptions of both approaches can sociological jurisprudence make its own contemporary subject matter intelligible or find the standard for measuring what to preserve and what to modify in that subject matter.

It remains to specify the distinction between "good" and "ought" in natural law ethics. "Good" is the name for the empirically verifiable theory of first-order facts when this theory is taken as the theoretical standpoint for guiding human behavior and evaluating its artifacts. The "good," therefore, is not a primitive concept, but is a predicate, applicable only to second-order artifacts, that is defined in terms of scientifically true theory of first-order facts. "Ought" is the *for-me-ness* of such theory. The making of a true theory mine occurs when, by appeal to first-order facts which are *mine*, I find the theory to be empirically verified *by* or *for me*. In short, goodness calls merely for empirically verified theory of first-order facts, whereas oughtness requires in addition the for-me-ness, by way of discovery, or rediscovery, and verification, of that truth.

Natural law ethics, because of its distinction between first- and second-order facts, and its thesis that second-order facts are the deposit, by way of art, of implicit or explicit theories of first-order facts, entails sociological jurisprudence and its living law. The living law, however, with its second-order facts can bring its inner norms to bear in deciding concrete disputes, especially in a technological law of contract society, only if its inner order is given operational definition in terms of a positive constitution, a bill of rights, legislative statutes and positive legal procedures. Hence, just as understanding of legal positivism leads to sociological jurisprudence, which in turn leads to natural law jurisprudence, so the latter needs first the living law of sociological jurisprudence and then the positive law of legal positivism to make itself effective.

XXI

The Method for Judging the Living Law

IN the previous chapters the important distinction was drawn between first-order and second-order facts. Theoretically considered, first-order facts *qua* fact are what they are independently of the beliefs of men and hence are the same in all cultures. For example, the immediately sensed sequence of lightness and darkness which we call natural day and night comes when and where it comes regardless of the beliefs of men. Second-order facts vary from culture to culture and within any culture from person to person as the beliefs of men vary. A Hindu temple, for example, is quite different in both its physical form and its religious function from a Quaker meeting-house. Likewise, the law of status codes of Manu, which specify the norms of the living law of ancient Aryan Hindu India, are different from the liberal democratic anti-patriarchal and anti-caste positive legal rules of the Constitution of present Free India and of the new living law in accord with this Constitution which the present political leaders of India are trying to bring into being. Clearly these two quite different second-order facts express two similarly different cultural philosophies. Empirically considered, facts of the first order are the subject matter of the natural sciences, whereas those of the second order are the subject matter of the social sciences, history and the humanities generally.

Scientific method applies to both types of facts. When referred to facts of the first order, the theories of natural science and their epistemological and operational criteria of the cognitively meaningful result. In any culture, and also in the case of empirical scientists in different cultures, the application of empirical scientific methods to the same first-order facts *qua* fact may result, and does in fact result, in different empirically testable theories. For example, Einstein's theory of the first-order facts of mechanics differs from Newton's; as the empirical theory of the first-order facts of chemistry of the Charvakian materialistic scientists of ancient India differs from the theory of these same first-order facts of Gibbs or of Dirac. Nevertheless, theory in natural science is significantly true or false, and hence cognitive, because, the first-order facts *qua* facts of natural science being what they are and where they are independently of man's theory about them, there are always non-question-begging facts to which to appeal to test any theory.

With respect, however, to different normative theories of the goal values which define the good and the just for second-order facts, an appeal to such facts to test rival normative theories, say the Hindu patriarchal theory of caste or the secular liberal democratic theory, is question-begging. This is the case because the second-order facts themselves, for example the Hindu temples and patriarchal and caste customs, are what they are because of the people's belief in one of the theories being tested. This is why the culturalistic fallacy referred to in Chapter XIX is a fallacy.

Suppose, however, that the reason for belief in the goodness and justice of patriarchalism and caste, upon the part of the sages and social leaders who initiated this specific second-order factual normative community, was an empirically testable theory which they held concerning first-order facts in the natural science of genetics and in the cognitive science of epistemology. Suppose also that the reason why the first formulators of the secular liberal democratic normative theory of the good and the just for second-order facts believed this normative theory to be the correct one because of a different theory in the cognitive sciences of genetics and epistemology concerning first-order facts. In short, suppose any normative theory which defines the good and the just for second-order facts contains within itself explicit or implicit premises which are empirically confirmable statements about first-order facts. Then by bringing out the latter first-order factual theoretical premises of any second-order factual normative theory, one would have the empirical and cognitive scientific method for putting any normative theory and the descriptive norms of any particular living law community to a non-question-begging empirical test. One would merely have to devise some crucial experiment with respect to first-order facts which would enable anyone to decide whether the theoretical first-order factual premises of normative second-order factual theory (A) or those of second-order fact theory (B) are the empirically confirmed premises. In short, one would have a cognitive method for judging and reforming any living law and for scientifically deciding between rival ideological and cultural theories of goal values.

It is the purpose of this chapter to show that this is the case. We shall attempt to do so by examining specific, incompatible legal and cultural philosophies. By way of preparation, consideration of some further concrete implications of the distinction between first-order and second-order facts is advisable.

Without this distinction the difference between physics and the history of art in any particular culture would not be clear; also within anthropology, the difference between physical anthropology and cultural anthropology would have no empirical or theoretical meaning. Since anthropology is the science of man, the distinction between its physical and its cultural branches reminds us that the difference between first-order and second-order facts applies to the science of psychology also. To the extent that the observable and experimentally determined facts of human nature are independent of the beliefs of human beings about either themselves or other things, psychological facts are of the first order. To the extent, however, that they are a function of (a) the beliefs of a particular person concerning himself and his universe, or (b) the living-law norms and philosophical beliefs of the culture in which a person is located, the facts of psychology are of the second order. It is because so many of the psychological characteristics of human beings are facts of the second order that comparative studies in cultural anthropology and the comparative philosophy of the world's cultures have shown personality structure and the normative "pattern of a culture" to be essentially connected.

That any human being has a nervous system is a first-order psychological fact. That a specific human being, say Judge Learned Hand, delivers the Holmes Lectures in the Harvard Law School in 1958 in which he affirms the psychological theory of ethics of William James and the positivistic theory of law of Thayer and Austin and then proceeds to interpret the Bill of Rights in the light of this ethical and legal philosophy is a psychological fact of the second order. Similarly, that there are biological animals called "cows" is a first-order fact, the same for Hindu Indians as for Americans. That the orthodox Hindus have a religious belief which prompts them frequently to slay anyone who kills a cow or a bull, whereas the Mexicans are transported into frenzied raptures of ecstasy over the slaying of such animals in a bull fight and most North Americans experience pleasure, rather than sacrilegiously laden irritation and pain, over the eating of a juicy beefsteak — these are second-order psychological facts.

Likewise, it is a first-order fact that any person in any culture directly inspects colors, sounds, odors, flavors, pains, pleasures and the images of dreams. The theory or belief, however, in terms of which a given person or a group of people in a single normatively homogeneous living law culture conceive of the relation of these first-order facts to their conception of themselves and of objects and events in nature is a second-order psychological and epistemological fact. The people may, for example, believe, as do all radical empiricists, such as Hume, William James, Judge Learned Hand, the nihilistic Mahayana Buddhists and the non-dualistic Vedanta Hindus, that only words referring to nothing but such directly inspected sensuous qualities and images are meaningful. Forthwith, all normative words are required to find their meaning solely in terms of such immediately experienced first-order facts. Also, all systems of belief which refer the aforementioned sensed qualities to supposedly external persisting common-sense objects or to persisting determinate substantial selves are regarded as words about the meaningless. Such a radically empirical belief, in both its positive and its negative implications, is a second-order fact.

Suppose, on the other hand, as Chapter XV has shown to be the case, for all systems whose living law is that of the law of status, the sensed first-order qualities given empirically are referred to the external common-sense objects which they seem to qualify and that introspected pains, pleasures and the images of dreams are referred to a determinate, substantial self or mental substance. Then one has the system of beliefs of a naïve realistic epistemology and a dualistic body-mind ontology. This belief system also is a second-order fact. Under such a naïve realistic type of purported meaningfulness, it becomes possible and natural to identify good and just man with directly sensed color-of-skin biologically bred familial and tribal man.

Thus, for people with such a purely naïve realistic epistemological mentality, the ethics of a law of biological status seems to be a scientifically meaningful theory of *the* good and *the* just living and positive law.

Let us suppose, also, that in the biological theory of such a people their empirical scientists came to the conclusion, as was the case in ancient Greece and Rome, that the genetic traits of people are transmitted to the next generation only by the male, the female serving merely as a receptacle. Then, since it is assumed that such naïve realistic biological concepts with respect to sex and to breeding define the good and the just, it follows that a good and just political and legal system must locate all responsibilities for administering the law and the affairs of the family and of the political community in its male members. Thereby justice and goodness take on the normative content of not merely a law of biological status, but also a patriarchal kinship society. In this connection the following quotation from Aeschylos' *Eumenides* and the conclusions reached by C. W. Westrup in his study of the *Patria Potestas* in his *Introduction to Early Roman Law* are interesting:

> "The mother of what is called her child is not its parent, but only the nurse of the newly implanted germ. The begetter is the parent. She, a stranger, doth but preserve the little creature, except God shall blight its birth." In the Syro-Roman Lawbook (5th century B.C.) the inferior position of women in the law relating to inheritance is directly traceable to the doctrine of Greek natural philosophy that the power of procreation is present in the father alone. The mother merely protects and nourishes the seed, as does the earth the seed sown in it.[1]

We now know, however, from contemporary experimentally verified genetic theory that the foregoing theory of the relative contributions of the male and the female to the determination of the inherited traits of children is false. Both sexes make their contribution to the genetic characteristics of the offspring. Since the living law of any patriarchal, law of biological status society rests on the experimentally testable scientific theory that only the male is significant genetically, we now have scientifically verified cognitive reasons which permit us to judge the living law of any patriarchal law of status community to be a false second-order factual ethical, political and legal state of affairs since the theory of first-order genetic facts which it assumes as the justification for its specific norms is false. This is the case, moreover, regardless of whether or not, in a particular society, such as early Filmerian seventeenth-century England or the present living law of the Old South,[2] a majority of the people believe in and practice normative Christian patriarchalism. In other words, by appeal to experimentally verified theory of the first-order facts of human experience, it is now possible to show that the particular theory of these first-order facts which defines the good and the just for the second-order living-law customs of any patriarchal law of status society is a false theory. For the same reason, this is true also of any matriarchal law of status society.

The naïve realistic epistemological assumption of any law of status community can be shown to be equally false. As the founders of Democritean and Platonic and of modern mathematical physics have shown, and as the ancient Oriental Mahayana Buddhists and the non-dualistic Vedantists showed before them, all sensed qualities or introspected images, whether they be the so-called primary or the so-called secondary or tertiary qualities, are relative not merely to the percipient but to the different sense organs of the same percipient. Witness the sensed "water" which is sensed as hot by a right hand that has come to it from a cake of ice and which is sensed as cold by the left hand which comes to it from the room's over-all temperature. Clearly, as shown in Chapter XVI, objects which purport, as the realism of the naïve realistic epistemology affirms, to possess scientific properties which exist independently of their relation to the perceiver cannot be defined in terms of directly sensed properties which are relative to the perceiver and to his sense organs. Hence the living law of a people whose beliefs concerning the first-order facts of nature and of human nature require a naïve realistic epistemology for their meaningfulness and cognitive justification is an inner order, or pattern, of second-order facts whose cognitive justification is self-contradictory, and hence false. Again, this is the case regardless of whether or not a majority of the people in the culture in question believe in and practice such a theory.

Put more concretely, the considerations of the previous paragraph mean that both Asian and Western epistemological analysis shows that any living law which, in the substantive content of its normative rules and non-normative beliefs, identifies the scientific defining

properties of either atoms or human beings with sensed qualities expresses a false theory. This is the case because all sensed qualities and
images are relative to the percipient and to the percipient's different
sense organs and to the particular perishing momentary occasion and
are, consequently, an accidental accompanying effect of, but not an
essential defining property of either an inorganic scientific object or a
human being. Hence any living law which identifies the essential —
that is, the scientific defining — properties of a person with his
sensed effects upon the observer and forthwith makes goodness and
justice a function of the color of skin of the person being evaluated is
a false second-order factual theory of first-order facts.

In short, both (1) contemporary experimental genetics and (2)
classical Oriental and classical and contemporary Western epistemological analysis provide cognitive criteria for judging the second-
order facts of any law of status society to be "false" and, in this sense,
bad. The second-order facts of such a living law are bad and unjust
because they rest on a theory of genetics and an epistemological theory
of the relation between sensed qualities and the defining properties
of knowable objects which is false. The foregoing conclusion applies
to any law of status society which rests on a patriarchal or matriarchal
genetics. Examples are (1) the Christian Filmerian patriarchalism
of early seventeenth-century England and of the First Families of
Virginia and the Old South; (2) the German *Herrenvolk* of Hitler's
frenzied living law Germans; (3) the color of skin tribal patriarchalism of the African ancestors of contemporary American Negroes; (4)
the high caste patriarchalism of the right-wing contemporary orthodox Hindu Brahmans of North India; and (5) the law of status
matriarchalism of the southern orthodox Hindus of Cochin-Travin-
core Province in South India.

This conclusion applies equally also, though for epistemological,
rather than genetic, scientific reasons, to any living law which embodies the beliefs of a naïve realistic epistemology. Examples are (1)
Aristotelian and Thomistic living law and natural law jurisprudence;
(2) Marxist naïve realistic materialistic Communism; (3) the essen-
tialist "mode of being" in Professor Paul Weiss' contemporary naïve
realistic ontology (fortunately his existential mode of being avoids
this error); or (4) the intuitive theory of ethics and law when
coupled with G. E. Moore's "common-sense" realism.

It appears, therefore, that our method for judging the living law provides a clear cognitive criterion for affirming some of the living law of the contemporary world to be bad and unjust. What, however, does this method have to say about the substantive content of the good and the just new positive law which is the criterion for creating a new good and just living law to replace the old?

This is too big a question to answer here. Two suggestions of previous chapters, which have been developed more fully elsewhere,[3] can, however, be noted. One has to do with the radically empirical epistemology of nihilistic Mahayana Buddhism, unqualified non-dualistic Vedanta Hinduism and modern British empirical philosophy. The other concerns the "constructs" of Western mathematical physics which are now captivating and being mastered by the ablest Oriental minds.

As noted at the end of Chapter XVI, both (1) the classical Oriental and the modern radical empiricists and (2) the Western mathematical physicists reached the conclusion that a naïve realistic epistemology with its supposedly common-sense external objects that are defined in terms of directly sensed qualities is a false theory of scientific knowledge. Hence it is a false basis for the substantive definition of the good and the just in the man-made second-order facts which are the world's legal, political and social institutions and First Constitutions. Thus, the Buddha, though of the second Hindu caste, unqualifiedly rejected the ethics of caste. Similarly no modern British empiricist, to the writer's knowledge, affirms a law of biological status patriarchal or matriarchal ethics or law. Similarly the Stoic Roman lawyers, influenced by the concepts and epistemological philosophy of Greek mathematical physics, initiated the legal and social shift from status to contract. Nevertheless, between (1) the Oriental and Western radically empirical epistemologists and (2) the Western mathematical physicists and Roman Stoic lawyers, all of whom reject naïve realism and the ethics of the law of status, there was one very important difference. As indicated in Chapter XVII, the classical Western mathematical physicists and the Stoic Roman lawyers discovered a new type of cognitively meaningful concept which many scholars today call a "construct" and which the writer has called a "concept by postulation which is a concept by intellection" [4] because its meaning is given without recourse to any images, whether of the outer senses or of the imagination. The importance of the discovery of this new type of cognitively meaningful scientific concept is that it provides determinate, objective and lawful knowledge which may escape relativity to different percipients and to the different sense organs of the same percipient. Ethically and legally it also makes the shift possible from status to contract.

The classical Oriental and the modern Western radical empiricists failed either to make this discovery or to appreciate its significance for epistemology and for normative subjects after the discovery had been made by the mathematical physicists. The consequence was that the Oriental radical empiricists, having discovered the self-contradictory and hence illusory character of naïve realistic epistemological thinking and its ethics, were forced to find the "first-best" ethic which was to supplement the "second-best" ethic of their previous law of status customs and codes, within the meaningfulness provided by radically empirical immediacy alone. The result was that they discovered that factor in the continuum of radically empirical immediacy which remains when all its relativistic, transitory, sensed and imageful differentiations are abstracted away. What remains is the undifferentiated continuum of immediacy itself, which the Buddhist calls "Nirvana" and the Vedantist terms "Brahman" or the "chit" consciousness and which the writer called, in Chapter XVI, the "undifferentiated aesthetic continuum." This common cognitive factor, being undifferentiated, cannot be said either in propositions or in legal codes. It can merely be experienced with immediacy when, by Zen Buddhist, Yogic or other experimental psychological methods, all its imageful differentiations are as far as possible removed. Nevertheless, because it is an immediately experienceable factor common to all determinate human experiences and disputes, it provides a common item in human experience, the same for all disputants, to which appeal can be made in the settling of any dispute. Thus the normative prescription arose with the Confucian, Buddhist and Gandhian non-Aryan Hindu Oriental moralists that the superior moral man does not settle a difference with his adversary by recourse to litigation and its law of status codes, but instead brings out the common, inexpressible man-to-manness of the disputants (which Confucius called *jen*) by recourse to mediation.

The reader will have to examine radically empirical immediacy

for himself to determine whether this radically empirical undifferentiated continuum of immediacy is a first-order fact. Elsewhere reasons have been given for believing that it is.[5] In any event one thing
is clear. According to this radically empirical theory of first-order
facts there is one factor in any radically empirically known natural
object or human being which is the same for all, namely the all-
embracing, undifferentiated field consciousness in its indeterminate
formlessness. Consequently, according to this field theory of first-
order facts, all human beings are, in their elemental, irreducible
selves, not merely equal but identical. It follows that any positive
and living legal community which is compatible, therefore, with this
theory of first-order facts would seem to be one which is egalitarian
in its most primitive and basic criterion of the good and the just, and
in which each person is intuitively sensitive emotively to the different relative radically empirical determinate feelings of all other creatures. Put negatively, this radically empirical common factor in human experience requires for its cognitive recognition and practical
expression an ethics of personal conduct in which if I completely
deny or condemn everything about another person, his undifferentiated as well as his differentiated deeds and consciousness, I in part
deny and condemn myself. Such is the first suggestion of our method
for prescribing a new positive and living law which is good and just
to replace the positive and living law of status which the method con-
demns. This positive constructive suggestion of our method for
measuring norms has the merit of finding something in the old living
law and positive legal procedures of Asia which is good and just.

The constructs of Western mathematical physics and the new type
of cognitive meaningfulness which they provide for the solution of
normative questions are equally significant in giving us positive substantive content for defining a new positive domestic and international law and a reformed living law which is good and just in the
sense of the method of this chapter. The discovery of concepts by
formal axiomatic postulation which are concepts by intellection, made
first by the Greek mathematical physicists, had, as Chapter XVII has
shown, its effect upon the Roman lawyers who created the novel type
of legal concepts which make the legal science of the West unique.
The essential point in the discovery of this new type of cognitive concept is that it provides a meaning for the scientific definition of a sci-

entific object and its laws without any recourse to the images of the senses or of the imagination. Thereby it provided a means of obtaining determinate, publicly valid propositional meanings which are the same for all human beings. The heart of the technique of constructing such cognitive concepts centers in the laying of imageless, merely formal, logical or mathematical properties on the relations between otherwise undefined entities, in such a way that the axiomatically and formally constructed relations define laws governing the related individuals which hold universally for any individual whatever which instances the entity variables of the theory.

Applied to ethics and to law, this theory of cognitive meaningfulness gives the normative concept that moral man and just man is cosmopolitan, or universal, or catholic man — that is, any human individual person whatever standing equally with any other human being as a term in a contractually constructed universal law to which each party to the contract has implicitly or explicitly given his consent. By the legal means of these contractually and axiomatically proposed constructs, such as those which are expressed in (*a*) the Declaration of Independence, the Federal Constitution of the United States and its Bill of Rights, (*b*) the present constitutions of Free India and Burma or (*c*) the new legal and political institutions of Continental European Union, men who do not know one another empirically and who have no person-to-person, genetically or tribally defined relations with one another can, nonetheless, build a common living law community, a common political nation and a common positive legal system. Moreover, with this law of constructs freely consented to, beliefs, even utopian beliefs, rather than codes which purport merely to describe the sensed facts of biological breeding and primogeniture of status, really matter.

In other words, as men become convinced epistemologically and cognitively that sensed qualities are accidental rather than essential properties of truly known objects, naïve realistic thinking and its sensuous color-of-skin ethics of familial or tribally bred status begins to lose its initial plausibility. Furthermore, as man in his theories of natural science comes to think of first-order facts about himself and nature in genetics, psychology, astronomy or terrestrial mechanics, in terms of formally constructed cognitive concepts which are the concepts by postulation of universally quantified laws, the possibility is open to the human mind and to its normative imagination of ordering human relations normatively by such conceptual means. Since, moreover, such normative proposals are axiomatically introduced, and in this sense utopian, consent is of the essence so far as obligation to be measured by them is concerned, as the previous chapter has shown, and with respect to consent to any hypothetically constructed contract, all parties are born free and equal. In short, to be aware of the existence of cognitively meaningful constructs and their universally quantified rules for ethics, law and politics is to realize that the statement of the American Declaration of Independence to the effect that all men are born free and equal before the law is a cognitive proposition in the epistemology of concepts by postulation and in the law of contract, and not a proposition in biology.

Such is the way in which (1) the distinction between first-order and second-order facts and (2) the two cognitively meaningful epistemological species of concepts for thinking about first-order facts and normatively ordering second-order facts prescribes the method of judging and reforming the living law. With this conclusion our problematic approach to the complexity of contemporary legal, political and ethical experience comes to its end. What we have achieved, if anything, is a suggestion of the reasons why the recent theories and methods in these normative subjects fall short and why the particular naturalistic method indicated in this chapter may meet the most basic and pressing problem of contemporary value theory generally. This problem is: How does one evaluate goal, or intrinsic, values? In other words, what is the cognitively meaningful and operationally practical method for judging the living law?

It remains to put the method of this chapter into graphical analytic form by giving its matrix specific substantive content. Then several important implications for both national and international law will become evident.

XXII

Some Domestic and International
Legal Implications

THE scientific method for evaluating (as distinct from merely describing) ethical, legal and political norms was specified in the previous chapter. In 1947, in an article in *Social Science* [1] which was reprinted as Chapter XXI in *The Logic of the Sciences and the Humanities*, the writer gave an analytical graph of this method. This graph is reprinted again here as Diagram II. It is now possible to make its skeletal form take on a little more of the flesh and blood of a living and effective instrument which has considerable domestic and international legal and political import. To make this evident, let us identify Normative Theories A and B in Diagram II with two specific theories of legal and ethical experience which the previous chapters have described.

For Normative Social Theory A and its epistemological and other cognitive premises of *xRyz* in Diagram II, substitute the patriarchal theory of heredity and its epistemological premise of naïve realism, i.e., the basic cognitive assumptions concerning first-order facts of a patriarchal law of status society. Let Normative Theory B in Diagram II be identified with the following complex theory: (1) The ethics and law of the most basic cognitive concept common to Confucian, Buddhist and Hindu cultures. (2) The ethics of the law of contract as formulated initially by the Stoic Roman lawyers and philosophers and given modern legal and political expression in the three major earlier treatises of John Locke,[2] in the American Declaration of Independence and in the legally conceived Bill of Rights of the Constitution of the United States. (3) The compatibility of (1) and (2), as shown in Chapter XI.[3]

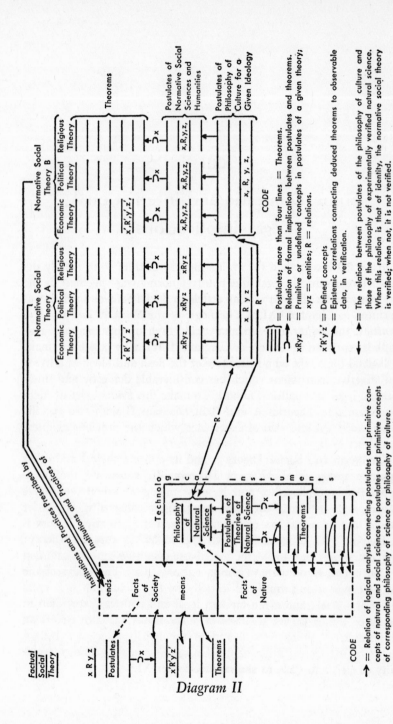

DIAGRAM OF THE RELATION BETWEEN FACTUAL SOCIAL THEORY, NORMATIVE SOCIAL THEORY AND NATURAL SCIENTIFIC THEORY

Diagram II

Analysis of Normative Theory B gives the following non-normative cognitive premises: Premise (1): Any radically empirically known person is not merely his differentiated immediately experienced self, which varies from one person to another and perishes, but also his all-embracing indeterminate field consciousness self. Premise (2): The scientifically known person, like any other scientifically known individual entity, is also a directly unobservable, theoretically known individual which is an instance of an imageless formal and constitutively constructed and procedurally defined determinate universal law. Premise (3): The complete first order factual cognitive (i.e., scientifically known) person is the epistemic and ontological correlation of the two components of personality specified in Premises (1) and (2). Premise (2) assumes also the epistemological thesis that there are the imageless concepts by postulation (the formal constructs and incomplete symbols of Chapter III) of a logically realistic epistemology of first-order facts, as well as the nominalistic concepts by intuition * of a radically empirical epistemology.

Applied to ethics and law, the assumption of the cognitive truth of Premise (1) of Normative Theory B gives the thesis that all human beings and all other natural objects in their intrinsic nature (as distinct from their accidental sensuous *esse est percipi* effects upon the observer) are not merely equal, but also identical. This is why, as shown in Chapter XI, the most basic beliefs and practices of the living law of classical Confucian, Buddhist or non-dualistic Vedanta Hindu Asian societies, though different, are compatible with the contractual morality and law of a modern, freely democratic society.

Applied to ethics and law, cognitive Premise (2) of Normative Theory B gives the following criterion of the ethically good and the legally just. For any person p, for any object of *intrinsic* (goal value as distinct from instrumental value) normative judgment x and for any substantive content s of either personal conduct or the living or positive law, to say that s of x is morally good and legally just is equivalent to saying that:

(i) x is in accord with a concept by postulation contractually constructed, determinate law L, which is universal in the sense that the

---

* A concept by intuition is one whose entire meaning refers to something immediately experienced with radically empirical directness. See Chapter V of *The Logic of the Sciences and the Humanities.*

law holds for all persons, i.e., is preceded by, to use the language of symbolic logic, the universal quantifier (p), where (p) means "for any one person whatever."

(ii) The substantive content s of this universal law (p) L is such that if its substantive content s confers specified rights, privileges and duties upon one person, or one group of people p, then any other person or group of persons whatever must enjoy the same specified *intrinsic* normative rights, privileges and duties; that is, not merely the law as a whole must be preceded by the universal quantifier (p) but also the substantive content s within the law must be accompanied by a second universal quantifier (p).

(iii) Being postulationally and contractually constructed, and hence merely hypothetical, the validity of any (p) L in which (p) s must rest on free implicit or explicit consent of the parties concerned.

(iv) There are the concepts by formal imageless postulation of a logical (as distinct from a naïve) realistic epistemology.

The italicized word *intrinsic* in the criterion given by Premise (2) when applied to ethics and law is important. It signifies that Requirements (i), (ii) and (iii) apply only to goal values and not to instrumental values, thereby not outlawing a division of labor for instrumental values with respect to which the skills of all human beings may not be equal.

Requirement (i) gives the formal lawfulness of Kant's categorical imperative as usually interpreted due perhaps to Kant's, and certainly to his critics', failure to specify unmistakably whether the substantive content within the law as well as the law itself considered as a whole has to be universally quantified for all persons. Requirement (i) *alone* permits law of contract to be filled in, quite inconsistently, with naïve realistic epistemological law of status, color of skin, tribal and first familial religious, moral, social and political content.

The living social and educational customs and positive state law of the Southern States of the United States, when combined with their acceptance of its Federal Constitution, is an instance of trying to interpret that document and its Bill of Rights, against the Southerners' own Jefferson, Madison and Marshall, as meaning Premise (2) of Normative Theory B with Requirement (i) but without (ii) and also, so far as Negroes in the South are concerned, without Requirement (iii). The issue between the elder Southern politicians today and the unanimous decisions of the Justices of the Supreme Court of the United States is precisely this.

As shown in the previous chapter, this inconsistent combination of the law of contract and its concept by postulation epistemology with the law of status content of a naïve realistic epistemology characterized Western contractual law, both Protestant and Roman Catholic Christian, Jewish and Islamic, following the fragmentation [4] of Stoic Roman Europe. It also characterizes in considerable part the living law and much of the positive law of most religions, nations and peoples today, especially those of Africa, Israel, Islam and Shinto Japan as well as caste India, and the positive and living law of the Old South in the United States. In the European and Pan-American West, Aristotle, St. Thomas, Hooker and Sir Robert Filmer, with their naïve realistic epistemologies and their patriarchalism, were undoubtedly in major part responsible, as the medieval Jewish and Arab Aristotelians were in Spain, Israel and Islam.

In any event, following the decline of the influence of the Stoic Roman lawyers and philosophers, it was only with the rejection of the naïve realistic epistemology by modern mathematical physicists such as Galilei, Descartes, Newton, Leibniz, Kant, Einstein and Heisenberg and with the influence of Bacon, Newton and Locke on Jefferson * that a serious attempt was again made to fill in law of contract statutes and political constitutions with concept by postulation formally contractual, rather than naïve realistic sensuous law of biological status content. Thereby the attempt was made to carry out consistently the cognitive epistemological Requirement (iv) of Premise (2) above of the law of contract and its ethic, while meeting also Requirements (i) and (iii). The result was the Declaration of Independence, which Jefferson wrote, and the addition to the first draft of the Federal Constitution of the United States of the legal Bill of Rights upon which he insisted.

The ethic of the law of contract, let it be recalled, is that cognitive, truly known man is not naïve realistic epistemological, color of skin, tribal and first familial religious, moral and political man, but is instead, as the Stoic Roman lawyers first realized, universal,

---

* This is what Jefferson meant when, in a letter to Dr. Benjamin Rush dated January 16, 1811, he referred to "Bacon, Newton and Locke" as "my trinity of the three greatest men the world had ever produced." [5]

cosmopolitan or catholic human being, whether man or woman. The importance of Requirement (ii) in Premise (2) of Normative Theory B above is that it insures this thesis.

Requirement (ii) is also necessary to warrant any United States Federal Court's rejecting majority passed legislation. Furthermore, without Requirement (ii) Locke's and Jefferson's religious and civil liberties, which even democratic legal and political governments cannot take away from the individual, are left legally and culturally unprotected. In other words, Requirement (ii) of Premise (2) is the criterion which distinguishes the Lockean living law of Great Britain, as described in Chapter X, and the Lockean positive and living law of the United States as a whole from the following forms of democracy: (a) The merely positive legal system of Great Britain in which, following Hobbes and Austin, rather than Locke and Jefferson, political sovereignty is left undivided [6] and hence is located entirely in the legislative branch, with no judicial review of acts of the House of Commons and with the executive merely the leader of the majority party in the legislative branch without the veto power over its majority approved statutes which Presidents of the United States exercise. (b) The Rousseauian type of democracy of even pre-Communist modern Continental Europe, in which justice is similarly identified with the social will of the majority.[7] (c) The aforementioned Filmerian democracy of the social customs of the Old South in the United States, in which law of contract universal laws are filled in with the patriarchal Christian early seventeenth-century English law of status content which is described in Sir Robert Filmer's *Patriarcha*.[8] (d) The "People's Democracy," i.e., "the dictatorship of the proletariat" democracy of the Marxist Communists. In short, Requirement (ii) is the differentiating criterion of (1) Stoic Roman law of contract cosmopolitan democracy, (2) the American Lockean and Jeffersonian Declaration of Independence and its legally interpreted Bill of Rights democracy and (3) the democracy of the living, but not the positive, law of Great Britain's unwritten constitution.

So much for the cognitive and normative premises and their legal, political and other cultural consequences when postulates of x_1 R_1 y_1 z_1 of Normative Social Theory B in Diagram II are given the content specified by Premises (1) and (2) (i), (ii), (iii) and (iv) above. The "cultural consequences" of Normative Theory B appear as the second-order facts at the end of the top arrow in the upper left-hand portion of Diagram II. The segregated educational and other social customs of the Old South in the United States exemplify the second-order facts at the end of the lower arrow from Normative Theory A, when interpreted as democratic rather than theocratic Filmerianism.

It remains to relate Normative Theories A and B, when given the respective content described above, to the lower left-hand portion of Diagram II and to follow the rules prescribed there and in the previous chapter for determining whether the second-order living law facts at the end of the top arrow from Normative Theory B, or those at the end of the lower arrow from Normative Theory A, are the cognitively true or false ones. In short: Is the Supreme Court's judgment in the desegregation cases, which requires Normative Theory B for its cognitive validity, or the Southern elder politicians' position, which requires Normative Theory A for its cognitive validity, the cognitively correct one?

The method prescribed by Diagram II is to compare the respective cognitive assumption $x_1 R_1 y_1 z_1$ of Normative Theory B and $x R y z$ of Normative Theory A with the natural scientists' and first-order factual psychologists' scientifically verified theory of the first-order naturalistic facts of the lower left-hand portion of Diagram II, when the latter theory has been philosophically analyzed to bring out its cognitive epistemological and other theoretical assumptions. That Normative Theory (and its second-order facts) in the central portion of Diagram II is the cognitively true one, if its cognitive epistemological and other theoretical assumptions are identical or compatible with those of the empirically confirmed naturalistic theory of first-order facts in the lower left-hand portion of Diagram II. That Normative Theory is the false one which is either self-contradictory or incompatible with the natural scientists' verified theory of first-order facts and its analytically determined cognitive epistemological and other assumptions.

The contemporary experimentally verified theories of first-order facts are those of Einstein, Planck, Schrödinger and Heisenberg. Philosophical analysis of these theories gives the following result: Even though some analysts initially believed the contrary, it is now agreed by recent scientists and philosophers such as Einstein, Carnap, Reichenbach, Margenau, Nagel, Hempel, Pap and the writer that the empirically verified theories of Western mathematical physics require (1) the concepts by intuition of a radically empirical epistemology in (3) epistemic correlation with (2) the formally constructed, universally quantified laws and scientific objects of a concept by postulation, or axiomatically constructed, epistemology.[9] The latter is precisely the kind of epistemology which Normative Theory B, as interpreted above, assumes and requires. This theory is, therefore, cognitively verified.

What of Normative Theory A? As shown in Chapter XV, its naïve realistic epistemological premise is self-contradictory. Hence, it is cognitively false on purely logical grounds. Furthermore, the naïve realistic epistemological science of Aristotle and of classical Asia lacks the assumptions and the deductive fertility necessary to account for the radically empirical observable experimental data. Hence, when put to a more rigorous observational and experimental test, it turns out to be false also on empirical grounds.

We conclude, therefore, as follows with respect to the desegregation cases in the recent domestic law of the United States. First, the unanimous decisions of the Justices of the Supreme Court in these cases are the cognitively verifiable correct judgments. Second, the position of some of the elder Southern governors, such as Governor Faubus of Arkansas and Governor Almond of Virginia, is the cognitively verifiable false position. Third, the thesis of Judge Learned Hand that the Justices should have kept their hands off these cases because the unified Hobbesian federal legislative political sovereign (Congress) has not issued a command to be used by the Federal Courts to declare in the matter is empirically and cognitively false for three reasons.

(a) It requires the legal positivists' philosophy of law for its validity. Let us call this philosophy Normative Theory C. This theory, because of its radically empirical epistemology, is valid so far as Premise (1) of the cognitively verified Normative Theory B is concerned. It is, however, quite incapable of providing the meanings of legal language in any modern contractual legal and political system. For this the concepts by postulation of Requirement (iv) of Premise (2) of Normative Theory B are necessary. Because, as just noted, the epistemology of first-order facts of the latter theory is the cognitively verified one, it follows that Judge Hand's interpretation of the Con-

stitution of the United States and its Bill of Rights, which requires
the restriction of the meaning of legal words to concepts solely of the
radically empirical type, is cognitively false.

(b) Judge Hand's opinion assumes, following the legal positivism
of Hobbes and the English jurist Austin and the American Thayer,
that the American democratic legal and political system is like the
positive legal system of Great Britain which, keeping political sovereignty undivided as prescribed by Hobbes, places the whole of it
in the legislative branch; whereas, in fact, the American legal system
is one in which, following Locke and Jefferson rather than Hobbes,
political sovereignty is divided, thereby producing a democracy of
checks and balances in which the independently elected executive can
veto the majority approved legislative commands for any reason he
chooses to give * and the courts in judicial review can declare any
majority approved legislative statute to be unconstitutional if its
substantive content is incompatible with the substantive content of
the Bill of Rights, i.e., is incompatible with Requirement (ii) in
Premise (2) of Normative Theory B above.

Judge Hand himself tells us that he (and he believes Holmes, too)
is a legal positivist, "so strictly Austinian." [10] He tells us also, in his
article in Volume LVII of the *Columbia Law Review* (1946) entitled "Chief Justice Stone's Concept of the Judicial Function," that
his (Judge Hand's) legal philosophy entails the "notion . . . that
the Bill of Rights could not be treated like ordinary law; its directions were to be understood rather as admonitions to forbearance." [11]
A page later, in accepting and describing his critics' conception of
this "notion," he adds that it is "an abdication of the admitted premise that the Bill of Rights was law, and not merely a counsel of perfection and an ideal of temperance; always to be kept in mind, it is
true, but whose infractions were to be treated only as matter for re-
gret." Two pages earlier Judge Hand tells us that this conception of
the American legal system was not the original one, but was instead
a "new approach" which did not become influential until the 1920's,
of which "at Harvard, Thayer had already become the prophet."
Thayer began his professorship at the Harvard Law School in 1873
and died in 1902. It is this Thayerian-Austinian and Hobbesian

* Why Judge Hand does not turn this also into a deceptive red herring
called "the introduction of a fourth legislature," he fails to make clear.

philosophy of Normative Theory C which, due to Thayer's influence on Mr. Justice Frankfurter, as well as on Justice Learned Hand, is the living law source of the legal philosophy of that group of Justices on the present Supreme Court of the United States who have been described as focusing around Mr. Justice Frankfurter. In any event, it follows on Judge Hand's own evidence that his opinion with respect to the desegregation cases and his oft-quoted thesis that some of the present Supreme Court Justices have "introduced a third legislature" rests on confusing the positive legal and political system of Great Britain, which is correctly described by the legal positivists' Normative Theory C, with the legal and political system of the United States, which requires Normative Theory B for its description.

There is, of course, no *a priori* reason why the American legal system as created by its Founders in accordance with the Lockean and Jeffersonian Normative Theory B should not be the cognitively false one and that the Hobbesian and Austinian philosophy of Normative Theory C, that came into the United States near the end of the nineteenth century, should not be the cognitively true one. As shown under point (a) above, this, however, is not the case; it is Normative Theory B which is cognitively verified.

(c) The third reason why Judge Learned Hand's position is cognitively false is that, following the radical empiricism of his Harvard College philosophy professor William James and of Hume and Bentham, Judge Hand identifies the meaning of the word "good" with "preferences, arbitrary and imperative." [12] Since all such introspective psychological preferences are relative to the percipient, as Judge Hand recognizes,* he, like Hume or William James before him, is able to obtain a meaning for the publicly good, that is, the legally just, only by adding up these private preferences in the laissez-faire legislative market place. This makes the judicial review of legislative statutes self-contradictory, since on this theory justice is equated with what the majority in the legislative affirm. This gives Hobbes' undivided theory of political sovereignty and the British rather than the American positive legal and political system.

---

* Referring to Holmes, Judge Hand writes, "He knew that outside ourselves there is no value; what we desire is the sole measure of right and wrong." [13]

Also an additional difficulty arises. Since everything rests on the "arbitrary preference" of the individual legislator and the individual voter, what justification is there for applying the statute which the majority prefer and approve to the minority who vote against it and who disapprove of it? In other words, assuming this introspective psychological theory of ethics and law, what meaning is there for the legal obligation of the minority to accept the majority approved statute as binding? Clearly there is no reason. To have seen this is Kelsen's great merit, as Professor H. L. A. Hart in his critique of Austin [14] has noted. From where, then, does the universally applicable "ought-ness" of the law derive to make it binding even upon those who do not prefer or approve it? Obviously, something objective and public is needed. But, as Berkeley and Hume showed, in a radically empirical theory of cognitive meaning there are no publicly meaningful substances, either material or mental. This is why Hume, Austin [15] and Judge Learned Hand have to draw upon Hobbes. For Hobbes' naïve realistic epistemology and its ontology of material substances gives meaning to the physical power of the political sovereign to inflict pain on those who dissent from his commands. This, of course, is the legal positivist Austin's famous definition of "law, proper so-called." Thus it is that thinkers such as Hume, Bentham, Austin, William James and Judge Learned Hand start out to be radical empiricists in their theory of ethics and law only to be forced in the end to the naïve realism and the metaphysical materialism and power politics of Hobbes in order to provide any meaning for legal obligation.

But naïve realism, as was proved in Chapter XV, is a self-contradictory theory of conceptual meaning. Furthermore, the radical empiricists themselves, thinkers such as Berkeley, Hume and William James, have shown unequivocally that if one refers all meaning to factors given with radically empirical immediacy, there is no meaning to the notion of a substantial self or the notion of a Hobbesian materialistic external object. Consequently, the legal positivist's Normative Theory C, which combines a radically empirical introspective psychological theory of the meanings of the words "good" and "just" with a naïve realistic Hobbesian physical power theory of legal obligation, is a doubly self-contradictory theory. Since Judge Hand's

conclusion concerning the desegregation cases requires Normative
Theory C for its justification, it follows that his conclusion with respect to these cases is false also.

Our method for cognitively deciding between alternative normative legal philosophies is equally decisive with respect to two more
recent cases: *Barenblatt v. U. S.* and *Uphaus v. Wyman.*[16] Analysis of these two cases shows that the majority opinions, written
respectively by Justice Harlan and Justice Clark with Justices Frankfurter, Stewart and Whittaker concurring, require the legal positivist's Normative Theory C, with its interpretation of the Bill of Rights
as merely "admonitions to forbearance," for their justification;
whereas the dissenting opinions, written respectively by Justices
Black and Brennan, in which Chief Justice Warren and Justice
Douglas concurred, require for their validation Normative Theory B,
which interprets the Bill of Rights as law. In his dissent, Mr. Justice
Black makes the latter identification unequivocally clear when, referring to the reason for the majority opinion, he writes:

> Not only does this violate the genius of our written *Constitution,*
> but it runs expressly counter to the injunction to Court and Con-
> gress made by Madison when he introduced the Bill of Rights
> . . . [that] "they [the first ten amendments] . . . will be an im-
> penetrable bulwark against *every* assumption of power in the Legis-
> lative or Executive . . ." Unless we return to this view of our ju-
> dicial function, unless we once again accept the notion that the Bill
> of Rights means what it says [i.e., is law as Normative Theory B
> prescribes] and that this Court must enforce that meaning, I am of
> the opinion that our great charter of liberty will be more honored
> in the breach than in the observance.[17]

Since our cognitive method tells us that Normative Theory C is the
cognitively false theory and that Normative Theory B is the cognitively correct one, we conclude, therefore, that the majority opinions
in these two cases not merely confuse the American positive legal
system with the British but are cognitively in error, and that the dissenting opinions, upon which Mr. Chief Justice Warren and Justices
Black, Brennan and Douglas were in agreement, were not merely the
only opinions compatible with the American legal system as conceived by its Founding Fathers, but also the cognitively correct
judgments.

It appears, therefore, that only Premise (2) (i), (ii), (iii) and (iv) of Normative Theory B can accurately describe the American positive political and legal system with its democracy of checks and balances. Its four requirements also serve to document what Jefferson must have meant when he suggested that he and his fellow Americans had created something unique in the history of mankind.[18]

His probable appreciation of the importance of the conceptual Requirement (iv) is shown in two of his statements. (1) "What probably fixed the destinies of my life," he tells us, was his professor of mathematics at William and Mary, Dr. William Strong, who undoubtedly acquainted him with the "fluxions," or incomplete dx/dy symbols of Newton's calculus. And "I have given up newspapers in exchange . . . for Newton and Euclid." [19]

The cognitive verifiability of Normative Theory B has similar significance for international law. Its Requirements (i), (ii) and (iii) were first announced, in modern times at least, in the basic "self-evident" proposition of the American Declaration of Independence. This was a foreign policy document. Furthermore, it shook the world then as it still shakes it today.

The present results have been described in Chapters II, XI, XII and XIII and may be summarized as follows: (1) Western imperialists are being forced to withdraw throughout the world. (2) The medieval law of status Asian maharajas, Judaic patriarchs, caliphatic sultans and African tribal chieftains are being forced out also. (3) To implement this world-wide declaration of independence, the technology of formally constructed mathematical physics and the democratic political and legal institutions of a law of contract society are being introduced from the modern West into Africa, the Middle East and Asia. The latter fact means that Premise (2) of Normative Theory B and its epistemological assumption (iv) is now an international premise that is world-embracing in its significance.

Needless to say, these modern technological and legal instruments are modifying, if not threatening to destroy, the traditional civilizations of the non-modern Western world. The question is often asked with respect to the great cultural traditions of Islam and Asia, as well as with regard to those of the Old South: Is this good? Our method for verifying evaluative, as distinct from merely descriptive, normative theory tells us that Normative Theory B rather than the patriarchal law of status ethics of Normative Theory A is the cognitively correct one. Hence, the cognitively verifiable answer is Yes.

Premises (1) and (3) in Normative Theory B tell us, however, that the rejection of the old living law of status and its values must be made in a most sensitive and cautious way. That portion of the world's medieval and classical living law which cognitively requires Premise (1) for its validity is to be retained. This means that political leaders in Africa, Islam and Asia do not have to reject all of their traditional living law in order to obtain the modern freely democratic contractual legal, political and economic institutions which they are today insisting upon having for themselves. This retention of some of the old living law as prescribed by its Premise (1), while modernizing as specified by Premise (2), gives Normative Theory B a prodigious advantage over its Communistic or other rivals in capturing the loyalties of the majority of mankind to become effective both domestically and internationally. Or, to be more precise, this would be the case were the voters and political leaders of the free world to become thus clear and consistent with respect to their intrinsic goal and their particular political decisions.

Normative Theory B is of international significance in an even deeper sense. The substantive content of its premises is international in meaning as well as with respect to the popular support they enjoy. The radically empirical field consciousness of the person, which its Premise (1) affirms, if true for one person or some people, is true for all human beings. Furthermore, the field factor in radically empirical immediacy to which this concept of the person refers, embraces all immediately apprehended natural phenomena as well as the transitory, differentiated consciousness of all men and women the world over. The two universal quantifiers (p) and (p), meaning "for any person whatever," of its Requirement (ii) have the same effect for Premise (2) of Normative Theory B.

The American Declaration of Independence expresses precisely this point. It does not read, "We hold it to be self-evident that only American men are created free and equal before their legal and political obligations, rights and duties." Instead, it affirms this to be the case for Americans only because it is the case for all humanity. In other words, the domestic legal and political system of the United

States, which was born of its creators' Declaration of Independence, embodies within itself an appeal to international law.

But this is the case for any law of contract legal system whatever, when its meaning is clearly understood. As noted previously, the self-evident proposition affirmed in the Declaration of Independence — Premise (2) of Normative Theory B — is true tautologically because it is a proposition in the law of contract and not one in the comparative biology and psychology of newly born babes. This is so because, in the concept of the person of the law of contract, to be a law of contract person is to be an instance of a determinate, contractually introduced and constructed law which both as a whole and also with respect to its intrinsic or goal value substantive content is universally quantified for any person whatever.

The concept of "nation" or of "national law" in the law of contract is similar. To use the language of Chapter III, in any contractual national legal system "nation" or "national law" are incomplete symbols, after the manner of the concept of "corporate personality" in contractual corporation law. This means that such expressions as "nation" or "national law" are the concepts of a formally constructed concept by postulation cognitive theory of conceptual meaning; they are not the concepts of either a radically empirical or a naïve realistic epistemological interpretation of the meaning of legal language.

It was shown in Chapter III that an incomplete symbol has no meaning by itself. Its meaning is to be found, consequently, only by examining the formal properties or the syntax of the basic premises of the theoretically constructed system in which it occurs. Consequently, as Regius Professor H. L. A. Hart has noted,[20] it is an error to ask, as most traditional legal theorists have done, for a definition of such legal words. Instead, to find out what incomplete symbols such as "nation" and "national law" mean, one must turn to the basic axioms or premises concerning intrinsic, or goal, values of the contractual legal system in question. When this is done, one finds that these goal value premises are universally quantified for any human being whatever and hence are principles of international rather than merely biologically, geographically or culturally restricted national law. The situation is not, therefore, as the seventeenth-century Hobbes, the nineteenth-century English jurist Austin and those contemporary foreign policy "experts" who write carelessly about "the national interest" would have us suppose, that "law, proper so-called" exists only within the absolutely sovereign nation, above and beyond which there is no law. Instead, the situation is: (a) All modern national legal systems are of the law of contract type. (b) All entities in the law of contract, such as "the nation," "the national law" and "the national interest," are incomplete symbols. (c) The basic syntactical goal value sentence, within which the aforementioned incomplete symbols function as variables, is the tautological truth of the law of contract which the American Declaration of Independence affirmed and to which Premise (2) — especially its Requirement (ii) of Normative Theory B — gives analytically precise and complete expression. (d) The latter basic tautological premise of the law of contract, apart from which the expressions "nation," "national law" or "national interest" are meaningless marks, is both empirically and tautologically true for any human being whatever. In short, in any modern national legal or political system, the meaning of its most commonplace words is not correctly understood except as these words are elucidated by reference to a basic premise of the law of contract which is true for any human being whatever and which is therefore a principle in international law.

It is only because Austin followed Hobbes, and because Hobbes, due to his naïve realistic epistemology and its metaphysical ontology of material substances, confused the incomplete symbol "nation" in the sense of the "tribe" of a naïve realistic epistemology and its law of biological status with the quite different concept of "nation" in the law of contract, that both Hobbes and Austin and the contemporary legally trained secretaries of state and foreign policy "experts" who have followed them [21] reach the erroneous conclusion that the notion of international law is theoretically meaningless and therefore practically impossible.

We are now prepared to appreciate the significance of the quotation from Locke which appears on the motto page of this book. Until we clarify and cognitively confirm our theory of the meaning of the words we use, it is futile to talk about religious, legal, moral or political problems. The plain fact is that contemporary law, morality and politics, both domestic and international, theoretical and applied, are a mass of confusions because legal and ethical theoreticians as able as Hobbes, Austin, Thayer and Judge Learned Hand and practicing lawyers, judges and statesmen are applying to nations and to national legal systems, whose law is that of the law of contract, theories of conceptual meaning and of political action in foreign policy which are appropriate only for the tribal nations of a geographically localized law of status society. For a "nation" in the latter sense, it is true as Austin maintained [22] that international law is a theoretically self-contradictory notion and hence practically impossible.

Three things cannot be repeated too often, therefore. The first is that the legal systems of the modern nations the world over are of the law of contract type. Second, in contractual law all entities such as "citizen," "voter," "secretary of state," "chief executive," "nation," "national law," "national interest," or "great powers" are incomplete symbols which have no legal or political meaning apart from the basic tautologically true premise of the law of contract. This is why Premise (2) and its Requirements (i), (ii), (iii) and (iv) are essential if we are to become clear about what is meant by any of the foregoing expressions or by "the democracy of the free world." Third, *the goal value premise of any self-consistent * modern national legal and political system* is, because of the universally quantified basic premise (ii) of the law of contract, a principle of national law only because it is a principle of international law.

However, it does not follow automatically that this international law which exists in every modern law of contract nation can be effective in this atomic age in bringing disputes between nations under the rule of law rather than that of atomic war. To reach such an easy conclusion is to overlook two other factors: (a) The aforementioned conceptual confusion in the minds of contemporary legal theorists and practicing jurists, lawyers and statesmen, and (b) the persisting law of status ethical beliefs and habitual behavior in the living law of the contemporary world.

It is factor (a), inherited from Hobbes and Austin in Great Britain by way of Thayer in the United States, which causes so many important contemporary leaders in the free world to believe that international law is meaningless theoretically and impossible practi-

---

* One that does not fill in law of contract statutes with law of status content or one that does not give to the concept by postulation legal language of the law of contract meanings that are appropriate only for a language which is of either the radically empirical or the naïvely realistic type.

cally. This in all likelihood is what former Secretary of State Acheson meant when he suggested, after President Eisenhower's appeal to international law in the Suez crisis, that the international law to which the President had appealed was "spurious." [23] This also is part, at least, of what Secretary of State Dulles meant when he told Professor William Ernest Hocking, "There is no such thing as international law." [24] George F. Kennan, who was Chairman of the Planning Board of the Department of State under Secretary of State Acheson, tells us similarly that Hobbes or Austin rather than Locke or Jefferson defines the American national interest when he writes that the legal-moral mentality is misplaced in foreign policy.[25] It is not an insignificant consequence of the cognitively verifiable truth of Normative Theory B that it shows these prevalent beliefs of those Democrats and Republicans who have determined the foreign policy of the United States since World War II to be cognitively false.

The first prerequisite, therefore, for making the positive international law which already exists in every modern law of contract nation an effective instrument for avoiding war is the removal of the aforementioned conceptual *confusion*. To this end two things seem necessary. The first is a legal, political and public education which makes everyone the world over aware of the differences between any word in its (R) radically empirical epistemological meaning, in its (NR) naïve realistic epistemological meaning, and in its (CP) concept by postulation incomplete symbolic meaning. The second necessary change is that it be made equally clear that the law of every modern nation, being contractual, is of the (CP) type, in which the most basic premise of the national law and the national interest is the international legal premise expressed in (ii) above. It then will be seen to follow that a foreign policy official or a voting citizen only understands and serves the national interest when he respects this international legal premise.

It is to be emphasized, moreover, that the national legal systems of the Soviet Union and of Mao's China, insofar as the latter nation copies Soviet law, contain Premise (2) of Normative Theory B just as unequivocally as do the national legal systems of the free nations. This is the case because Soviet law rejects the law of status and is, therefore, contractual. Furthermore, its political and legal system of the law of contract type derives directly from Stoic Rome through

Justinian by way of Constantinople. That the Communists have written such logically inconsistent content into their law of contract is
due to the fact that they commit the same error with respect to the
meaning of legal obligation that occurs, as shown above, with Hobbes,
Austin and the Anglo-American legal positivists. For both the Communists and the Anglo-American legal positivists, the theoretical
meaning of legal obligation (as distinct from its police power imple-
mentation) is the physical power of the political sovereign to enforce
his command. The English legal positivist Austin states this explicitly in his famous definition, taken from Hobbes, of "law, proper
so-called" as "a *command*" of a political sovereign who has "the
power . . . to inflict an evil or pain in case [his] desire be disre-
garded." [26] Furthermore, in both the legal positivists' and the Communists' philosophies of politics and law, the cognitive error is identical. The contractual concept of legal obligation, in which contract
and consent are of the essence, has been confused, due to the materialistic metaphysics or a naïve realistic way of thinking, with the
naïve realistic biological and tribal notion of legal obligation of a law
of status nation. In the case of the Anglo-American legal positivists,
the source of their naïvely realistic metaphysical materialism is
Hobbes by way of Austin and Thayer; in the case of the Communists, it is Feuerbach by way of Marx and Engels. [27]

What has to be realized is that in any modern legal system expressions such as "legal obligation" are incomplete symbols in the sense
described in Chapter III. More specifically, they are what the writer,
in his *Logic of the Sciences and the Humanities,* called "concepts by
postulation which are concepts by intellection." [28] Such a symbol
derives its meaning grammatically and syntactically from the formal
properties of the sentence in which it functions as a term. More specifically, it derives its meaning from the formally constructed, most
basic or logically primitive indicative sentence in the system of indicative sentences in which it functions as a term.

This is why modern mathematicians were unable to give the meaning of their incomplete symbol dx/dy of the infinitesimal calculus,
which we described in Chapter III, until a philosophical analysis of
the symbols of the language of mathematics was carried through
which revealed the most basic or logically primitive propositions of
the science. Since, as was shown in Chapters XV and XVIII, West-

ern legal science arose with the discovery of the self-contradictory character of the complete symbols of a naïve realistic epistemology and its law of status, two things follow similarly for modern political and legal language: First, any abstract expression in this language, such as "legal obligation," is given a false interpretation if either a radically empirical or a naïvely realistic epistemological meaning is read into it after the manner of Hobbes, Austin, Thayer and Judge Learned Hand or Feuerbach, Engels and Marx. Second, all the abstract nouns of modern legal and political language, such as "obligation," "sanction," "nation," "the national interest," "the great powers" or "law, proper so-called" are incomplete symbols whose meaning is made evident only by reference to the tautologically self-evident basic sentence of the law of contract. This is why the meaning of modern and contemporary political and legal language could not be given until the philosophical analysis, completed at the beginning of this chapter, had specified the basic or logically primitive sentences of the law of contract in Premise (2) of Normative Theory B.

Its Requirements (ii) and (iii) specify the meaning of legal obligation in the law of contract. Let us pursue the significance of (iii) first, coming to (ii) afterwards.

Requirement (iii) tells us that *for-me-ness* or consent is essential. This, let it be recalled, is a tautologically true or self-evident proposition of the law of contract, the reason being that, until consent is given, what is put into the contract by the contracting parties is merely a fanciful or hypothetical "might be," it is not an obligatory for-me-binding imperative.

It is precisely at this point that sociological jurisprudence or philosophical anthropology, in the merely descriptive and statistically quantitative component of its method as described in Chapter VII, becomes essential for an effective positive international law. Even though this international law now exists in the contractual national law of every modern nation, *on its own principles* it cannot be and should not be effective in bringing these nations under the control of their own international principles unless the majority of mankind consent. The reason, let it be emphasized, is that in the law of contract the physical power of the political sovereign to enforce his commands is not the sanction for law; instead, physical power is merely the police instrument for implementing the community authorized prescriptions of the law once its sanction has been assured in a quite different way, as prescribed by Requirements (ii) and (iii) above. At this point, the previous quotation from Sir Arthur Goodhart, the Regius Professor of Jurisprudence (Emeritus) at Oxford merits repeating: "It is because a rule is regarded as obligatory that a measure of coercion may be attached to it: it is not obligatory because there is coercion." [29]

Only descriptive sociological and philosophical anthropological jurisprudence can tell us, therefore, whether Requirement (iii) of Premise (2) of Normative Theory B is empirically the case or not. As noted earlier in this chapter, and as suggested more extensively in Chapter XI, such, in all probability, is the case. If so, then the international law which now exists in every modern Oriental, Middle Eastern, African or Western nation's natural law as defined by Premise (2) of Normative Theory B not only cognitively *ought to be in theory,* but also, because of the empirical satisfaction of its Requirement (iii), *can be in fact.*

It might be thought that the admission of these empirical sociological implications of Requirement (iii) of the law of contract means that there is no international law after all, since Requirement (iii) may well have the practical effect of not making effective international law exist in fact until a majority of mankind transform their beliefs and unconscious social habits and customs to conform to Premise (2) of Normative Theory B. Such a conclusion would be, however, erroneous. It confuses the existence of international law in the sense of one part of its theory of obligation as given in Requirement (iii) of Premise (2) with the existence of natural law in any modern nation's national law in the sense of the substantive content of that natural law as specified by Requirement (ii) of Premise (2). Certainly if a law of contract nation exists, and there are many of them in Africa, the Middle East, and Asia as well as in the West today, then the substantive content of its international law of contract exists also. Since, as Requirement (ii) insures, the substantive content of every law of contract legal and political nation is international, it follows in the sense of Requirement (ii) that international law also exists.

Hence, even if we should be wrong in our estimation of the quantitative popular, world-wide living law support which Normative

Theory B now commands, it would still be true, since law of contract nations exist, that positive law of contract international law with substantive content also exists. All that would be lacking is the education and the persuasion of the majority of mankind to make explicit in their foreign policy, through the United Nations, the international law which is already implicit in their present modern national law.

It is at this point that the aforementioned cognitive truthfulness of Normative Theory B gives it a prodigious advantage. Because this theory can be shown to be cognitively true and its rivals can similarly be shown by the method of Diagram II to be cognitively false, the task of persuading the majority of mankind to accept its authority as the basis for effective international legal and political institutions is less difficult or time-consuming than one might at first suppose.

Providing, therefore, that the leaders of the modern nations, and especially the modern free nations whose citizens comprise an overwhelming majority of mankind, will put a clear understanding and statement of the international implications of their own present national law in the foreground of what they are doing and will push their atomic bombs and pocketbooks into the background, where instrumental values, necessary though they be, belong, there certainly is no *theoretical reason,* as Austin and Marx supposed, *and in all probability there is no practical reason* why disputes between nations cannot be brought under the rule of law rather than of war in this atomic age. Both the cognitively verifiable qualitative theoretical principles as given in Normative Theory B and the quantitative world-embracing living law support necessary for success seem to be at hand if we will but take advantage of them.

Even so, the most telling theoretical reason for success still remains to be noted. This reason becomes evident when we examine Requirement (ii), the second of the two conditions that define the meaning of legal obligation in the law of contract.

Requirement (ii) tells us what the legal and political concept of the person is in the law of contract. More specifically, it tells us both what rights and privileges this contractual concept of the person implies and what obligations it entails. It is because of the latter implication that the concept of legal obligation in any contractual legal and political system is specified only when Requirement (ii) as well as Requirement (iii) is given. In other words, consent is a necessary but not a sufficient condition for legal obligation in the law of contract.

The rights and liberties which Requirement (ii) guarantee are truly remarkable. They hold regardless of the living law, the positive law or the majority approved statutes of even a democratically elected legislature. This is precisely what the American Declaration of Independence affirmed. Moreover, these personal rights and liberties are so universal and international in their reference that, as the creators of this first foreign policy document of the United States of America made clear, the law of contract concept of the person gives any person or any group of people the right to revolt if these rights and liberties are not satisfied.

But the obligations entailed by the concept of the person in the law of contract are equally remarkable and much less frequently noted. In fact, due to the reading of either (R) radically empirical or (NR) naïvely realistic meanings into the (CP) incomplete symbols of the law of contract, its concept of the person's legal and political obligations have been confused with the meaning of obligation in either a legal system of the mediational type or a legal system of the law of status type. Consequently, the concept of legal obligation in the law of contract has not been understood by contemporary legal theoreticians, nor has it been practiced by most of the citizens of the modern nations. This situation can well be serious. If people continue to demand the rights and liberties of a law of contract person while having no comprehension of such a person's obligations, not only will we be left adrift internationally, shaking atomic bombs at one another in this atomic age, but even our domestic legal and political institutions are likely to break down.

Certainly Requirement (ii) cuts both ways, entailing obligations upon *any* person the world *over* as well as similarly guaranteeing rights and liberties. The rights and privileges of a legal or political person in the meaning of the law of contract are worthless unless his or her obligations in the meaning of the law of contract are understood and practiced with the same declaration of independent assent and insistence that is put into the demand for one's contractually warranted rights and liberties.

What, then, does the concept of the legal and political person in the law of contract entail for anyone the world over with respect to his or her obligations? Requirement (ii) of Premise (2) of Normative Theory B gives the answer.

The first thing to note about this Requirement is that it is formally defined with its substantive content *s* left variable except as the formal quantification (*p*) of *s* restricts *s*. Requirement (ii) tells us, therefore, that the concept of the person in the law of contract is a (CP) incomplete symbol, since neither the rights and liberties nor the obligations of the person *p* are defined by recourse to the sensuous qualities of either a radically empirical or a naïvely realistic epistemology. Consequently, instead of some inductively known property of human beings defining what Requirement (ii) means, Requirement (ii), the most basic, or logically primitive, sentence in the law of contract, defines what it means to be a legal or political person in the sense of the law of contract.

What this involves concretely will become clear if we consider some implications of the three following historical suppositions: (1) Let us suppose that, rejecting legal and political systems of the law of status type because of their self-contradictory naïve realistic cognitive epistemological assumptions, the natural scientists and lawyers of the classical West discovered the (CP) incomplete symbols of Democritean and Eudoxian Greek mathematical physics and Stoic Roman Western legal science. (2) Suppose also that with Galilei's and Newton's rejection of the naïve realistic epistemology to which Aristotle returned Western physics and metaphysics, modern mathematical physicists rediscovered the (CP) language of incomplete symbols and that Jefferson, following two of his "greatest men," Newton and Locke, did the same for Western legal science. (3) Suppose finally, as is now occurring, that people and their political leaders the world over are demanding for themselves the concept of the legal and political person which the American Declaration of Independence affirmed to be the right of any human being whatever and which Requirement (ii) expresses in precise analytic form. It then follows that the assent to Requirement (ii), which insistence upon the rights and liberties of its concept of the person expresses, entails the similar obligation of any such assenter the world over to be measured by any law which (a) is universally quantified for any human being whatever, and (b) the substantive contents of which is similarly universally quantified.

It is to be noted, furthermore, that the latter obligation holds as universally for any human being whatever who appeals to the law of contract, irrespective of living law customs, positive law support or even majority approved democratic legislation to the contrary, as do the rights and liberties guaranteed by Requirement (ii). This reference to majority approved legislative statutes is important. It points up the twofold fact that (1) majority approved legislation must in judicial review pass Requirement (ii) before it is legal, thereby protecting religious and civil liberties against a "tyranny of the legislature," and (2) any dissenter or minority group has the legal obligation to be measured by merely majority approved statutes of the legislature, providing their substantive content is in accord with Requirement (ii).

At last the meaning of legal obligation in the law of contract is before us. It is given by Requirements (ii) and (iii) of Premise (2) of Normative Theory B, in which the otherwise unlimited rights and privileges guaranteed by (iii) are limited by the obligations imposed by (ii).

Without Requirement (ii) there would be no obligation of dissenters and minority groups to be measured by the majority approved statutes of a democratic legislature, which in judicial review pass the test with respect to their substance s that is prescribed by Requirement (ii). Otherwise the theory of legal obligation in the law of contract would fall into the same self-contradictory error, noted just above, into which the theory of legal obligation of the Anglo-American Hobbesian and Austinian legal positivists and the Feuerbachian and Marxist Communists fall. Otherwise, too, one could insist for oneself upon the religious and civil rights and liberties guaranteed by Requirement (ii) while appealing to Requirement (iii) to refuse to assent to majority approved legislative statutes meeting Requirement (ii) in judicial review, which make it a crime for one to interfere with the religious and civil liberties of other people. We conclude, therefore, that quite apart from its cognitive verification, demonstrated earlier in this chapter, Premise (2) of Normative Theory B is the only theory that accounts for the legal obligation of the minority to be measured by majority approved legislation which, in judicial review, satisfies Requirement (ii).

The foregoing analysis of the meaning of legal obligation in the law of contract solves what may be termed *the problem of legal induction* in an assent and contractual theory of law and government. The problem is how, in such a theory, to pass from the majority assent to a statute to the obligation of all — dissenters and assenters alike — to accept the statute.

On the radically empirical theory of legal language and its introspective psychological theory of the meaning of normative words, i.e., on a theory of legal obligation which contains only Requirement (iii), there is no solution to this problem. The reason, as the radical empiricist Hume showed, is that in radical empirical knowledge no relation of necessary connection is given. Hence there is no implication or obligation taking one from what is assented to by some, even a very large "some," to what is obligatory for all.[30] Since the naïve realist defines his purportedly realistic objects in terms of the directly sensed qualities, properties and relations of the radical empiricist, it follows that the problem of legal induction is insoluble for the naïve realist also.

Making Requirement (ii) as well as (iii) the criterion of legal obligation solves the problem of legal induction in legal science, precisely the same way in which Frege and Bertrand Russell [31] solved the problem of mathematical induction in mathematical science. In both instances the problem consists in passing from what is true for some to what holds for all.

The solution consists in pointing out that any individual person in the meaning of the law of contract, like any natural number in the modern science of arithmetic, is a (CP) incomplete symbol whose meaning is that of being an entity variable of the most basic, or logically primitive proposition of the science. In the modern science of arithmetic, this most basic proposition is Peano's Fifth Postulate.[32] Hence, to be *any* natural number is to be bound by this postulate. Consequently, there is no problem of going, so far as this postulate is concerned, from what is the case for some natural numbers to what is the case for all. Similarly, the basic postulate of any political and legal system of the law of contract type is Requirement (ii) of Premise (2) of Normative Theory B. Hence, to be *any* legal and political person in the sense of the law of contract is to be obligated by this postulate. Consequently, providing a majority approved statute in judicial review satisfies Requirement (ii), there is no problem of going from what is true merely for some to what is obligatory for all.

Furthermore, the proposition which is Peano's Fifth Postulate in the modern science of arithmetic and the proposition which is Requirement (ii) of Premise (2) of Normative Theory B in contractual legal science are cognitively true because they are analytic propositions. They are analytic because the subject term in both cases, being an incomplete symbol, has no meaning other than what the predicate term of the proposition assigns to it. Hence, to understand what is affirmed is to see that what is asserted is true self-evidently or tautologically, as contemporary mathematicians and mathematical logicians all now agree, in the case of mathematical science and as is here, for perhaps the first time, realized in the case of legal science.

But contractual legal science first discovered by the Stoic Romans is now the legal and political science of all the modern nations of the entire world — Asian, Middle Eastern, African and Western, Communist and non-Communist alike. People and their political leaders everywhere are demanding its rights, liberties and privileges. In short, people the world over are committing themselves to the concept of the legal and political person of the law of contract. But this concept of the person implies obligations as well as rights, liberties and privileges. Moreover, these obligations, like the correlative rights and liberties, are valid for some men only because they are valid for all men, following tautologically from what it means to be a person in the law of contract. Hence, once these commitments are admitted, the passage from an international law assented to by a very large "some" of the world's inhabitants to an internationtal law which, respecting Requirement (ii), is obligatory for all is, to use Jefferson's language, "self-evident."

To be sure, the latter self-evidence holds only for those whose legal system is that of the law of contract, rather than that of either a law of status society or one whose law is of the mediational type described in Chapter XV. The law of contract, however, requires the cognitive epistemological assumption (iv) of Premise (2) as well as its Requirement (ii) for its validity and, as shown at the beginning of the present chapter, this epistemological premise (iv) is empirically confirmed by the method of Diagram II. This empirical confirmation of (ii) by way of (iv) transforms the analytically self-evident premise (ii) of the pure theory of the law of contract into an empirical, synthetic proposition compounded of Requirements (ii) and (iv) which is empirically confirmed.

Legal and ethical experience is antecedent to all theory about it, as a great Justice observed. Also it is complex. Its complexity expresses a subtle combination of positive, living and naturalistic factors which cognitive epistemological theory relates in a non-eclectic manner, as Locke observed. Legal and moral experience is further complicated by the presence of rival epistemological theories of the meaning of any word in any subject whatever, and the fact that these alternative epistemological theories have their respective rival normative moral, legal and political counterparts.

Legal and moral experience is confused as well as complicated. The confusion arises because of the failure of people to distinguish the three major types of conceptual meaning which any word in their discourse may have. Consequently, as C. I. Lewis tells us, it is the business of philosophy to analyze experience, as this book has attempted to do, in order to disentangle the different types of conceptual meaning that at present confuse the discourse and the practice of not merely the normative but even the natural sciences.

Nevertheless, since any normative theory assumes and requires for its validity specific non-normative cognitive assertions concerning the first-order facts of any human being's experience, philosophical analysis, by distinguishing first-order and second-order facts and by disentangling the different types of conceptual meaning in normative discourse, is able to submit the rival de facto normative theories of our world (and their corresponding second-order factual living law cultural artifacts) to an empirical and hence a cognitive test. Hence, evaluative as well as descriptive law and ethics are sciences.

Furthermore, when this test is made, it appears that Normative Theory B is the cognitively correct theory. Fortunately, also, it describes a most significant part of the world's living law that now is. To be at once both the *is* of a significant part of the world's living law and the cognitively confirmable *ought* for the whole of it, is to be something of considerable domestic and international importance.

Notes

Works are referred to by a short title or as *op. cit.* only when full information is given previously in a note for the same chapter.

PREFACE

1. William Ernest Hocking, *Man and the State,* Yale University Press, New Haven, 1926, esp. Part I, "Facts, Theory, Problems."
2. Learned Hand, *The Spirit of Liberty, Papers and Addresses* Collected by Irving Dilliard, Knopf, New York, 1953, p. 58.
3. John Locke, *Essay Concerning Human Understanding,* A. C. Fraser, ed., Clarendon Press, Oxford, 1894.
4. Charles L. Stevenson, *Ethics and Language,* Yale University Press, New Haven, 1944; A. J. Ayer, *Language, Truth and Logic,* Gollancz, London, 1936 and 1948.
5. Alf Ross, *Towards a Realistic Jurisprudence,* Einar Munksgaard, Copenhagen, 1946; "On the Logical Nature of Propositions of Value," 11 *Theoria* 172–210; *On Law and Justice,* University of California Press, Berkeley and Los Angeles, 1959.
6. Hans Kelsen, *General Theory of Law and State,* Harvard University Press, Cambridge, Mass., 1946; *What Is Justice? Justice, Law, and Politics in the Mirror of Science,* University of California Press, Berkeley and Los Angeles, 1957; F. S. C. Northrop, "The Importance of Kelsen's Legal Positivism," 44 *Virginia Law Review* 815–819.
7. Alf Ross, *Towards a Realistic Jurisprudence.*
8. Ernest Nagel, "On the Fusion of Fact and Value: A Reply to Professor Fuller," 3 *Natural Law Forum* 77–82; "Fact, Value, and Human Purpose," *ibid.,* Vol. 4, 26–43.

II LEGAL PHILOSOPHY IN THE CONTEMPORARY WORLD

1. Roscoe Pound, "Toward a New Jus Gentium" in F. S. C. Northrop, ed., *Ideological Differences and World Order,* Yale University Press, New Haven, 1949, pp. 1–17.
2. For an introduction to what this means specifically and methodologically, see Northrop, *The Meeting of East and West,* Macmillan, New York, 1946; *The Logic of the Sciences and the Humanities,* Macmillan, New York, 1947, chaps. 14, 16–19, 21 and 22; and Pound, *op. cit.*

III SOME PHILOSOPHICAL ISSUES IN ANGLO-AMERICAN LAW

1. W. W. Cook, "Scientific Method and Law," 13 *American Bar Association Journal* 303–309; *The Logical and Legal Bases of the Conflict of Laws,* Harvard University Press, Cambridge, 1942.

2. A. N. Whitehead and Bertrand Russell, *Principia Mathematica,* second
    edition, Cambridge University Press, Cambridge, 1925, chap. III; Ber-
    trand Russell, *Introduction to Mathematical Philosophy,* Allen and Un-
    win, London, 1919, chap. XVII.
3. Bertrand Russell, *Portraits from Memory,* Simon and Schuster, New York,
    1956, p. 42.
4. Glanville Williams, "Language and the Law," 61 *Law Quarterly Review*
    71–86, 179–195, 293–305; 62 *Law Quarterly Review* 387–406; Gra-
    ham B. J. Hughes, *Jurisprudence,* Butterworth, London, 1955, chap.
    1; H. L. A. Hart, "Definition and Theory in Jurisprudence," 70 *Law
    Quarterly Review* 37.
5. G. H. Hardy, *Pure Mathematics,* Cambridge University Press, London,
    1928, p. 205.
6. Arthur L. Corbin, *Corbin on Contracts,* West, St. Paul, 1950, pp. iii–vi.
7. Wesley A. Sturges, *Cases on Arbitration Law,* Bender, Albany, 1953.
8. Harry Shulman, "Reason, Contract, and Law," 68 *Harvard Law Review*
    999–1024.
9. Ruth Benedict, *Patterns of Culture,* Houghton Mifflin, Boston, 1934;
    A. L. Kroeber, *Configurations of Culture Growth,* University of Cali-
    fornia Press, Los Angeles, 1944.
10. Eugen Ehrlich, *Fundamental Principles of the Sociology of Law,* translated
    by Walter I. Moll, Harvard University Press, Cambridge, 1936.
11. E. A. Hoebel, *The Law of Primitive Man: A Study in Comparative Legal
    Dynamics,* Harvard University Press, Cambridge, 1954. See also
    F. S. C. Northrop, *European Union and United States Foreign Policy,*
    Macmillan, New York, 1954, chaps. 3 and 6.
12. Learned Hand, "Chief Justice Stone's Concept of the Judicial Function,"
    57 *Columbia Law Review* 696, and "Thomas Walter Swan," 57 *Yale
    Law Journal* 167; also republished in *The Spirit of Liberty, Papers and
    Addresses* collected by Irving Dilliard, Knopf, New York, 1953, pp.
    201–219.
13. William O. Douglas, *We the Judges: Studies in American and Indian Con-
    stitutional Law from Marshall to Mukherjea,* Doubleday, New York,
    1956, p. 430, note 2.
14. John Austin, *The Province of Jurisprudence Determined and the Uses of
    the Study of Jurisprudence,* with an introduction by H. L. A. Hart,
    Weidenfeld and Nicolson, London, 1954, pp. 1–33, 123, 132–133,
    193–194, 253–254.
15. *Ibid.,* p. 254. See also Hughes, *op. cit.,* p. 71.
16. For a discussion of the latter problem, see Northrop, *The Taming of the
    Nations,* Macmillan, New York, 1952, especially chaps. 7 and 9.
17. Underhill Moore and Charles C. Callahan, "Law and Learning Theory: A
    Study in Legal Control," 53 *Yale Law Journal* 1–136.
18. See Albert Einstein, *The World As I See It,* Covici Friede, New York,
    1934, pp. 35–36; also Northrop, "Einstein's Conception of Science," in
    Paul A. Schilpp, ed., *Albert Einstein: Philosopher-Scientist,* Library of
    Living Philosophers, Evanston, 1949, chap. 14.
19. Underhill Moore and others, "Institutional Studies," 38 *Yale Law Journal*
    703–719; 40 *Yale Law Journal* 381–400, 555–575, 752–778, 928–
    953, 1055–1073, 1219–1250 and Appendix 1251–1272; 41 *Yale Law*

Journal 566–576, 1109–1133; 42 *Yale Law Journal* 817–862, 1198–1235; 45 *Yale Law Journal* 1–38, 260–292. See also Charles E. Clark, "Fact Research in Law Administration," 38 *Connecticut Bar Journal* 211–233; William E. Hocking, *Present Status of the Philosophy of Law and of Rights*, Yale University Press, New Haven, 1926.

20. See Austin, *op. cit.*, pp. 184, 260–261.
21. C. L. Hull, *Principles of Behavior*, Appleton-Century-Crofts, New York, 1943.
22. C. L. Hull, C. I. Hovland, R. T. Ross, M. Hall, D. T. Perkins and F. B. Fitch, *Mathematico-Deductive Theory of Rote Learning*, Yale University Press, New Haven, 1940.
23. Thomas Jefferson, *The Papers of Thomas Jefferson*, Julian P. Boyd, ed., Princeton University Press, Princeton, vol. XII, 1955, pp. 34, 189, 440. See also Claude G. Bowers, "Jefferson and the Bill of Rights," 41 *Virginia Law Review* 709–729 esp. p. 720.
24. Sol Tax, Loren C. Eiseley, Irving Rouse and Carl F. Voegelin, eds., *An Appraisal of Anthropology Today*, University of Chicago Press, Chicago, 1953, p. 373.
25. Clyde Kluckhohn, "The Philosophy of the Navaho Indians," in Northrop, ed., *Ideological Differences and World Order*, Yale University Press, New Haven, 1949, chap. XVII.
26. Cornelius Osgood, "Culture: Its Empirical and Non-empirical Character," 7 *Southwestern Journal of Anthropology* 202–214.
27. See note 11, *supra*.
28. Northrop, *The Meeting of East and West*, Macmillan, New York, 1947; "The Importance of Deductively Formulated Theory in Ethics and Social and Legal Science," in Paul Henle, Horace M. Kallen and Susanne K. Langer, eds., *Structure, Method, and Meaning: Essays in Honor of Henry M. Sheffer*, Liberal Arts Press, New York, 1951, pp. 99–114.
29. Thomas Jefferson, *The Life and Selected Writings of Thomas Jefferson*, Adrienne Koch and William Peden, eds., Modern Library, New York, 1944, p. 609.
30. John Locke, *Of Civil Government*, Everyman's Library, London, 1940, p. 183.
31. *Ibid.*, p. 187.
32. Adler v. Board of Education of the City of New York, 342 *U. S. Supreme Court Reports* 496–497, 508–511.
33. See Austin, *op. cit.*, pp. 260–261.
34. See note 13, *supra*.
35. 342 *U. S. Supreme Court Reports* 497–508.
36. Northrop, *Meeting of East and West*, p. 71.
37. Sir Robert Filmer, *Patriarcha*, edited with introduction by Peter Laslett, Basil Blackwell, Oxford, 1949, pp. 1–46.
38. See F. H. Lawson, *A Common Lawyer Looks at the Civil Law*, University of Michigan Law School, Ann Arbor, 1953; see also chap. XVII of this book.
39. Chiang Monlin, *Tides from the West*, Yale University Press, New Haven, 1947, pp. 255–256; Northrop, *Taming of Nations*, chap. 7; and Chapter XV of this book.

40. M. K. Gandhi, *Gandhi's Autobiography: The Story of My Experiments with Truth*, Public Affairs Press, Washington, 1948, pp. 167–168. See also Northrop, *Taming of Nations*, chap. 4.

IV   CULTURAL VALUES

For references on the legal theories of this chapter, see the following works:

Roscoe Pound, *Outlines of Lectures on Jurisprudence*, Harvard University Press, Cambridge, 1943.

W. Friedmann, *Legal Theory*, 2nd ed., Stevens, London, 1949.

F. S. C. Northrop, ed., *Ideological Differences and World Order*, Yale University Press, New Haven, 1949.

Joseph Needham, *Human Law and the Laws of Nature in China and the West*, Oxford University Press, London, 1951.

Hu Shih, "The Natural Law in the Chinese Tradition," in Edward F. Barrett, ed., *University of Notre Dame Natural Law Institute Proceedings*, University of Notre Dame Press, Notre Dame, vol. V, 1953, pp. 119–156.

Sir Henry S. Maine, *Ancient Law: Its Connection with the Early History of the Society and Its Relation to Modern Ideas*, John Murray, London, 1908.

Hans Kelsen, *General Theory of Law and State*, Harvard University Press, Cambridge, 1946.

Eugen Ehrlich, *Fundamental Principles of the Sociology of Law*, Harvard University Press, Cambridge, 1936.

Underhill Moore and Charles C. Callahan, "Law and Learning Theory: A Study in Legal Control," 53 *Yale Law Journal* 1–136.

Chiang Monlin, *Tides from the West*, Yale University Press, New Haven, 1947.

William E. Hocking, *Present Status of the Philosophy of Law and of Rights*, Yale University Press, New Haven, 1926.

V   LEGAL POSITIVISM, INTUITIVE ETHICS AND SOCIOLOGICAL
JURISPRUDENCE

1. Roscoe Pound, "Toward a New Jus Gentium," in F. S. C. Northrop, ed., *Ideological Differences and World Order*, Yale University Press, New Haven, 1949, p. 7; *Social Control through Law*, Yale University Press, New Haven, 1942.

2. Myres S. McDougal, "The Law School of the Future: From Legal Realism to Policy Science in the World Community," 56 *Yale Law Journal* 1345.

3. P. E. Corbett, *Law and Society in the Relations of States*, Harcourt, Brace, New York, 1951.

4. *Ibid.*, p. 70.

5. *Ibid.*, p. 73; Hans Kelsen, "The Pure Theory of Law," 50 *Law Quarterly Review* 474–498; 51 *Law Quarterly Review* 517–535.

6. Hans Kelsen, *General Theory of Law and State*, Harvard University Press, Cambridge, 1946, pp. 115 *et seq.*; Corbett, *op. cit.*, pp. 72–73.

7. Corbett, *op. cit.*, p. 73.

8. *Ibid.*

9. *Ibid.*

10. *Ibid.*

11. John Austin, *Lectures on Jurisprudence, or The Philosophy of Positive Law*, Robert Campbell, ed., Murray, London, 1873, pp. 16–18.
12. *Ibid.*, p. 17.
13. Kelsen, *General Theory of Law and State*, p. 110.
14. *Ibid.*, p. 113.
15. *Ibid.*, p. 114.
16. Eugen Ehrlich, *The Fundamental Principles of the Sociology of Law*, Harvard University Press, Cambridge, 1936, pp. 81, 369, 388, 401, 499; chaps. XX, XXI.
17. Hans Kelsen, *Die Verfassungsgesetze der Republik Deutsch-Österreich*, vols. 1–3, 1919, vol. 4, 1920, vol. 5, 1922, Deuticke, Wien and Leipzig, 1919–1922.
18. Kelsen, *General Theory of Law and State*, p. 115.
19. *Ibid.*
20. *Ibid.*, p. 116.
21. Hans Kelsen, "Causality and Imputation," 61 *Ethics* 1–11.
22. Kelsen, *General Theory of Law and State*, p. 116.
23. Morris R. Cohen, "Philosophy and Legal Science," 32 *Columbia Law Review* 1103–1127; *Reason and Nature: An Essay on the Meaning of Scientific Method*, Harcourt, Brace, New York, 1931, pp. 333–457; *Law and Social Order: Essays in Legal Philosophy*, Harcourt, Brace, New York, 1933. Felix Cohen, *Ethical Systems and Legal Ideals: An Essay on the Foundation of Legal Criticism*, Falcon, New York, 1933; "The Problems of a Functional Jurisprudence," 1 *Modern Law Review* 5. And see Rudolf Stammler, *The Theory of Justice*, Isaac Husik, tr., Macmillan, New York, 1925.
24. Pound, "Toward a New Jus Gentium"; "The Scope and Purpose of Sociological Jurisprudence," 24 *Harvard Law Review* 591–619, 25 *Harvard Law Review* 140–168, 489–516; "Law and the Science of Law in Recent Theories," 43 *Yale Law Journal* 525; "A Survey of Social Interests," 57 *Harvard Law Review* 1; *An Introduction to American Law*, Dunster House Papers No. 3, Cambridge, 1919; *An Introduction to the Philosophy of Law*, Yale University Press, New Haven, 1946, pp. 1–143; *Outlines of Lectures on Jurisprudence*, 5th ed., Harvard University Press, Cambridge, 1943, chaps, IV, V, VI. See also Julius Stone, *The Province and Function of Law: Law as Logic, Justice and Social Control, A Study in Jurisprudence*, Harvard University Press, Cambridge, 1950.
25. Ehrlich, *Fundamental Principles*, chaps. XX, XXI.
26. *Ibid.*, p. 473.
27. Kelsen, *General Theory of Law and State*, p. 391.
28. Kelsen, "Causality and Imputation," 61 *Ethics* 1–11.
29. Underhill Moore, with Theodore S. Hope, Jr., "An Institutional Approach to the Law of Commercial Banking," 38 *Yale Law Journal* 703–719; with Gilbert Sussman, *Legal and Institutional Methods Applied to the Debiting of Direct Discounts*: I. "Legal Method, Banker's Set-Off," 40 *Yale Law Journal* 381–400; II. "Institutional Method," 40 *Yale Law Journal* 555–575; III. "Connecticut Studies," 40 *Yale Law Journal* 752–778; IV. "South Carolina and Pennsylvania Studies," 40 *Yale Law Journal* 928–953; V. "The New York Study," 40 *Yale Law Journal*

1055–1073; VI. "The Decisions, the Institutions, and the Degrees of Deviation," 40 *Yale Law Journal* 1219–1250; and "Appendix," 40 *Yale Law Journal* 1251–1272; with Gilbert Sussman, "The Current Account and Set-Offs Between an Insolvent Bank and Its Customer," 41 *Yale Law Journal* 1109–1133; with Gilbert Sussman, "The Lawyer's Law," 41 *Yale Law Journal* 566–576; with Gilbert Sussman and C. E. Brand, *Legal and Institutional Methods Applied to Orders to Stop Payment of Checks:* I. "Legal Method," 42 *Yale Law Journal* 817–862; II. "Institutional Method," 42 *Yale Law Journal* 1198–1235; "Drawing Against Uncollected Checks," 45 *Yale Law Journal* 1–38; with Gilbert Sussman and Emma Corstvet, "Drawing against Uncollected Checks," 45 *Yale Law Journal* 1–38 and 260–292; with Charles C. Callahan, "Law and Learning Theory: A Study in Legal Control," 53 *Yale Law Journal* 1–136; "My Philosophy of Law," in *My Philosophy of Law: Credos of Sixteen American Scholars*, Boston Law Book, Boston, 1941, pp. 201–228; Northrop, "Underhill Moore's Legal Science: Its Nature and Significance," 59 *Yale Law Journal* 196–213.
30. Ehrlich, *Fundamental Principles,* chaps. III, IV.
31. *Ibid.*
32. McDougal, "Law School of the Future"; "The Role of Law in World Politics," 20 *Mississippi Law Journal* 253–283; Harold D. Lasswell and Myres S. McDougal, "Legal Education and Public Policy: Professional Training in the Public Interest," 52 *Yale Law Journal* 203–295; Lasswell, *The Analysis of Political Behaviour,* Kegan Paul, Trench & Trubner, London, 1948.
33. Moore and Callahan, "Law and Learning." See also Northrop, "Underhill Moore's Legal Science."
34. Karl R. Popper, *The Open Society and Its Enemies,* Princeton University Press, Princeton, 1950.

VI   PETRAZYCKI'S PSYCHOLOGICAL JURISPRUDENCE

1. Leon Petrazycki, *Law and Morality,* Hugh W. Babb, tr., with an introduction by Nicholas S. Timasheff, 20th Century Legal Philosophy Series, Harvard University Press, Cambridge, vol. VII, 1955.
2. *Ibid.,* p. 27.
3. H. L. A. Hart, "Definition and Theory in Jurisprudence," 70 *Law Quarterly Review* 37, 39.
4. See F. S. C. Northrop, ed., *Ideological Differences and World Order,* Yale University Press, New Haven, 1949, chap. XIX.

VII   THE METHOD OF RECENT CULTURAL ANTHROPOLOGY

1. E. Adamson Hoebel, *The Law of Primitive Man: A Study in Comparative Legal Dynamics,* Harvard University Press, Cambridge, 1954.
2. F. S. C. Northrop, *European Union and United States Foreign Policy,* Macmillan, New York, 1954, chaps. 3, 6–8.
3. Hoebel, *op. cit.,* p. 14.
4. *Ibid.*
5. *Ibid.,* p. 15.
6. See Northrop, "Underhill Moore's Legal Science: Its Nature and Signifi-

cance," 59 *Yale Law Journal* 196–213; see also Chapter VI of this book.

7. See Chapter XV of this book; also Northrop, *The Taming of the Nations,* Macmillan, New York, 1952, pp. 56–65.
8. Hoebel, *op. cit.,* p. 176.
9. *Ibid.,* p. 140.
10. *Ibid.,* pp. 131, 138, 142, 144, 145, 224–225, 264–265.
11. *Ibid.,* p. 167.
12. *Ibid.,* pp. 285–291.
13. *Ibid.,* p. 145.
14. A. R. Radcliffe-Brown, "Patrilineal and Matrilineal Succession," 20 *Iowa Law Review* 286.
15. Hoebel, *op. cit.,* p. 181.
16. *Ibid.,* p. 217.
17. *Ibid.,* p. 181.
18. *Ibid.,* p. 28.
19. A. L. Goodhart, *English Law and the Moral Law,* Stevens, London, 1953, p. 17.
20. Leon Petrazycki, *Law and Morality,* Hugh W. Babb, tr., with an introduction by Nicholas S. Timasheff, 20th Century Legal Philosophy Series, Harvard University Press, Cambridge, vol. VII, 1955. See also Northrop, "Underhill Moore's Legal Science" and Chapter VI of this book.
21. Hoebel, *op. cit.,* p. 333.

VIII THE METHOD AND NEUROPHYSIOLOGICAL BASIS
OF PHILOSOPHICAL ANTHROPOLOGY

1. F. S. C. Northrop, *European Union and United States Foreign Policy,* Macmillan, New York, 1954; see also the recent study by Julius Cohen, Reginald A. H. Robson and Alan Bates, *Parental Authority: The Community and the Law,* Rutgers University Press, New Brunswick, 1958.
2. W. Friedmann, Review of *European Union and United States Foreign Policy,* 64 *Yale Law Journal* 469.
3. Chiang Monlin, *Tides from the West,* Yale University Press, New Haven, 1947.
4. Pitirim A. Sorokin, *Social and Cultural Dynamics,* American Book, New York, 1937–1941; *Society, Culture and Personality: Their Structure and Dynamics,* Harper, New York, 1947; *Sociocultural Causality, Space, Time: A Study of Referential Principles of Sociology and Social Science,* Duke University Press, Durham, 1943; see also Jacques J. Maquet, *The Sociology of Knowledge: Its Structure and Its Relation to the Philosophy of Knowledge,* Beacon, Boston, 1951.
5. See Northrop, *The Logic of the Sciences and the Humanities,* Macmillan, New York, 1947, pp. 219–226.
6. Northrop, "Philosophical Anthropology and World Law," 14 *Transactions of the New York Academy of Sciences* 109–112.
7. Clyde Kluckhohn, "The Philosophy of the Navaho Indians," in Northrop, ed., *Ideological Differences and World Order,* Yale University Press, New Haven, 1949, chap. XVII.

8. Warren S. McCulloch and Walter Pitts, "How We Know Universals," 5 *Bulletin of Mathematical Biophysics* 115–133; McCulloch, "A Hierarchy of Values Determined by the Topology of Nervous Nets," *ibid.*, 89–93. See also Arturo Rosenblueth, Norbert Wiener and Julian Bigelow, "Behavior, Purpose and Teleology," 10 *Philosophy of Science* 18–24. For a summary of the foregoing material see Northrop, "The Neurological and Behavioristic Psychological Basis for the Ordering of Society by Means of Ideas," 107 *Science* 411–417, *Ideological Differences,* chap. XIX.

9. Northrop, "Philosophical Anthropology and World Law."

10. John von Neumann, *The Computer and the Brain,* Yale University Press, New Haven, 1958.

11. *Ibid.,* pp. 31 and 32.

12. *Ibid.,* p. 33

13. Adler v. Board of Education of the City of New York, 342 *U.S. Supreme Court Reports* 485–511. The Feinberg Law makes membership in any organization which advocates overthrow of the government by violence prima facie evidence of disqualification for employment in the public school system.

14. For further specification of the scientific method of philosophical anthropology, see Northrop, "The Importance of Deductively Formulated Theory in Ethics and Social and Legal Science" in Paul Henle, Horace M. Kallen and Susanne K. Langer, eds., *Structure, Method and Meaning: Essays in Honor of Henry Sheffer,* Liberal Arts Press, New York, 1951, pp. 99–114.

15. Northrop, *European Union and United States Foreign Policy.*

IX   CULTURAL DYNAMICS AND HISTORICAL JURISPRUDENCE

1. Pitirim A. Sorokin, *Social and Cultural Dynamics,* American Book, New York, 1937–1941; *Society, Culture, and Personality: Their Structure and Dynamics,* Harper, New York, 1947.

2. Clyde Kluckhohn, "The Philosophy of the Navaho Indians" in F. S. C. Northrop, ed., *Ideological Differences and World Order,* Yale University Press, New Haven, 1949, chap. XVII.

3. Northrop, "Philosophical Anthropology and World Law," 14 *Transactions of the New York Academy of Sciences* 109–112.

4. Vilfredo Pareto, *Traité de Sociologie Générale,* Librairie Payot, Lausanne, 1919.

5. Underhill Moore and Charles C. Callahan, "Law and Learning Theory: A Study in Legal Control," 53 *Yale Law Journal* 1–136; and Northrop, "Underhill Moore's Legal Science: Its Nature and Significance," 59 *Yale Law Journal* 196–213; and Chapters V and VIII of this book.

6. Northrop, "Evolution in Its Relation to the Philosophy of Nature and the Philosophy of Culture," in Stow Persons, ed., *Evolutionary Thought in America,* Yale University Press, 1950, pp. 44–84.

7. Lionel Robbins, *An Essay on the Nature and Significance of Economic Science,* Macmillan, London, 1935; Northrop, "The Impossibility of a Theoretical Science of Economic Dynamics," LVI *Quarterly Journal of Economics* November 1941, pp. 1–17.

8. Northrop, *The Meeting of East and West*, Macmillan, New York, 1946, especially chaps. VIII and XI.

X   EUROPEAN POLITICAL EXPERIENCE SINCE WORLD WAR II

1. Paul-Henri Spaak, "England Tiptoes into Europe," 7 *United Nations World* No. 4, April 1953, p. 18.
2. Northrop, *European Union and United States Foreign Policy*, Macmillan, New York, 1954, chap. 9.
3. "Europe After London," *The Economist*, Vol. CLXXIII, No. 5798, October 9, 1954, p. 103.
4. *Ibid.*, p. 101.
5. "Europe in 4–D," *The Economist*, Vol. CLXXII, No. 5796, September 25, 1954, p. 954.
6. Spaak, *op. cit.*, p. 18.
7. A. L. Goodhart, *English Law and the Moral Law*, Stevens, London, 1953, p. 127.
8. *The Century Dictionary and Cyclopedia*, Century, New York, Vol. I, 1895, p. 794.
9. Lord Lindsay of Birker, "The Philosophy of the British Labour Government" in Northrop, ed., *Ideological Differences and World Order*, Yale University Press, New Haven, 1949, p. 251.
10. *Ibid.*, p. 255.
11. Based on figures from *The World Almanac and Book of Facts 1958.*
12. For evidence of this see *Dod's Peerage, Baronetage and Knightage of Great Britain and Ireland* for 1910, Simpkin, Marshall, Hamilton and Kent, London, pp. 44–92.
13. T. D. Weldon, *A Vocabulary of Politics*, Penguin, Harmondsworth, Middlesex, 1953, p. 57.
14. For a more detailed study of these matters, see Northrop, *European Union*, chaps. 1–9.
15. *Ibid.*
16. "Atlantic Assembly," *The Economist*, Vol. CLXIX, No. 5757, December 26, 1953, pp. 943–944.
17. Eugen Ehrlich, *Fundamental Principles of the Sociology of Law*, translated by Walter I. Moll, Harvard University Press, Cambridge, 1936.

XI   PHILOSOPHICAL ANTHROPOLOGY AND INTERNATIONAL LAW

1. See Northrop, "Einstein's Conception of Science" in Paul A. Schilpp, ed., *Albert Einstein: Philosopher-Scientist*, Library of Living Philosophers, Evanston, vol. VII, 1949; also Northrop, *The Logic of the Sciences and the Humanities*, chap. XII; Henry Margenau, *The Nature of Physical Reality*, McGraw-Hill, New York, 1950.
2. See Plates XIII and XIV in Northrop, *The Meeting of East and West*, Macmillan, New York, 1946, p. 406.
3. For evidence supporting this point and a designation of its precise content and meaning, see Gray L. Dorsey's investigation of the source of verification of Confucian Chinese legal norms in his chapter, "Two Objective Bases for a World-Wide Legal Order," in Northrop, ed., *Ideological Differences and World Order*, Yale University Press, New Haven, 1949.
4. *Ibid.*, p. 451.

5. Marcel Granet, *La Pensée Chinoise*, La Renaissance du Livre, Paris, 1934.
6. P. V. Kane, *History of Dharmasastra*, vol. I, Bhandarkar Oriental Res. Inst., Poona, 1930, pp. 244–245.
7. Fritz Berolzheimer, *The World's Legal Philosophies*, translated by Rachel S. Jastrow, Boston Book, Boston, 1912, pp. 37–38.
8. Kane, *op. cit.*, p. 829.
9. F. Max Müller, ed., *The Laws of Manu*, vol. 25 of *The Sacred Books of the East*, Clarendon, Oxford, 1886, chaps. I, II.
10. David Nasmith, *Outline of Roman History*, Butterworths, London, 1890, p. 200.
11. Arthur Nussbaum, *Concise History of the Law of Nations*, Macmillan, New York, 1947, p. 19.
12. E. Vernon Arnold, *Roman Stoicism*, Cambridge University Press, Cambridge, 1911.
13. *Ibid.*, p. 66.
14. *Ibid.*, p. 67.
15. *Ibid.*, p. 64.
16. *Ibid.*, p. 74.
17. B. Jowett, ed., *The Republic of Plato*, Clarendon Press, Oxford, 1888, Bk. 7, line 533, p. 236.
18. H. Rackham, Introduction to Cicero's *De Natura Deorum, Academica*, Loeb Classical Library, Heinemann, London, 1933, p. vii.
19. Arnold, *op. cit.*, chap. VI.
20. *Ibid.*, p. 129.
21. *Ibid.*, p. 131.
22. *Ibid.*, pp. 132–133.
23. For a detailed account of the different stages of scientific inquiry and their respective scientific methods, see Northrop, *Logic of the Sciences*, chaps. I–XII.
24. See Arnold, *op. cit.*, p. 140.
25. Northrop, *Meeting of East and West*, chaps. VIII, XII and XIII.

XII   NATURAL LAW IN CHINA AND THE WEST

1. Joseph Needham, *Human Law and the Laws of Nature in China and the West*, Oxford, London, 1951.
2. F. S. C. Northrop, *The Meeting of East and West*, Macmillan, New York, 1946, chaps. IX and X; *The Logic of the Sciences and the Humanities*, Macmillan, New York, 1947, chaps. I–VII.
3. Alfred North Whitehead, *Process and Reality*, Macmillan, New York, 1929.
4. Henry Margenau, *The Nature of Physical Reality*, McGraw-Hill, New York, 1950, chaps. III and XIII; Northrop, *Logic of the Sciences*, chaps. VI and XI.

XIII   THE RELATIVITY OF NATURAL LAW THEORIES

1. Edward F. Barrett, ed., *University of Notre Dame Natural Law Institute Proceedings*, University of Notre Dame Press, Notre Dame, vol. V, 1953.
2. See Sir Ernest Barker, translator, Introduction, *Politics of Aristotle*,

Clarendon, Oxford, 1946, chap. IV; also E. Vernon Arnold, *Roman Stoicism*, Cambridge University Press, Cambridge, 1911; also H. Rackham, Introduction to Cicero's *De Natura Deorum, Academica*, Loeb Classical Library, Heinemann, London, 1933.

3. Thomas Jefferson, *The Living Thoughts of Thomas Jefferson*, presented by John Dewey, Longmans, Green, New York, 1940, pp. 61–62.

4. Thomas Jefferson, *The Writings of Thomas Jefferson*, edited by H. A. Washington, Taylor and Maury, Washington D.C., vol. V, 1853, p. 559.

XIV   LINGUISTIC SYMBOLS AND LEGAL NORMS

1. F. S. C. Northrop, *The Meeting of East and West*, Macmillan, New York, 1946.

2. Alfred North Whitehead, *The Concept of Nature*, Cambridge University Press, London, 1920; *Dialogues of Alfred North Whitehead* as recorded by Lucien Price, Atlantic-Little, Brown, Boston, 1954.

3. Sir Henry S. Maine, *Ancient Law: Its Connection with the Early History of Society and Its Relation to Modern Ideas*, John Murray, London, 1908, p. 151.

4. Lin Yutang, *My Country and My People*, John Day, New York, 1939, p. 83.

5. Ludwig Wittgenstein, *Tractatus Logico-Philosophicus*, Kegan Paul, Trench & Trubner, London, 1922.

XV   THE PHILOSOPHY OF NATURAL SCIENCE AND COMPARATIVE LAW

1. Sir Henry S. Maine, *Ancient Law: Its Connection with the Early History of Society and Its Relation to Modern Ideas*, John Murray, London, 1908.

2. *Ibid.*, p. 151.

3. *Ibid.*, p. 151.

4. Shih-Fang Liu, "Westernized Administration of Justice and Chinese Racial Characteristics," translated from the Chinese by Alfred Wang, Yale Law Library; Chiang Monlin, *Tides from the West*, Yale University Press, New Haven, 1947.

5. Nalinakasha Dutt, *Early Monastic Buddhism*, Calcutta Oriental Series No. 30, Calcutta Oriental Press, Calcutta, vol. I, 1941, vol. II, 1945.

6. H. G. Creel, *Confucius: The Man and the Myth*, John Day, New York, 1949, p. 221.

7. M. K. Gandhi, *Gandhi's Autobiography: The Story of My Experiments with Truth*, Public Affairs Press, Washington, D. C., 1948, pp. 323–324.

8. Satischandra Chatterjee and D. Datta, *An Introduction to Indian Philosophy*, University of Calcutta Press, Calcutta, 1948, p. 431.

9. Chiang Monlin, *op. cit.*, p. 251.

10. Morris R. Cohen and I. E. Drabkin, *A Source Book in Greek Science*, McGraw-Hill, New York, 1948, p. 1.

11. Albert Einstein, *The World As I See It*, Covici Friede, New York, 1934, pp. 31–32.

12. Edwin A. Burtt, *The Metaphysical Foundations of Modern Physical Sci-*

ence, A Historical and Critical Essay, Harcourt, Brace, New York, 1925, p. 75.

13. E. Vernon Arnold, *Roman Stoicism,* Cambridge University Press, Cambridge, 1911; H. Rackham, Introduction to Cicero's *De Natura Deorum, Academica,* Loeb Classical Library, Heinemann, London, 1933. See also Northrop, "Criterion of Universal Ethical and Legal Norms" in Ruth Nanda Anshen, ed., *Moral Principles of Action: Man's Ethical Imperative,* Harper, New York, 1952, pp. 128–139.

14. Charles L. Stevenson, *Ethics and Language,* Yale University Press, New Haven, 1944.

XVI COMPARATIVE ETHICS AND EPISTEMOLOGICAL THEORY

1. See Northrop, "Complementary Emphases of Eastern Intuitive and Western Scientific Philosophy" in Charles A. Moore, ed., *Philosophy — East and West,* Princeton University Press, Princeton, 1944, chap. VIII; also Northrop, *The Meeting of East and West,* Macmillan, New York, 1946, p. 447; and *The Logic of the Sciences and the Humanities,* Macmillan, New York, 1947, chap. V.

2. E. A. Burtt, "Basic Problems of Method in Harmonizing Eastern and Western Philosophy," Charles A. Moore, ed., *Essays in East-West Philosophy,* University of Hawaii Press, Honolulu, 1951, pp. 103–123.

3. S. C. Chatterjee and D. M. Datta, *An Introduction to Indian Philosophy,* University of Calcutta Press, Calcutta, 1948, p. 54.

4. See Northrop, *Meeting of East and West,* pp. 447–454; also "Complementary Emphases of Eastern Intuitive and Western Scientific Philosophy" in Charles A. Moore, ed., *Philosophy: East and West,* Princeton University Press, Princeton, 1944, pp. 168–234; and *Logic of the Sciences and the Humanities,* chaps. III–VIII.

5. *Ibid.*

6. *Ibid.* See especially *Meeting of East and West,* chap. XII; and *Logic of the Sciences and the Humanities,* chaps. VII–VIII.

7. D. M. Datta, "Epistemological Methods in Indian Philosophy" in Moore, *Essays in East-West Philosophy,* chap. III.

8. S. C. Chatterjee and D. M. Datta, *op. cit.,* p. 54.

9. *Ibid.,* p. 53.

10. E. A. Burtt, *op. cit.,* note 2, pp. 103–123.

11. G. W. Leibniz, *Philosophical Writings,* Everyman's Library, Dent, London, and Dutton, New York, 1934, p. 191.

12. Sir Henry S. Maine, *Ancient Law: Its Connection with the Early History of Society and Its Relation to Modern Ideas,* John Murray, London, 1908, p. 151.

XVII COMMON LAW, ROMAN LAW AND THE CIVIL LAW

1. F. H. Lawson, *A Common Lawyer Looks at the Civil Law,* University of Michigan Law School, Ann Arbor, 1953.

2. Lawson, *op. cit.,* p. 69.

3. A. P. d'Entrèves, "Case for Natural Law Re-Examined," 1 *Natural Law Forum* 5–52.

4. Lawson, *op. cit.,* p. 45.

5. *Ibid.*, p. 46.
6. *Ibid.*
7. *Ibid.*, p. 116.
8. *Ibid.*, pp. 116–117.
9. *Ibid.*, p. 126.
10. *Ibid.*
11. *Ibid.*
12. *Ibid.*, p. 127.
13. E. Vernon Arnold, *Roman Stoicism,* Cambridge University Press, Cambridge, 1911, pp. 383 ff.; also chap. 12.
14. *Ibid.*, chap. 6.
15. *Ibid.*, chaps. 6 and 7. See also H. Rackham, Introduction to Cicero's *De Natura Deorum, Academica,* Loeb Classical Library, Heinemann, London, 1933, p. vii.
16. Lawson, *op. cit.,* pp. 88–89.
17. *Ibid.*, p. 95.
18. *Ibid.*, p. 96.
19. *Ibid.*
20. *Ibid.*, p. 99.
21. *Ibid.*, p. 123.
22. Thomas Jefferson, *The Writings of Thomas Jefferson,* edited by H. A. Washington, Taylor and Maury, Washington, D. C., vol. VII, 1854, p. 139.

XVIII   CONCERNING THE SOCIOLOGY OF KNOWLEDGE

1. Jacques J. Maquet, *The Sociology of Knowledge: Its Structure and Its Relation to the Philosophy of Knowledge,* Beacon, Boston, 1951.
2. Clyde Kluckhohn, "The Philosophy of the Navaho Indians" in Northrop, ed., *Ideological Differences and World Order,* Yale University Press, New Haven, 1949.
3. Northrop, "Ideological Man in His Relation to Scientifically Known Natural Man" in *Ideological Differences and World Order,* chap. XIX. See also Northrop, "The Neurological and Behavioristic Psychological Basis for the Ordering of Society by Means of Ideas," 107 *Science,* No. 2782, pp. 411–417.
4. Gray L. Dorsey, "Two Objective Bases for a World-Wide Legal Order," in Northrop, *Ideological Differences,* chap. XXI.
5. Henry Margenau, "The Meaning and Scientific Status of Causality," 1 *Philosophy of Science* 133–148; "The Critical Points in Modern Physical Theory," 4 *Philosophy of Science* 337–370.
6. Northrop, *The Logic of the Sciences and the Humanities,* Macmillan, New York, 1947, chaps. 11 and 12.

XIX   THE THEORY OF TYPES AND THE VERIFICATION
OF ETHICAL THEORY

1. Northrop, *The Logic of the Sciences and the Humanities,* Macmillan, New York, 1947, p. 279 ff.
2. Y. P. Mei, "The Basis of Social, Ethical, and Spiritual Values in Chinese Philosophy," in Charles A. Moore, ed., *Essays in East-West Philosophy,* University of Hawaii Press, Honolulu, 1951, pp. 301–316.

3. Edward H. Carr, *Soviet Impact on the Western World,* Macmillan, New York, 1947, p. 94.
4. A. S. Ferguson, "Plato's Simile of Light," 15 *Classical Quarterly* 131–152, 16 *Classical Quarterly* 15–28, "Plato's Simile of Light Again," 28 *Classical Quarterly* 191–210.
5. E. Vernon Arnold, *Roman Stoicism,* Cambridge University Press, Cambridge, 1911.
6. *Ibid.,* p. 133.

XX   ETHICAL RELATIVISM IN THE LIGHT OF RECENT LEGAL THEORY

1. Jerome Frank, "A Conflict with Oblivion: Some Observations on the Founders of Legal Pragmatism," 9 *Rutgers Law Review* 425–463.
2. Learned Hand, *The Spirit of Liberty,* Papers and Addresses Collected by Irving Dilliard, Knopf, New York, 1953, pp. 41, 58.
3. *Ibid.,* pp. 51, 54, 209–219.
4. *Ibid.,* p. 73. See also James B. Thayer, "The Origin and Scope of the American Doctrine of Constitutional Law," 7 *Harvard Law Review* 129–156.
5. Beauharnais v. Illinois, 343 *United States Supreme Court Reports* 250–306, esp. pp. 267–268. Adler v. Board of Education of The City of New York," *ibid.,* vol. 342, pp. 485–512, esp. pp. 485, 496–497, 508–511.
6. Eugen Ehrlich, *Fundamental Principles of the Sociology of Law,* translated by Walter I. Moll, Harvard University Press, Cambridge, 1936.
7. Roscoe Pound, "Law and the Science of Law," 43 *Yale Law Journal* 525–536; *An Introduction to the Philosophy of Law,* Yale University Press, New Haven, 1946, pp. 1–143; "The Scope and Purpose of Sociological Jurisprudence," 24 *Harvard Law Review* 591–619; *ibid.,* vol. 25, pp. 140–168, 489–516.
8. Underhill Moore and others; see the following references in note 29 to Chapter V: 38 *Yale Law Journal* 703–719; vol. 40, pp. 381–400, 555–575, 752–778, 928–953, 1055–1073, 1219–1250; vol. 42, pp. 817–862, 1198–1235; vol. 45, pp. 1–38, 260–292; vol. 53, pp. 1–136.
9. Ehrlich, *op. cit.,* p. 37.
10. *Ibid.,* p. 493.
11. Clyde Kluckhohn, "Universal Categories of Culture" in *Anthropology Today,* prepared under A. L. Kroeber, University of Chicago Press, Chicago, 1953, pp. 507–523; also A. L. Kroeber, *Configurations of Culture Growth,* University of California Press, Los Angeles, 1944.
12. F. S. C. Northrop, "Philosophical Anthropology and World Law," 14 *Transactions of the New York Academy of Sciences* 109–112.
13. A. L. Kroeber, "Concluding Review," in Sol Tax, Loren C. Eiseley, Irving Rouse and Carl F. Voegelin, eds., *An Appraisal of Anthropology Today,* University of Chicago Press, Chicago, 1953, p. 373.
14. Ehrlich, *op. cit.,* pp. 39–136.
15. Chiang Monlin, *Tides from the West,* Yale University Press, New Haven, 1947, pp. 137–140. Cf. Northrop, *The Taming of the Nations,* Macmillan, New York, 1952, pp. 108–148.

16. Underhill Moore and Charles C. Callahan, "Law and Learning Theory: A Study in Legal Control" 53 *Yale Law Journal* 1–136, esp. p. 61 ff.

17. Clyde Kluckhohn, "The Philosophy of the Navaho Indians" in Northrop, ed., *Ideological Differences and World Order,* Yale University Press, New Haven, 1949, p. 356. Cf. Pitirim A. Sorokin's "logico-meaningful causality" in his *Society, Culture, and Personality: Their Structure and Dynamics,* Harper, New York, 1947.

18. A. L. Kroeber and Clyde Kluckhohn, *Culture: A Critical Review of Concepts and Definitions,* Papers of the Peabody Museum of American Archaeology and Ethnology, Harvard University, vol. XLVII, 1952, p. 181.

19. Clyde Kluckhohn, "The Philosophy of the Navaho Indians," pp. 356–384.

20. F. S. C. Northrop, *European Union and United States Foreign Policy,* Macmillan, New York, 1954, pp. 75–137.

21. *Ibid.,* pp. 126, 133; see also E. Adamson Hoebel, *The Law of Primitive Man: A Study in Comparative Legal Dynamics,* Harvard University Press, Cambridge, 1954, chap. I, especially p. 14.

22. For suggestions of how this is to be done, see Chapters V and VIII, and Northrop, *Taming of Nations,* pp. 259–309.

23. A. P. d'Entrèves, *Natural Law,* Hutchinson's University Library, London, 1952.

24. Lon Fuller, *The Law in Quest of Itself,* Foundation Press, Chicago, 1940; Roscoe Pound, "Toward a New Jus Gentium," in Northrop, *Ideological Differences,* pp. 1–47.

25. Friedrich Kessler, "Natural Law, Justice and Democracy," 19 *Tulane Law Review* 32–61; also "Theoretic Bases of Law," 9 *University of Chicago Law Review* 98–112.

26. Mortimer J. Adler, *What Man Has Made of Man,* Longmans, Green, New York, 1937.

27. Sir A. L. Goodhart, *English Law and the Moral Law,* Stevens, London, 1953. Note also John Wild, *Plato's Modern Enemies and the Theory of Natural Law,* University of Chicago Press, Chicago, 1953.

28. Karl Mannheim, *Ideology and Utopia,* Routledge and Kegan Paul, London, 1948; *Man and Society,* Routledge and Kegan Paul, London, 1948; Jacques J. Maquet, *The Sociology of Knowledge: Its Structure and Its Relation to the Philosophy of Knowledge,* Beacon, Boston, 1951.

29. See Chapter XIX.

30. For contemporary scientific theories of how this can be, see Northrop, *Ideological Differences,* pp. 407–428; also Chapter XIII above.

31. For a description and analysis of the scientific method by which the norms of culture are related to the philosophy of nature, see Northrop, *The Logic of the Sciences and the Humanities,* Macmillan, New York, 1947, pp. 328–347.

32. F. S. C. Northrop, *The Meeting of East and West,* Macmillan, New York, 1946, pp. 312–404.

XXI THE METHOD FOR JUDGING THE LIVING LAW

1. C. W. Westrup, *Introduction to Early Roman Law,* vol. III, Patria Potestas, Oxford University Press, London, 1939, pp. 228–229.

2. For a description of this Christian patriarchal living law see the following studies by Peter Laslett: "The Gentry of Kent in 1640," 9 *Cambridge Historical Journal* 148–164; "Sir Robert Filmer," 5 *William and Mary Quarterly* 523–546; the Introduction to *Patriarcha and Other Political Works of Sir Robert Filmer*, edited with an Introduction by Peter Laslett, Basil Blackwell, Oxford, 1949.

3. Northrop, *The Meeting of East and West*, Macmillan, New York, 1946, chap. 12; "The Mediational Approval Theory of Law in American Legal Realism," 44 *Virginia Law Review* 347–363; *The Taming of the Nations*, Macmillan, New York, 1952, chaps. 5, 10 and 16.

4. Northrop, *The Logic of the Sciences and the Humanities*, Macmillan, New York, 1947, chaps. 5 and 21.

5. Northrop, *Meeting of East and West*, chaps. 10, 11 and 12; *Taming of Nations*, preface and chap. 5; "The Mediational Approval Theory of Law in American Legal Realism."

XXII   SOME DOMESTIC AND INTERNATIONAL LEGAL IMPLICATIONS

1. F. S. C. Northrop, "The Scientific Method for Determining the Correct Ends of Social Action," *Social Science*, Vol. 22, July 1947, p. 226.

2. John Locke, *Essays on the Law of Nature*, edited by W. von Leyden, Clarendon, Oxford, 1954; *Letter Concerning Toleration*, edited by C. L. Sherman, Appleton-Century, New York, 1937; *Of Civil Government*, Everyman's Library, Dent, London, and Dutton, New York, 1940.

3. Roscoe Pound, "Toward a New Jus Gentium," in Northrop, ed., *Ideological Differences and World Order*, Yale University Press, New Haven, 1949, chap. I; Gray L. Dorsey, "Two Objective Bases for a World-wide Legal Order," in Northrop, ed., *Ibid.*, chap. XXI; see also Northrop, *The Taming of the Nations*, Macmillan, New York, 1952, chaps. 7–16; Northrop, *The Meeting of East and West*, Macmillan, New York, 1946, chaps. III, IV, VIII–XII.

4. Northrop, *Taming of the Nations*, chap. 11.

5. Thomas Jefferson, *The Life and Writings of Thomas Jefferson*, Adrienne Koch and William Peden, eds., The Modern Library, New York, 1944, p. 609.

6. Thomas Hobbes, *Leviathan or the Matter, Forme and Power of a Commonwealth, Ecclesiasticall and Civil*, Michael Oakeshott, ed., Blackwell, Oxford, undated, chap. 18; John Austin, *The Province of Jurisprudence Determined*, introduction by H. L. A. Hart, Weidenfeld and Nicolson, London, 1954, pp. 235 and 246.

7. For an excellent and concise account of (a) the difference between a democracy based on Locke and Jefferson and one based on either Hobbes or Rousseau and (b) the ease with which the latter types of democracy prepare the way for dictatorship and Communism, see E. H. Carr, *The Soviet Impact on the Western World*, Macmillan, New York, 1947, chap. I.

8. Sir Robert Filmer, *Patriarcha*, edited with Introduction by Peter Laslett, Basil Blackwell, Oxford, 1949, pp. 1–43.

9. R. M. Martin, "On Semantical Rules and Definable Predicates" in *Philosophical Studies*, Vol. X, April 1959, pp. 33–38; Northrop, *The*

Logic of the Sciences and the Humanities, Macmillan, New York, 1947, chaps. VII, VIII, XI, XII and VI; Northrop, "Einstein's Conception of Science," in Paul Arthur Schilpp, ed., *Albert Einstein: Philosopher-Scientist*, The Library of Living Philosophers, Vol. VII, Evanston, Ill., 1949, pp. 387–408 and p. 683; Hans Reichenbach, *Philosophie der Raum-Zeit-Lehre*, Walter de Gruyter, Berlin and Leipzig, 1928, chap. 4, "Die Zuordnungsdefinition," pp. 23–29; Henry Margenau, *The Nature of Physical Reality*, McGraw-Hill, New York, 1950, esp. chap. 4.

10. Learned Hand, *The Spirit of Liberty*, Papers and Addresses Collected by Irving Dilliard, Knopf, New York, 1953, p. 58.

11. As reprinted in *ibid.*, p. 204.

12. *Ibid.*, p. 58.

13. *Ibid.*, p. 61.

14. John Austin, *The Province of Jurisprudence Determined*, pp. xi and xii.

15. *Ibid.*, pp. 13–14.

16. *Barenblatt* v. *U. S.* and *Uphaus* v. *Wyman*, 360 *U. S. Supreme Court Reports* 109, *ibid.* 72.

17. *Ibid.*, pp. 143–144.

18. Thomas Jefferson, *The Living Thoughts of Thomas Jefferson*, Presented by John Dewey, Longman's, Green, New York, 1940, pp. 61–62.

19. Thomas Jefferson, *The Life and Selected Writings of Thomas Jefferson*, pp. 4 and 617.

20. H. L. A. Hart, "Definition and Theory in Jurisprudence," 70 *Law Quarterly Review* 37–60.

21. Cf. Northrop, "Neutralism and United States Foreign Policy," *The Annals of the American Academy of Political and Social Science*, Vol. 312, July 1957, pp. 42–68.

22. John Austin, *The Province of Jurisprudence Determined*, p. 201.

23. As quoted in the *New York Times* at that period.

24. Letter from Professor William Ernest Hocking to the writer, dated November 24, 1957. For further documentation of this point, see Northrop, "Neutralism and United States Foreign Policy," *op. cit.*

25. George F. Kennan, *American Diplomacy, 1900–1950*, University of Chicago Press, Chicago, 1951, p. 95.

26. John Austin, *The Province of Jurisprudence Determined*, pp. 13–14.

27. Cf. Northrop, "The Theory and Practice of Soviet Russian Communism" in *The Taming of the Nations*, chap. 12.

28. Northrop, *The Logic of the Sciences and the Humanities*, chap. V.

29. A. L. Goodhart, *English Law and the Moral Law*, Stevens, London, 1953, p. 17.

30. David Hume, *A Treatise on Human Nature and Dialogues Concerning Natural Religion*, edited by T. H. Green and T. H. Grose, Longman's, Green, London, 1886, Vol. I, p. 389 and Vol. II, pp. 245–246.

31. Gottlob Frege, *The Foundations of Arithmetic*, English translation by J. L. Austin, Basil Blackwell, Oxford, 1953, 2nd rev. ed.; Bertrand Russell, *Introduction to Mathematical Philosophy*, Allen and Unwin, London, 1919, chaps. 1, 3 and 4.

32. Bertrand Russell, *ibid.*, p. 5.

Index